FIGHTING CHANCE

For Dad.
We sat by the wireless and it felt
like being at ringside.

fighting chance

Winners and Losers in the Ultimate Risk Business

DERICK ALLSOP

MAINSTREAM
PUBLISHING

EDINBURGH AND LONDON

First published in Great Britain in 2003 by
MAINSTREAM PUBLISHING (EDINBURGH) LTD
7 Albany Street
Edinburgh EH1 3UG

ISBN 1 84018 691 7

A catalogue record for this book is available from the British Library

Typeset in Ehrnhardt

Printed in Great Britain by
Mackays of Chatham

CONTENTS

ACKNOWLEDGEMENTS

THIS BOOK DEVELOPED FROM CONCEPT TO REALITY ONLY BECAUSE so many people were willing to open their doors, hearts and minds. Their co-operation and candour are testimony to the nature of the boxing fraternity, a breed set apart from others in more ways than the obvious.

Since it would be impossible to list or even recall every single person who has contributed, in some way, to the telling of this tale, a sincere thanks to those who are not named below. Some were so generous in their assistance that expressions of gratitude are inadequate, but here goes anyway.

Martin Jolley, who reveals his remarkable story in the opening chapters, fittingly has the final word, too. His personality, humility and honesty were inspirational. Brian Hughes and his gym were ever-welcoming, even through the most trying of circumstances. His Collyhurst and Moston stable was a mine of precious material, forthright opinion and enthusiasm. His boxers, notably Robin Reid, Michael Jennings, Thomas McDonagh, Matthew Hall and David Barnes, have enriched this book. Anthony Farnell and Michael Gomez were equally helpful before and after they parted company with Collyhurst and Moston. Gomez shares the experiences of his extraordinary young life with disarming frankness. Billy Graham, who now trains Farnell and Gomez, gave unconditional access to his Phoenix Camp and other fighters, among them Ricky and Matthew Hatton and Steve Foster Jnr.

Jack Doughty was similarly accommodating at his gym, offering also his observations and suggestions, while Nobby Nobbs served up food for serious thought as well as a helping of his fabled humour. Frank Warren, Richard Maynard and all at Sports Network have been compliant throughout.

The forbearance of Paul Ingle and his mother, Carol, is especially appreciated. It is impossible to comprehend what they have endured, but they were prepared to talk about their ordeal and give a moving insight.

Thanks, also, to Bobby Vanzie, Des Gargano, Wayne and Charles Shepherd, Phil Williams and Mike Goodall at StarSports Promotions, Steve Pollard, Frank Maloney, Robert Battersby, Ray Hatton, Mike Jackson, Steve Goodwin, Glyn Rhodes, Darren Rhodes, Pat Barrett, Eamon Vickers, Ray Ashton, Tracey Pollard and Jonathan Greening.

Sky's boxing coverage and the excellent service provided by Claude Abrams and *Boxing News* have been invaluable sources of ideas and information. Colleagues have rallied round with advice and encouragement, none more so than Martin Leach and Kevin Garside, who also cast expert eyes over the manuscript. Stan Piecha, Kevin Francis and Peter Keeling gave their input, too. Thanks to all at Mainstream, whose faith and backing made this venture possible, and finally to my own corner team, Sue, Natalie and Kate, for seeing me through it.

INTRODUCTION

THE ABOLITIONISTS POUNCED ON BOXING LIKE THE YOUNG MIKE Tyson laying into a groggy opponent. It was bound to happen again, they said. How many more times must it happen? The accusations and demands battered the doors of the boxing authorities and the consciences of those who purport to be humanitarians yet still condone this base and brutal activity, presented for public consumption in the name of entertainment.

This latest victim was Paul Ingle, a 28-year-old featherweight from Scarborough. He had entered the ring at the Sheffield Arena, on the night of 16 December 2000, for the second defence of his International Boxing Federation (IBF) title against a South African, Mbulelo Botile. He was carried away on a stretcher by paramedics, an oxygen mask over his face, after being knocked unconscious in the 12th and final round of a gruesome contest. Within an hour he was prepared for surgery. A blood clot was removed from his brain.

As Paul Ingle lay in an induced coma, clinging to life, boxing was forced to adopt its familiar, defensive stance. Once more it had to fend off the claims that it was barbaric, immoral and an anachronism in a self-proclaimed civilised society. The charges were, and remain, difficult to refute. Pictures of the wretched Ingle, on television and in the newspapers, provided powerful evidence for the prosecution's case. The rebuttal was equally well-worn: that professional boxers were consenting adults and any ban would drive the sport underground. Contests were now, generally, more readily stopped at any sign of a boxer's distress and safety precautions had been greatly improved following earlier tragedies.

The swift response to Ingle's plight gave him a chance and he pulled through. He had further surgery 11 months later to have the right side of his skull, cut out in the original operation, replaced by a titanium plate. He is still recovering but may never fully regain his mobility and memory. He recalls nothing of that fateful night in Sheffield, or the build-up to the fight. However, he is clear and unequivocal in his support of the sport that almost killed him.

'I have no regrets about getting into a boxing ring,' Ingle says. 'If I could box next week I would. I would always defend boxing.'

The object of this book is neither to persecute nor to exonerate boxing. It merely attempts to give an insight into a trade that has survived the pressure campaigns in Britain to sustain a presence into the twenty-first century. But the shadow of death and serious injury is evident every time a boxer climbs through the ropes and those involved can never hide from the inherent risks.

Jack Doughty, a manager and trainer in north-west England, confesses: 'Whenever somebody is badly knocked out and hurt I say to myself, "What are you doing in this business?" But then there are other sports and pastimes that are just as dangerous.'

The difference, of course, is that in those other, often cited pursuits of peril, such as motor-racing, horse-riding and mountaineering, the objective is not to deliberately hit and disable the opponent.

Brian Hughes, another respected trainer in the north-west, maintains that boxing is, first and foremost, the 'noble art of defence'. But he, too, has agonised over his participation in a game that can be just as uncompromising and traumatic out of the ring. Hughes has endured a maelstrom of emotions over the past couple of years, as we shall discover in subsequent pages. He has been tormented by what he calls a 'dirty, rotten, stinking business'. He has talked of retirement.

Nobby Nobbs, a comical figure from Birmingham, who is famed for training journeymen boxers, contends Hughes cannot walk away from the sport 'because it's in his blood'. Billy Graham, Hughes' rival on the intensely competitive Manchester scene, claims he is the target of jealousy-fuelled abuse and 'bitchiness'. Two of Hughes' best boxers,

Anthony Farnell and Michael Gomez, recently defected to Graham's Phoenix Camp.

Rancour and recrimination come with the territory in most businesses. Bloodletting is another matter. Boxers accept the potential consequences of their trade and are willing to risk the ultimate price. Doughty suggests social deprivation is no longer the spur that it was. 'I don't think poverty and hunger are issues as much as they used to be,' he says. And yet we shall hear from boxers at all levels of the sport that they found hope, dignity and a chance of prosperity in the ring. The alternative for many was entrapment in society's underbelly; a life of crime, drugs and squalor. Michael Jennings, from Chorley, Lancashire, is convinced boxing spared him the fate of his brother, killed by an overdose. Gomez, whose life story is barely credible, teeters on the edge of self-destruction but at least has a choice, thanks to his boxing ability.

The cynics will counter, perhaps with justification in some instances, that inherently violent men will proffer any excuse to indulge their bloody obsession. Undoubtedly fighters – and promoters, managers and trainers – will take what financial gain they can from boxing. But then they argue it is a legitimate business and they are harnessing their talent and knowledge.

This book does not seek to pass judgement, but to present British boxing the way it is. We shall hear from journeymen such as Martin Jolley and Wayne Shepherd, Britain's oldest professional boxer, and champions, including Ricky Hatton, acknowledged as the most exciting young fighter in the country. From the stereotypical dingy environs of their gyms, trainers and managers share their experiences and express their forthright opinions. Frank Warren, Britain's leading promoter, reveals what it is like knowing you are always there to be shot at. He has survived a would-be assassin's bullet as well as the sniping of competitors and pundits. Warren now operates in the major arenas and on television, but boxing still goes on show in small halls and in front of black-tie dinner audiences.

Boxing will always have its critics and maybe some day it will die. Those who work in the game are normal human beings in the sense that they represent all shades of morality, compassion, mood and conduct. However, what is striking about boxing people is a candour and openness rarely so apparent in other sports. Humour and camaraderie illuminate their forbidding workplace, perhaps even providing a lifeline. Darkness, they know, can descend at any time, yet the laughter and optimism are indomitable. The risks are ever present but so, too, are the potential rewards. Boxers accept the deal on those terms and take their fighting chance.

1 ☆ POINTS OF PRINCIPLE

MANCHESTER IS A MELANCHOLY PARODY OF ITSELF THIS OCTOBER evening, a sitting duck for the carload of men arriving from the other side of the Pennines. 'It's always piddling down in this miserable dump,' one of them mocks. The response from a native is as tired as the old jibe. 'Yeah, yeah. Get back over them bloody 'ills if you don't like it.'

The five men, clutching sports bags and suitably smug after their wind-up success, swagger into the forbidding, cavernous foyer of the Palace Hotel, one of Manchester's new wave of four-star establishments, created from the shells of long-obsolete business and industrial buildings. The five men are steered to room 154. It is spacious, with two double beds and pseudo-plush décor. One of the men puts on the TV and is instantly immersed in *The Bill*. Another, bigger man, with red hair and a flat nose, looks around the room and nods approvingly.

'Normally, at a leisure centre, we have a room about the size of this bed,' he says. 'And that's for three or four of us.'

The red-haired man is called Martin Jolley. He works as a printer but he is also a professional boxer. Two of the other men are boxers, another their trainer, the fifth the cornerman. They have been allocated this unusually luxurious changing-room because tonight Jolley and one of the other fighters, Kevin England, are on show at a boxing dinner in the hotel. Another fighter and his aides step into Room 154 and suddenly it no longer seems so spacious.

13

Jolley, who drove from his home in Chesterfield to Sheffield to pick up the other four from a boxing club, is matched with a local fighter, Wayne Pinder, in a super-middleweight bout of four three-minute rounds. Jolley is not expected to win. He is rarely expected to win. He is a journeyman boxer; a jobber. He is 33 and has won only 13 of his 75 contests. He is booked as cannon fodder for boxers on the way up, or to fill in when another fighter pulls out. He was given two days' notice for this fight. Yet he betrays no sign of an inferiority complex or self-consciousness. 'I'm in good shape,' he says. 'I weighed in down in Nottingham yesterday. Twelve stone two. The other lad's undefeated, but . . .' The sentence tails off and he shrugs his shoulders.

The ring is erected in the middle of a ballroom, which occupies the basement of the hotel. Jolley goes on a reconnaissance mission.

'I like to check out wherever I'm fighting. I like to get the feel of it and not let my opponent think I'm uneasy in any way,' he says and winks.

The ballroom is airy, the ceiling high. Men in dinner jackets are seated at round tables, sating their appetites for food, wine and gossip. Jolley, conspicuous in casual clothes, is apparently unnoticed as he scans his workplace.

'I'm glad it's a high ceiling,' he says. 'You can't breathe in some places, especially if it's smoky. This is okay. I prefer a leisure centre to a dinner show. Sometimes you'll hear somebody shout in a half-hearted way, "Come on, Ginger," but you'll often leave a place like this and wonder if they even realised you were in there fighting.'

Palpably, it would take more than disinterested diners in black ties to discourage Jolley. He accepts the knocks in any form. He appears open, affable, and self-assured.

'People think I'm really confident but that's put on. The truth is I'm a pretty nervous sort but you don't want the guy in the other corner knowing that,' he confides with another wink. 'They call me "Cooler" or "Jollster". Everybody thinks I'm calm and pleasant, which I am most of the time. Jolley by name . . . But I've got a temper and it's landed me in trouble in the past. I'm a street-fighter, not a boxer. Getting into the ring kept me out of trouble. I was bullied when I was a kid. When I laughed a lot they thought I was a bit simple. If I see somebody getting picked on now I'll step in and throw a punch without thinking twice. That's the way I am. But I don't get in bother the way I used to.

'Boxing has helped me and I've learned how to survive in the ring. Just little things. Referees don't like to see you take six punches without throwing one back so I always keep count and make sure I get one in, a jab, any sort of punch, before the six are up. Refs have a difficult job. There's been so much bad publicity about boxing they know they can't take any risks and usually step in before anyone gets badly hurt. I can appreciate their position.'

Back up in room 154, Jolley and the other two boxers due to fight tonight stretch out on the beds, perhaps dreaming of a winning combination of punches. Their shiny trunks are laid out beside them.

Glyn Rhodes, who runs the Sheffield Boxing Centre, is sipping a cup of tea. 'Martin's the kind of bloke who'll fight anywhere, any time. As long as the money's right. Win, lose or draw, it makes no difference to him. He'll move on to the next one. He's a good trainer and he's got something about him in terms of personality. It's a pity it's never really happened for him.'

The slumbering figures are roused by the entrance of a dinner-jacketed official, who checks their names against his list and issues a general 'good luck' message. Weighing scales are placed on the floor of the room and a voice asks: 'Who wants weighing?'

Suddenly there is another question in the air. It comes from Jolley and it conveys agitation. His scheduled opponent has dropped out and he faces a replacement fighter. 'Who is he?'

'Alan Page,' is the coy reply.

'Who's he?' Rhodes wants to know.

As the other two fighters strip to briefs and boxer shorts and step on the scales, Jolley prowls the room, shaking his head. 'I don't give a toss who I fight, but they always do this to me,' he growls. 'If my mate here wasn't fighting I'd be off. This is the fifth time this has happened to me since I came back last October.'

He prowls some more and growls some more: 'I'm mad now.'

The room falls silent until Jolley turns to his stable-mate and tells him: 'Don't you be as daft as me. Get your money and make sure they don't mess you.'

Rhodes offers to glean some intelligence on Page and Jolley sits down. 'They take advantage of my good nature,' he says. 'A good example – I had this fight a couple of months ago and weighed in at 12 stone 1lb, just right for the opponent I was supposed to have. Then I recognise this big black guy warming up. "What you doing, Clint [Johnson]?" I say to him. "I'm fighting you," he says. He was 13 stone and he'd known for two weeks that he was fighting me.'

Jolley is cut short by the announcement of another arrival: 'Doctor's here.'

The doctor is a woman, smartly dressed, mainly in black. She has blonde hair, cut to the level of her ear lobe. She says little but seems to have a foreign accent. She wields her stethoscope and Kevin England is the first to introduce himself. He is bare-chested and maintains his swagger even when he's standing still. His tattoos include an erotic image of a woman, on his right leg. The doctor consults her notes and mutters something about his pulse. She checks his eyes and ears before declaring her satisfaction. 'Brilliant, doctor,' says England, swaggering back to his bed.

Next up is the youngest of the three. He is slight of build, quiet, almost reticent. But he still has the apparently obligatory tattoos. His display features a tiger.

'How long since you were knocked out?' the doctor asks.

'Two months.'

The doctor pauses for a moment before sanctioning his next bout.

Jolley marches forward and obeys the instructions to take deep breaths. 'No Pain' is the defiant declaration tattooed on his right arm. The doctor examines his hands and teeth. Rhodes playfully calls over: 'Don't get too familiar with the doctor, now.'

The doctor patently has no intention of trading banter. She manages a thin smile, or maybe it is a smirk. She picks up her bag and heads for the door.

The cornerman, Andy Manning, pulls a bucket and his own medical equipment from a bag. He starts to bandage the hands of the young fighter, a meticulous routine he could presumably accomplish blindfolded.

Jolley has put his shirt back on and gone to seek out the promoter and matchmaker. He agreed to fight Pinder for a purse of £550. He will fight his new opponent so long as they pay him an extra £150. This is not the mega-buck world of Lewis and Tyson. This is another world altogether.

'I'm telling them to pay me more or I'm off to the pub.' It does not sound like a hollow threat.

FIGHTING CHANCE

The young fighter goes through warming-up exercises as Jolley sits and broods. He still hasn't weighed and shows no sign of doing so. Rhodes, who has been scurrying in and out of the room for the past half-hour, is back again with the reply to Jolley's ultimatum. A short, sharp shake of the head delivers the verdict. 'Won't budge.'

Jolley will, but only to get out of the hotel as quickly as he can. He thrusts his arms into his jacket, snatches his bag, puts back his trunks and tells Rhodes he will see him at the car later. 'Tell them we've come in two cars and I'm off home.'

Jolley bolts out of the room and out of the hotel. Manchester's stereotypical weather provides him with suitably sombre accompaniment. He dumps his bag into the boot of his car and seeks out a pub where he can sit and collect his thoughts.

The very nature of boxing would suggest its participants have strayed off life's regular path. However, Jolley has reached this pub in the centre of Manchester via a network of back alleys that would have led many to oblivion. He nearly went that way, too. And yet his starting point was nowhere remotely close to the archetypal environment that breeds prize-fighters. His father built up a successful business in painting and decorating. The family lived in a nice house in a smart part of Chesterfield. Martin was sent to a highly reputable school. Then the business collapsed and the family lost just about everything. They moved to a council house in a less-smart part of town. It was during those formative years that Martin Jolley encountered his first experiences of bullying. Illness compounded his vulnerability and sense of foreboding.

'You know how cruel kids can be,' he says, swirling his orange juice around the glass. 'About the age of 13 I had bad asthma and whooping cough. I was in an oxygen tent and actually died for five seconds. But for me it was a psychological problem as much as a physical one. We went from a posh area, where people talked a bit la di da, to a rough area. That was when they started to pick on me. I was a bit different, you see. The trouble was mainly outside school but it affected me in school as well. They looked on me as a bit of a wimp and used that against me.

'Because I was suffering I took it out on my brother and bullied him. I used to beat him up. Because of that, and unbeknown to me, he went to an amateur boxing club. One day he said, "Here. You want a fight, put them on." So he threw me these gloves and there I was, waving my arms like a windmill. I couldn't touch him. He's there doing the Queensberry Rules and he busts my nose. He was actually twice as good as me technically, very talented, but he wasn't bothered about boxing when he was older.'

Fighting back struck him as the solution and the boxing gym presented him with the means. But that ready supply of ammunition was triggered too easily and the inevitable street fights led to inevitable brushes with the local constabulary.

'I did some amateur stuff, but packed it in. I found women and beer. Then I started going to another boxing gym, sparring. I was 17 or 18, and these other guys were 25 or 26. I got involved with them and got a bit streetwise. Being the young and naïve one, I was chucked into the middle of the punch-up every time. I got some fist but I learned the technique of street-fighting. I hardened up.

'I spent a few nights in the police cells,' he recalls. 'Actually it was quite funny because I knew the duty sergeant. I painted his house when I was working for my dad, after he started on his own again. So I got looked after all right. But I was getting myself a reputation around Chesterfield. It made more sense to do my fighting in the ring and make some extra money out of it.'

Working in a paint factory bizarrely contributed to his first win in the ring, in 1992. He was fighting one Gypsy Johnny Price, in Bury, when he reeled away from a clinch and threw up.

'Because I'd been working in that factory my throat was full of crap and I just had to puke it up.'

A bemused Price was transfixed. Jolley hit him with a right and the hapless Gypsy was done for.

Another of Jolley's blows landed him in big trouble with the police after a domestic squabble with his then partner got out of hand. He was 23.

'She created a bit of a scene in Chesterfield town centre, pulling my hair and generally getting a bit volatile. Suddenly I felt this hand on my shoulder and I automatically snatched it, threw this guy over the top of me and hit him. Then I realised I'd decked a policeman. Before I knew it, they were swarming out of the woodwork. I had a fight with three of them and they got me in handcuffs. In court they said I'd butted this policeman first, but I swear on my kid's life he butted me first. I'd hit him and he was getting his own back. He was six foot four, 17 and a half stone. He took his helmet off and butted me. Needless to say I got some fist in the cell. When I was in handcuffs I was jumping about like Zebedee, trying to butt all eight of them. The court verdict, to me, proved they knew there was more to the case than the police said, otherwise I would have gone down for bumping three policemen. I got community service instead.'

This all-too-close encounter with the law led Jolley to improbable work as a probation officer. The authorities were so impressed with his resourcefulness and communication skills that, two years on, they invited him to harness his obvious talent again.

'I never wanted to be a probation officer, but they asked me to do it. I did three areas, Derby, Chesterfield and Nottingham, and they all said I was one of the best they'd had because I could relate to the people I was dealing with. I could talk to them and calm them down.'

And yet he could not prevent the course of his own life veering into the back alleys. Any pain he suffered in the ring was insignificant compared with the emotional agonies that blighted his personal relationships. A broken romance with the woman he fought in Chesterfield town centre turned into a harrowing and recurring nightmare when he began to doubt he was the father of her two children. The absence of any obvious physical resemblance, in particular ginger hair, caused the initial anxiety. Later he was advised to read a certain edition of the *Derbyshire Times* because it contained an article that should be of interest to him.

'It was all about her. It said she'd been an escort. Well, a prostitute. That's what it was really saying. Our relationship was over but I loved those kids like my own son and daughter and still do. They call me Daddy. But I don't know if that's what I am.'

His morale and self-esteem were restored when he met a woman he thought would be the perfect partner. She came from a wealthy family, was strong-willed and demanded he give up boxing. Reluctantly, he complied, but their marriage lasted less than a year.

'She told me I didn't need to box again because we'd be financially secure. We lived at my house, a little terraced place, but once we got married it wasn't good enough. Like a fool, I agreed to move in with her parents at their farm. Worst mistake of my life. It all went pear-shaped one night when I got involved in a fight with her parents. Her father clipped me and her mother slapped me three times, and I couldn't control my temper any longer. I turned round and knocked both of them out. My wife ran off screaming and phoned the police. They came and it all calmed down. I was standing outside, explaining everything to the police and the next thing I know is the father's come out with a shotgun, telling the police if I don't get off his land he's going to shoot me. I now despise my wife because she turned her back on me.'

This latest body blow reduced him to alcohol-fuelled, suicidal despair. In a state of mental turmoil, he walked for miles, from the home his wife had rejected to the stable where she kept a horse he had bought her for £6,000.

'I was highly intoxicated and walked all the way up to the farm, near where I live now. I lay beside the horse, stroking it and telling it I couldn't go on. I fell asleep but when I woke up I was still under the influence of alcohol and decided I'd had enough. I'd lost the kids because my ex-partner wouldn't let me see them, I'd lost my wife and I'd packed in boxing. I'd lost everything I'd worked to achieve. So I stood up on a breezeblock in the stable, put a noose around my neck and jumped.

'I'm not a church-goer but I've always believed there is somebody up there, that we are here for a reason, and when I jumped my foot got stuck in the hole at the top of the breeze block. I'm bloody glad it did because I butted the girder and knocked myself out. I was trapped between the girder and the breezeblock and when I came round – I don't know how long later – I managed to free myself and walked home.

'From that day I said to myself, "Right, I'm going to get my life on track." I'd been binge drinking and feeling sorry for myself, looking through wedding albums and photos of the kids. I would watch old boxing videos and basically trashed myself. Then I tried to hang myself. I saw other drunks and realised how pathetic I must have looked. Enough was enough, and boxing helped me get myself together again. I put on my tracksuit, went on a six-mile run and got myself back into shape. I got into boxing again and to be honest I became more popular than ever.'

The Rocky-like comeback was enhanced by other changes in his life. 'Now I've got a better job, a better house and I'm happy with my new girlfriend, Joanne. We met about a year ago and, touch wood, it's working OK. She's 30 and very sensible, nothing like the blonde dolly birds I usually go for. She has a daughter from a previous relationship, which turned out to be a bit of a bad one. I wanted her to move in with me but

I can't be too influenced by love and everything. I've been hurt too much over the last five years and I've got to make sure it's right and that I don't make another mistake. She doesn't like me boxing either, but I made my comeback before we got together, and at the moment I want to continue – in spite of what's happened tonight and has happened to me four times before in the last year.

'People always ask me why I do it, especially with my record. You start out with great ideas about becoming a world champion but I knew from my first fight I was never going to be anything special. I just love boxing and training. I know it sounds corny but it's the truth. If I'm working on the day shift I'll train late afternoon, if I'm on nights I'll go to the gym early afternoon. I've sparred with eight fighters in a session for Glyn. I'll train till I bleed.'

He has bled a lot over the years, literally and metaphorically, although he maintains his most serious cuts were sustained outside the ring.

'I was in a pub in Chesterfield and because they knew me, I got served before this bloke who was at the bar. I went back to my seat but he got the monk on and the next thing I knew a glass was smashed on my head and blood was pouring down my face. I lost three pints of blood. Even worse was a time I put my hand out to stop a plate-glass door blowing in the wind. My hand went straight through the glass and severed an artery.

'I've had my nose bust, my ribs broken and a few cuts around the eye in the ring, but I know how to look after myself. I've never been knocked out. I can take a punch, because when you have a medicine ball thrown into your stomach in training a normal punch is nothing.'

Jolley's distinctive, hoarse and slightly drawling voice has given some of his friends and associates concern about the cumulative effect of the punches. If Muhammad Ali can be ravaged so appallingly, the inherent dangers for a journeyman like Jolley are transparent.

He replies: 'I know my voice sounds a bit strange and people do wonder if I might get punchy but I've got a broad tongue and that's what makes me talk like this. My throat has also been affected by working with paints and chemicals. I had an operation only recently. Of course I'm aware of the dangers and I don't intend to stay around too long. I don't have the evil eye some of the younger lads have, I know that, but I'm no pushover for anybody. Ali has Parkinson's disease. Anyone can get that. Boxing may have contributed to his condition but we don't know that for certain.

'If I was ever like Ali, I know I've got friends who would help me take my life. I wouldn't want to be a burden on anyone. You see the medical checks we have before each fight. They weigh you again to make sure you're not dehydrated. You put back the food and liquids after the official weigh-in and are expected to be heavier. I'm probably 12 stone 10 lb now. But I wasn't going to get weighed tonight until we were sorted with the money. They knew better than to try and mess with me. They could see I'd got the monk on so when I told them to get stuffed that was it. Nobody was going to argue with me. We have full scans every year and you have to have scans again before title fights. So really the precautions are thorough.'

Jolley concedes the money is useful and has helped him buy and improve a home that is a testament to personal vindication and achievement against the odds.

'But hey, don't think I'm picking up £550 clear from a fight. I'll average a fight a month. My various costs for the gym, equipment and petrol come to £200 a month. Twenty-five per cent goes to Glyn and then there's tax. I'm left with about £150. That's why I won't be taken for a sucker tonight. They knew earlier in the day about the change and could have called me. I gave up the chance of a fight in Sheffield tomorrow to take this one. I know I'm in the right and that eventually I'll get the £550 anyway. It can take months because the case has to go backward and forward, to the area Board and then the national Board. I'm still waiting for the money from my first scheduled fight after I came back. But you see, this way I could still fight tomorrow and double my money.'

He winks again and rings the Sheffield matchmaker. He leaves a message on the answer machine, informing him he is available if required. Moments later Jolley's phone rings but he does not answer.

'It's them across the road. If I answer and go over they'll put an arm around me and sweet-talk me. They'll try to get me on a guilt trip. There's no way I'm going back. Besides, I wouldn't be in the right frame of mind to fight now. That's when you can get hurt. I'd share my last penny with anybody. People who know me will tell you that. I'm like that; I always try to help people. But I won't go on being a sucker for promoters and matchmakers. They are taking me for a mug and I won't have it. I'm there as cannon fodder, I know that. They don't want me there to win. I've even gone into the ring at the last minute with no tapes on my hands. They're supposed to check that, but there wasn't time. Some fighters avoid weigh-ins. Their people say, "Don't worry, he's fine," and they get away with it. These things happen in the game. I once had a six-rounder and put the other guy down in three of the rounds. I won by a mile. But the points verdict went to him. It was such a scandalous decision that they wouldn't allow the fight to be shown on TV.

'There are decent people in the game – a lot of decent people. A lot of my opponents are friends and I'll go and have a drink with them. I bet I can count on one hand the number of opponents whose phone number I don't have. But there are the con-men, as well.'

Again his mobile rings. Again he does not answer. Again he winks.

'Unless I get a fight tomorrow I'll probably be low and sulk for a week and hardly train. But then I'll pick myself up and start working really hard for the British Masters fight I've got in Chesterfield next month. Somebody like me doesn't usually get a shot at a title but the Masters is a way of giving us all a chance. I'm fighting a lad from just down the road, in Belper. I think I'm fit but he's a fitness fanatic. Even so, I'm sure I'll win. I'll look on it as my destiny, that I was fated to do it. I'll get myself up as never before. I'll throw punches from everywhere. I'll be all over him like a rash. He won't know what's hit him.

'I am a fatalist. I do believe that whatever happens is pre-ordained. Death doesn't scare me or anything because I know that after death I'll be going to a better place.'

Any minute now he'll be going home. The phone rings again and this time, he knows, it's Glyn Rhodes. They're finished and are on their way over. Jolley jumps to his feet and pulls his hood over his head as he walks to his car.

'Don't want anyone over there seeing me,' he says. And winks.

He reverses his J-reg Vauxhall Cavalier up the cobbled side street and waits for the others. One of his reversing lights is out.

'It hasn't been the sort of night I was hoping for, but it happens. Not just to me, and not just at this level. That's the sort of game it is. But you know, it can still make a bloke like me feel good occasionally. I was at a big fight night here in Manchester a while back and met all sorts of stars – the Gallaghers, Freddy Starr and Claudia Schiffer. She asked me for my autograph because I was a fighter. That made me feel I was somebody.'

2 ☆ LOCAL HERO

MARTIN JOLLEY'S CHANCE TO BE RECOGNISED AS SOMEBODY IN THE ring is six days away. The call to fight in Sheffield never came and he was quietly relieved. He wanted to focus on HIS big one, in front of HIS people, in pursuit of HIS destiny. He wanted to be better prepared than he had ever been, to trim off the pounds systematically and get down to 11 stone 6 lb without compromising his health or stamina, and to sharpen his reflexes to an irresistible peak. Belper's Gary Beardsley, his opponent for the British Masters middleweight title, had been warned.

Jolley is due to be training this afternoon in Sheffield, under the guidance of Glyn Rhodes. Visitors are told the gym is just off the road heading out from the city centre towards Hillsborough. 'Anybody in the area will know where we are,' Rhodes says with unbridled pride. 'The school we're at is the one where they filmed *The Full Monty*.'

At lunchtime, Jolley relays a mobile phone message: 'Bad news. Won't be training. Think I'm going to lose my licence.'

He sounds as though his world has been blown apart. It has. This may only loosely fit the description of a 'title' fight but the regulations require the contestants to undergo brain scans and Jolley's check has revealed a problem.

'It is on the left side of my head, where I was glassed,' he says in a solemn, breaking voice. 'I'm feeling depressed. They won't let me fight. It looks like the end. I don't know. I've got to keep going. I'll maybe come back in the New Year. I'll have to see. I don't really know what's going to happen.'

He is devastated and confused and his state of mind is not helped by second and third opinions that both confirm an abnormality, a potential risk and grounds for revoking his licence. By Friday he has to confront the reality.

'It's over. There's no way I can fight on Sunday. Trouble is I've sold a load of tickets for the fight. They'll get a replacement, but if I pull out now the show will collapse.'

Early on Sunday afternoon Jolley and a couple of friends drop into a pub before making their way to the Queen's Park Sports Centre, in Chesterfield. Jolley orders a vodka and coke and looks as though he is about to climb into the ring with his hands tied behind his back and face Mike Tyson. It is one of those modern, kit pubs: large, open plan, with an extensive lunch menu to lure families and middle-aged couples.

'My girlfriend, my family and all my friends have been brilliant,' says Jolley, seeking a table in the corner. 'One of my friends took me to one side and told me to forget about being depressed; life goes on, take every day as it comes. Even though I love fighting and it's been taken away from me, there's more to me than boxing, so keep my chin up. Things like that help. But it's still hard to take in.

'The Boxing Board rang me up to tell me about the brain scan. They asked me to retire but I didn't want to until the third specialist had looked at it. I was entitled to see three independent specialists and I thought the first one might be wrong. Even after the third one I didn't want to say that was it. I can't even spar. I've got a damaged area of tissue on the left side of my head. They say that if I repeatedly take shots to that side of my head there's a possibility I'll get knocked out and go into a coma.

'I've had 75 fights, fought 21 champions, 4 world champions, and I've passed every scan and medical test. Then a guy shoves a glass in my face and suddenly he's taken away my career. If I retire no one knows the truth. I suppose it's better for me, but I don't want to pack in. If I could go on I would try to get the world record for the most fights. If I could go on for 300, 400, 500 fights I would, I love the game so much. If it was a fight to the last person standing up at the end it would always be me. Robin Reid, Joe Calzaghe, Mike Tyson, forget them. Forget about Tyson

25

biting my tab off. He could put me down a hundred times, I'd keep getting back up. He wouldn't beat me. Sincerely. I've got 150 per cent mental attitude. I would beat anybody.'

His excited, almost frenzied flow is interrupted, if never stemmed, by well-wishers who do not appear to find it unusual that he should be in a pub hours before his appointment with destiny. 'Yeah, I'm fine . . . thanks.' He throws up his eyes and squirms only when the well-wisher has walked away.

'Ninety-five per cent of this town loves me, the other five per cent hate me, but that's because I've bumped them. They deserve it. They're wasters. They're druggies, piss-heads, wife beaters, men who swear in front of women and bully people. I can't stand them. I'm a genuine guy. I'm not two-faced. If I don't like you, I tell you. We've all got faults. I've got plenty, I'm the first to admit it. But like that last guy who came over, he's two-faced. He's a thug, a piss-head, he causes trouble. I tell him so. He's nice as pie with me now but that's because I bumped him a few years ago. When he has too much to drink he starts hitting innocent people and I won't stand for that.

'Nobody can truthfully say they aren't different when they've had a drink. I go soft on drink. I just sit there laughing, it doesn't make me aggressive at all. So I can't understand what they are about. But many do get aggressive on drink. I need this drink before I go to the show and they announce I'm retiring.

'To be honest my head's going a bit. I've trained that much and not had a drink for about six weeks. I need this to boost my confidence. My hands are shaking. I've never been nervous going into the ring before. I'm not scared of anybody. I wasn't even scared for my first fight because I knew what to expect. But I'm going in there today knowing that a thousand people are going to be watching me and I'm on my own. When I'm fighting it's me and him and I can do something about it. But on my own I can't do anything.'

This portrayal of a sensitive being with Victorian principles is at odds with the image of the fearless street-fighter and the contradiction is not lost on Jolley.

'There's going to be a full house, a really good atmosphere, and I'll find it hard to hold back the tears. I'm a bit macho, I suppose, that's why I'm deep with my emotions. I'm not one to break down and cry in front of the macho hard men in Chesterfield because I'm classed as a hard man and I don't want them to see my weak side. But then it takes a real man to cry. I hope I don't, but if I do and anybody laughs at me I shall go straight up to them and knock them out. I know that sounds a bit thuggish but if they can't appreciate what I'm going through and they start taking the Mickey out of me, then they are the ones who are childish. I need my friends to be close to me, not take the Mickey. Now I'll find out who my real friends are.'

The turmoil in his mind is unrelenting. He sees the compensations, the new beginning . . . but it still hurts to let go.

'I'm looking forward to living a normal life, spending more time with the kids, going out, eating what I want, when I want. But the future is, I don't know . . . a bit scary. Boxing has been my life for 18 years. I feel like I've had my arms cut off. I know I'm putting myself down because I have got a lot of qualities, but I'm thinking to myself, "I'm a nobody." Everybody tells me I've got a good job, I'm intelligent, I've got a lot of common sense, I'm well liked, I've got two beautiful kids, a lovely girlfriend, a nice house. Come on, Jolley, what are you moaning about? Stop being bitter. Stop being selfish. You want a kick up the backside. There are people who haven't even got a roof over their heads.'

Soon he must confront the ring without his gloves and still the memories and emotions are whirring in his head.

'You'll see how popular I am, even though people will be a bit down because I'm not fighting. People can maybe beat me technically, but in terms of attitude, forget it. I've really got boxing going in Chesterfield. It's starting to thrive here. We are the centre of the country, we've got the Crooked Spire. There is a bit of thuggery around the pubs of the town. Some of them have a bit of a reputation – what they call the "Town Lads", rough and ready lads. There's lots of encouragement to get stuck in. I think boxing gives kids like these a lot of discipline and self-respect.

'I can't totally defend boxing because I go in there to maim the other guy, and common sense tells you that's immoral. But I would tell people who condemn boxing that in life so many things are immoral. If I could look into the background of every person who makes comments about boxing, I guarantee I would be able to pick faults with nine out of ten of them. Whether it's going behind their wife's back, not going to work when they're supposed to, speeding in their car, drink-driving, swearing or whatever, they are doing something on those lines. So who are they to criticise boxing? It gives a lot of lads hope. It can make somebody who's nothing into something.

'It is a good sport, even though a lot of people deride it. There are many kind, genuine people involved in it. Yes, there is a corrupt side to it. It's political and money-orientated. But there is a corrupt side to everything. Look at rock stars, pop stars, film stars, TV stars . . . they are no different to anybody else. They are only human beings, same as us. I have people coming to me, shaking my hand and asking for my autograph. They put me on a pedestal but I know I'm no different to what they are.

'The local paper put a half-page piece in about me this week, with a big picture, and they called me "Chesterfield's Hard Man". OK, I'm strong, I'm durable, but comments like that in the paper make guys on beer and drugs have the extra confidence to say, "Look at me, I'm a hard man," and I'm an ideal target for the Friday or Saturday night crowd. If they can knock me out, well, they are somebody. "Wow, you didn't knock out Martin Jolley, did you?" I don't think they would knock me out but I don't want people coming up and being nasty to me. I want them to be nice.

'When they come up being nasty it gets my back up and I'll knock them out because I'm defending myself. I can see the signs coming so I might hit him first. Being a fighter, you know when somebody's going to hit you. So straight away I'm classed as the bad guy. But you look at anybody in showbiz, TV, pop – they get people hassling them because of who they are. Even at my lower level of popularity you've got to learn to take a backward step, stay in the shadows and keep out of the way.'

Jolley is also taking the trade press to task. After his refusal to fight against a replacement opponent in Manchester, *Boxing News* suggested it was time he hung up his gloves because he was taking too much punishment. Prophetic stuff.

'It hurts me, it hurts me a lot when people write things like that. You've got a reporter there who's never had a glove on in his life. He doesn't know what it's like. Speak to people who have boxed, who do know what it's like – people like Glyn Rhodes, Pat Cowdell. I get the odd headache, but not regularly. I've been knocked out and knocked round again while I've been standing up. I've been dazed and then hit again and come round. For that split second I must have been knocked out. People make silly comments, but the only people who can take the Mickey out of me are those who have had gloves on, and nobody who has had gloves on does that, because they know exactly how it feels.

'I would have won this title today and gone on from there. I'd have got another title in January. Then I would have had something to throw back at that reporter. They will deny it, but reporters always stick with the local hero. Even if the local hero loses, they will come up with every excuse in the book to explain why he's lost. That's what sucks.'

Jolley's boxing career is over, at least as a fighter. If he is to stay in the game he must pursue an already-developing interest in training or take up an offer from the Board to become an inspector, a classic case of poacher turned gamekeeper.

'It's a nice compliment,' he says. 'It shows a lot of respect. I'd definitely like to stay in boxing. I like training, passing on my knowledge. The only thing is that if I do something I want to do it 100 per cent, but I have a job, so I have to get another trainer to do the work when I can't. I'll have to see how that goes.'

His mind and heart are palpably not in training this Sunday afternoon.

'The sooner the MC makes that announcement the better. I know I'm going to have to repeat the story over and over. I just hope people don't pester me all day.'

Pestering is one of the prices of being a local hero and Jolley's stature in these parts is evident the moment he steps into the Queen's Park Sports Centre. He is showered with 'good luck' calls. A security man tells him: 'You're going to win, I'm not just saying that.' Again Jolley throws up his eyes and squirms as he turns away. A sometime fighter carrying too much weight around the middle to be serious shows Jolley his damaged hand and pledges to be back after Christmas. Jolley advises hot water and salt for his hand but resists telling him what he really thinks of his prospects. A small boy hovers to shake Jolley's hand. 'You all right, brother?' The boy nods. Jolley addresses almost everyone in the boxing fraternity as 'brother'.

Jolley's sister and real brother catch up with him in the café. She is agitated yet relieved.

'I was worried because I couldn't get him on his mobile,' she says. 'I thought he might have been locked up again.'

'I turned the phone off,' Jolley explains meekly. 'I didn't want to talk to anyone. I'm OK now.'

He slides into a seat close to the ring and fends off a barrage of 'What's up?' questions. Word has got around.

'You'll soon find out. The MC's going to make an announcement.'

The first contest goes ahead without any announcement about Jolley. The hall is almost full this Sunday tea-time. Vociferous fans become noisier still as the obligatory, scantily dressed ring-board girl climbs through the ropes. She returns the howls and leers with interest. Jolley smiles uneasily. The arrival of his father is instant therapy. Jolley Snr reels off a succession of jokes. His son has heard them all before but doubles up in laughter. This father has cause to be jovial today.

'I'm glad he's stopped,' Jolley Snr admits. 'His mother is, especially. She never wanted him to start. She's never been to any of his fights. She's just watched the videos when she knows he's not been hurt.'

Another fight is introduced and still there is no announcement about Jolley. 'It looks as if they're not going to say anything until the second half of the show. I have to get out of here for a bit. I'll be upstairs.'

The bar is no refuge from the questions, but at least he can find something to calm his nerves.

Jolley returns to the same seat, which has briefly been kept warm for him. 'Don't sit there,' the unwitting occupier was warned. 'That's Jolley's seat.' Jolley looks far from intimidating now. He is wearing a white, sleeveless T-shirt, which displays his ample biceps, and an earring, but nothing can disguise his terrified countenance.

Mike Goodall, a familiar MC on the boxing circuit, calls for the attention of the gallery. He informs the obliging audience that the local hero has had to stop boxing. He tells them no one is more disappointed than Martin Jolley but, without mincing his words, reminds them that 'men die in this ring'. He continues: 'If Martin was to box on a tragedy could happen. Unfortunately, the doctor says he can't box.'

Goodall asks Jolley to join him in the ring and the applause is deafening. This infamous, uncompromising street-fighter cuts a lonely, forlorn, vulnerable figure, struggling to hold back the tears. Goodall does not ask him to speak and it is perhaps just as well. 'He hopes to stop in boxing and we wish him all the best indeed,' adds Goodall, encouraging a final show of appreciation.

FIGHTING CHANCE

Jolley, head in hand, returns to his seat an ex-fighter. Those within handshaking distance reach out to him, literally and metaphorically. Johnny Nelson, the British No. 1 cruiserweight, seated a few rows behind Jolley, pays his respects: 'I would have been proud of a reception like that. A world champion wouldn't have got warmer applause. You stay in boxing.'

The day can only get easier. This evening Jolley will do a round of pubs and friends, all insisting on throwing farewell parties. 'It's incredible the way people have responded. It's overwhelming,' he says.

Another contest is underway, the ring-board girl is parading in her umpteenth scanty outfit, and the spectators are whipped into a tumult, baying for the decisive blow as two more pugilists ply their brutal trade.

Darkness has fallen and outside the main entrance a parked ambulance provides a sobering reminder of the price any boxer might have to pay. Not Martin Jolley, though. Not any more.

3 ☆ TEAM COLLYHURST AND MOSTON

AUTUMN GIVES WAY TO WINTER, BUT IN THE GYM ABOVE THE
Co-op Late Shop in Moston, an area of Manchester where quick hands,
feet or wits are essential survival equipment, the only meaningful
acknowledgement of passing time is the clock over the sparring ring. It
sounds the end of a round and the start of the next one. As it does the
two fighters are prompted and cajoled. 'Come on, you're too stiff,' calls
out the trainer, a short, stout figure, leaning on the ropes and resting a
foot on the edge of the ring.

The trainer's name is Brian Hughes. One of the fighters in the ring is
Michael Gomez, the British super-featherweight champion and a potential
world champion. Gomez, whose real name is Armstrong, provides all-
action proof of Martin Jolley's case that 'rough and ready lads' can find
hope in boxing.

Gomez's story is the stuff of legend and celluloid heroism. He was
destined for a turbulent life from the moment he was born in the back of
a car after his father crashed driving his mother to hospital near Dublin.
He was one of ten children born to the Armstrongs. When he was eight,
one of his two sisters, two-year-old Louise, died. The family sought a new
life in Manchester, only to be plunged deeper into strife. His father was
afflicted by fading eyesight and his mother left home. Michael, a serial
truant, was taken into care. He met a girl and found a kind of stability.
On the night he learned she was pregnant with their second child he

became involved in a fight outside a nightclub. He hit one of his assailants, who banged his head on the pavement and later died. Gomez was charged with murder, then manslaughter, and eventually acquitted.

That Gomez has come through his 23-year ordeal with the prospect of a settled family life and successful career is testament to his inner spirit and Hughes' paternal influence. Hughes has been giving youngsters like Michael Armstrong an escape from the hazards of the streets for almost 40 years. He hails from Collyhurst, another insalubrious district of the city, where he established a lads' club. The Collyhurst fabled for its footballers, boxers and Catholic connections was effectively erased from the cityscape by the planners. Hughes' club had to find new premises and moved to Moston, hence the Collyhurst and Moston Lads' Club that thrives to this day. Any youngster with genuine talent and application has the opportunity to graduate to Hughes' senior and professional ranks. His other current boxers include the former WBC super-middleweight champion, Robin Reid, the undefeated WBO Inter-continental light-middleweight champion, Anthony Farnell, and another promising, unbeaten light-middleweight, Thomas McDonagh.

On the wall opposite the round-timing clock is a plaque proclaiming the 'World-Famous Collyhurst Boxing Academy', with the rallying motto, 'Pride in Battle'. Another wall is dominated by a huge casting of a bare-knuckle fight scene. The spectators, as well as the participants, have patently changed over the years. Top hats and canes were the order of those distant days. Mike Tyson, who visited the gym when he came to Manchester to fight, was so impressed he wanted to buy it. Hughes explained it was a gift and not for sale. On the fourth wall hangs a picture depicting the Sacred Heart of Jesus. 'He's the guv'nor in here,' Hughes tells his new recruits. It's a wonder that Hughes has not given wall space to his beloved Busby Babes, but that might be a little too self-indulgent. Besides, United fans seem to be out-numbered by those with City affiliations in this gym.

Hughes, 62 and awarded the MBE for his services to the club and the community, is driven by the satisfaction of channelling raw aggression and moulding crude talent into champions and decent citizens. He watches intently as Gomez, a week away from his attempt to win the coveted Lonsdale Belt outright, flicks out his yellow gloves and forces his opponent to cower. The bell sounds and an animated Hughes issues instructions to the attentive Gomez. The fighter nods and resumes his sparring. Hughes, a gentler, Mancunian version of Bob Hoskins, tells two other boxers to pad up and shouts to Reid: 'Come on, Robbie, start moving.'

One of Hughes' old friends, a regular visitor to the gym, observes: 'A pity Robbie's not taller. He would have made a great heavyweight.' Reid, sometime model as well as boxer, has an awesome physique, the envy of the gym. However, his career has taken a couple of backward paces. He has an important fight coming up. He needs a convincing performance to force himself back into the major league.

The bell sounds again and Gomez hugs his opponent. This may be the ultimate sport for individuals but the sense of comradeship and common purpose in the gym are as striking as anything thrown by those yellow gloves. Gomez flings himself to the canvas to perform a few piston-like press-ups, then prowls the ring, sweat dripping from his brow and flat nose.

Gomez offers an apologetic glove for a low punch but all the grunts and groans are coming from the other main section of the gym, where a boxer is hammering away at the pads held up by a colleague. Another is burying his fists into a punch bag. Two more boxers are skipping. Yet another figure is using a piece of wood and a nail to chalk concentric circles on the wooden floor. The lines will be painted white and the patterns used in technical exercises. Reid, legs apart, shoulders forward, is silent as a young hopeful helps him glove up. Hanging on the walls here are posters and pictures of the sport's legends, doubtless inspiring the next generation of contenders. And from every pore comes the unmistakable stench of human endeavour.

The bell is a relief to Gomez's sparring partner, a slip of a lad, who can now climb out of the ring, his contribution completed. He is exhausted but smiles contentedly. 'Thanks for that, son,' Hughes says. Reid steps in and gets a playful cuff from Gomez before loosening up for his sparring session. Gomez and his partner embrace and compare notes.

Reid, wearing black tracksuit bottoms and a grey sweatshirt bearing the legend, 'The Grim Reaper', moves into his hefty, slightly ponderous partner with a flurry of shots. They are delivered with speed and stinging accuracy. Hughes approves but is distracted by noise next door. 'Who's messing about?' he barks, leaning through the hatch. Gentle but firm. 'You two, 20 press-ups.'

'But Brian . . .'

'Down, 20 press-ups.'

The regulation punishment is taken with smiles and served with ramrod-straight backs, chins to the floor and full extension of the arms. Gomez, skipping-rope in hand, giggles, but not too excessively. He could be next to fall foul of their all-seeing, all-hearing boss.

Hughes is back in Reid's corner, shadow boxing to illustrate a point. The fighter takes a swig of water and goes back to work, unloading combinations, then guarding against the counter. Hughes appears suitably satisfied and can afford to turn his attention to a solid, shaven-headed youngster on the other side of the hatch.

'See this lad here, he's only 14,' Hughes says. 'He's been suspended from school for causing trouble. He's a bit of a handful. To help them get back on track they are allowed to get involved in something that interests them, so he comes here and then goes back to school for a couple of hours. He's like a pussycat in here because there are lads bigger and rougher than him.'

Hughes wants to know why the youngster missed training a couple of days ago. The boy explains that three bus drivers wouldn't believe he was only 14 and insisted he must pay the full fare. In the end he gave up.

'Was you cheeky?'

'No, honest.' The grin casts doubt. He sheepishly retreats to a punch bag.

Reid is in full flow. He gives his rendition of the shuffle and wields a crunching upper cut. He is a man on a mission and his sparring partner might wish to be otherwise occupied right now.

The bell is like an act of mercy. Hughes applauds and calls for a change of partners. The redundant opponent is out of the ring in an instant. Reid clears his nose in a bucket in the corner and turns to face his next target. The new opponent is younger, leaner, and intent on coming forward. Soon he is replaced by a smaller, more compact boxer. These two alternate to test Reid's stamina as well as his technique. Reid, a sheen of perspiration over his remarkably undisturbed and handsome features, leaves the ring to his latest sparring partners, who receive the benefit of Hughes' coaching experience. 'Work inside. Come on, inside... Work to the body instead of holding.'

Two more boxers take over and Hughes continues to spurt the

instructions: 'Bend those knees, now spin him off, spin him off.' One of the fighters has the temerity to engage in banter with a colleague outside the ring. Hughes berates his sparring partner for pausing: 'You could have knocked him out while he was talking!'

They return to business but it degenerates into too much of a scrap for Hughes' liking. 'Come on box, box . . . You two have lost 50 brain cells fighting like that.'

They have also lost exclusive use of the ring. Reid is back in, this time aiming at a colleague's pads. He is on his toes, jabbing, hooking, then planting himself to release the upper cut. The pounding of the pads is ferocious. You shudder to think what one misdirected shot would do to his mate.

Hughes has joined one of his old sidekicks, who is coaxing a mountain of a young man through the rudimentary moves of the trade. Sam Rawlinson is Hughes' great British heavyweight hope. He is 19, 6 ft 5 in. and a genuine heavyweight. He is also untutored and untried. First things first.

Gomez and the suspended schoolboy are exercising on a mat, two others are skipping and another three are talking too much. 'Who's yapping?' Any response is futile. 'All three – twenty, up there.' Hughes points to a high bar and supervises as, one by one, they pull themselves up to the bar 20 muscle-aching times.

Everything about this dingy little gym appears to have an uplifting effect. The discipline and perspiration are essential but so are the humour and fellowship. That much-vaunted mantra of modern sport, 'work ethic', has relevance here only in a wider, more noble and humanitarian context. Those who descend the grimy stairwell at the end of training today dream of fame and fortune, or perhaps nothing more than comfort and dignity in life. For some it is a triumph that they can dream at all.

Gomez dreams of winning the Lonsdale Belt outright, which will become a reality if he successfully defends his British title for the third time, against the Scotsman, Ian McLeod, at the Kingsway Leisure Centre, Widnes. Hughes has told Gomez to stay at his hotel until mid-evening since his bout, the top of the bill, is scheduled for nine o'clock. Hughes and his assistant seconds, Steve Goodwin and Mike Jackson, arrive at the venue for the show to find their champion waiting for them.

'What are you doing here?' It is a rhetorical question. Hughes knows

Gomez as well as anyone. He knows his man is pumped up for the occasion and couldn't bear to kill time in a hotel room. Just being here makes the fight seem closer, the Lonsdale Belt loom larger in his imagination. Right on cue an official walks into the narrow dressing-room and opens a briefcase to reveal that ornate prize.

'We don't want that in here,' Hughes protests. 'He's got to win it.'

The official mutters apologetically but Gomez cannot resist cradling and then kissing the belt before it is placed back in the briefcase and taken away. There is scarcely room to swing a belt in here. Hughes has three other fighters – Thomas McDonagh, Michael Jennings and Darren Rhodes – on the bill and all are sharing this cramped room. The cornermen stick strips of tape on the tiled walls as Gomez selects a CD to feed into a portable stereo. Soothing music it is not. 'Who Let the Dogs Out?' reverberates around the Collyhurst and Moston bunker. The more Hughes screws up his face, the more Gomez turns up the volume. Fun and by-play are as evident here as they are back in the gym. McDonagh, just 20, is too much of a joker for Hughes' liking. The trainer and the other boxers attempt to wind him up with warnings that his opponent, Richie Murray, is intent on revenge. 'He's been bragging about what he's going to do to you,' Hughes cautions, barely attempting to hide the smirk.

McDonagh, dancing and shadow boxing at the end of the room, is unmoved. 'He'll never crack this chin,' he declares, throwing up his head in defiance. 'Cement can crack, but not this chin.'

A chorus of 'Oh, I wouldn't be so sure' comes back at him. He sneers and dances some more as the rest snigger. Hughes and his assistants are taping up Rhodes and Jennings. They wrap the hands in bandage, which is held firm and reinforced by those strips of plaster.

Rhodes, a middleweight from Leeds, is the club's first representative to take the walk along the corridor and into the hall. He is accompanied by Hughes, Goodwin and Jackson. More support is already in place, on the front row. Anthony Farnell, whose next fight is in the New Year, yells advice as Rhodes tries to run down the elusive Paul Wesley, a 38 year old from the quirky Nobby Nobbs' stable in Birmingham. The wisecracking Nobbs glories in mass defeat. His gym has been dubbed 'Losers Limited' – or 'Losers Unlimited', as some wag suggested would be more appropriate. He makes a living out of supplying cannon fodder for shows up and down the land. Nobbs' grin widens as his man sways out of Rhodes' range, showing scant interest in trading punches.

'Start boxing, you fairy,' bellows an exasperated punter from the back of the hall.

By the end of the four rounds, no one outside the Hughes camp appears to care any more. Rhodes has won clearly and duly gets the verdict. Congratulatory hugs and slaps welcome him back to the dressing-room. One down, three to go. Gomez is last on the club's schedule and he is straining at the leash. He contorts his face, smashes a fist into the metal lockers and follows up with a butt. 'Michael,' an anxious Hughes shouts. Gomez, saying nothing, laces up his red and blue boots.

Next on duty is Jennings, and his arrival cranks up the volume in the hall. The welterweight, from Chorley, has an enthusiastic fan club and he responds with a convincing win against a more competitive representative of the Nobbs camp, Paul Denton.

Gomez's supporters are now making their presence felt. It is a football-style following, the chants reflecting a common allegiance to Manchester City. Many of his fans wear City's light blue and white. More peculiarly, they wear sombreros. Gomez became Armstrong's nickname as he grew obsessed with the spectacular exploits of Wilfredo Gomez, WBC featherweight champion in 1984 and WBA super-featherweight title winner a year later. He decided to change his name to Gomez and his supporters captured the mood with what was deemed appropriate headgear. The fact that Wilfredo Gomez was not Mexican but Puerto Rican was presumably considered an irrelevant minor detail. The Michael Gomez roadshow was up and running.

McDonagh, from the Blackley district of Manchester, follows Jennings and faces Murray, an unsmiling, muscular Liverpudlian trained by Brendan Ingle, the Irishman who introduced Naseem Hamed to boxing. McDonagh, who beat Murray over four rounds in their previous meeting, prowls around the ring as the MC – the ubiquitous Mike Goodall – waits for Sky TV to give him the OK. Hughes winces as he climbs up to the corner. He fell and hurt his back in the shower during his trip to London for Reid's WBF title fight. Reid demolished Mike Gormley, a late substitute, to win in the first round but Hughes returned home in agony.

The normally assured McDonagh looks a mite uncomfortable as Murray bulldozes forward. 'Pick him off, Thomas, pick him off,' Hughes shouts. Thomas has to pick *himself* off the floor in the third round after Murray bowls him over with a move straight out of WWF RAW. McDonagh milks the situation for laughs, stretching himself out on the canvas in mock distress before jumping to his feet. Murray, meanwhile, is receiving a stern warning from the referee.

McDonagh draws blood from Murray's nose in the fourth and puts him down in the fifth. Murray conveniently loses his gum shield, earns some respite and survives the round. McDonagh crosses himself before the sixth and final round. 'Pick it up,' Hughes urges. 'Try and stop him.' McDonagh cannot finish his man inside the distance, but he gets the points verdict and Hughes gets a kiss from his protégé.

McDonagh sticks to the script in his TV interview, insisting he likes to entertain. Hughes is suitably dismayed. 'He's going on the building sites to learn about work,' the trainer says. 'Work to him is like a cross to Dracula. He's barmy. He's that lazy he turned down work as Father Christmas. He's got to get serious. He's telling jokes between rounds! He could be as big as Naz, but he's got to stop messing about.'

For all that, Hughes has three wins out of three. The fourth, and biggest, fight will soon be on. The atmosphere in the hall intensifies with the sense of anticipation. Farnell and another of Britain's rising stars, Ricky Hatton, here to support his brother, Matthew, sign autographs for a stream of well-wishers. Frank Maloney, one of boxing's more familiar figures, chats with members of the press. Mike Goodall tightens the ropes. The official with THAT briefcase arrives at ringside and places it on a table.

The stage is set and the challenger, McLeod, is the first to make his way to the ring. He is clad in tartan and has a white towel over his head. A volley of boos greets him. Sky's camera in the Gomez dressing-room catches the champion aiming another punch at the locker as he makes for the door. 'Look at that,' yelps a startled Ian Darke, Sky's commentator. A rendition of the 'Mexican Hat Dance' and thunderous applause greet Gomez. He is robed in the blue and white of Manchester City. His black shorts seem to reach his ankles. The shape of a shamrock has been shaved into the back of his head.

Chants of 'Gomez, Gomez, knock him out' almost drown out the sound of the first bell. Their hero, who has a record of 22 wins and 3 defeats from 25 contests, makes a confident start. McLeod, 31, is docked a point in the second round for holding and sustains a cut eye in the third. Gomez is assured, busy, on top. He has an excellent fourth round, leaving McLeod's corner with more work to do on the eye.

Suddenly, in the fifth, McLeod retaliates. He lures Gomez into a brawl and the champion emerges with a cut over his left eye. The mood and complexion of the fight change dramatically. McLeod is rejuvenated and his whirlwind start to the sixth stuns Gomez. Now the champion is warned about his use of the head. Farnell and another camp supporter, former boxer Pat Barrett, desperately scream advice. Hughes tells his man to weave, to move his head from side to side. The barrage of instructions reflects their concerns.

Gomez gathers his wits but he cannot contain the obdurate Scot. It is a brutal, bloody, ugly slog. Gomez is having to trade flailing shots. Barrett is near apoplectic. 'Tell him, tell him,' he shouts to the corner.

'We do, but he won't listen.'

McLeod is warned for a low punch in the tenth and Gomez finishes the round with a crisp combination to the head. That buoys him for the 11th, but it is still hard and gruesome. The referee's shirt is soaked in blood and sweat. 'I'm glad it's not me in there,' Barrett says.

Hughes tries to lift Gomez through the last round. Long before the end he is calling: 'Come on, Mike, last ten seconds.' Barrett smiles. He's heard that one before. 'I know he's Irish, Brian, but he's not stupid!'

The bell releases the tension. Gomez has won and the crowd, subdued for much of the fight, can acclaim their champion. Sombreros are tossed into the air. Some reach the ring. Gomez plants one on his head. So does McLeod. The referee, Richie Davies, climbs out of the ring, wiping himself down with a towel. He, too, has had a gruelling 12 rounds. He scored it 118–110, a comfortable margin. It scarcely felt comfortable for the Gomez camp. However, their man has his belt and he holds it aloft. Hughes wipes his eye and has City's blue and white draped over him for his trouble. Gomez is bubbly in front of the TV cameras, admitting he trained too hard for this fight, but he takes the bait when he is asked if he is ready to tackle Acelino Freitas, the WBO super-featherweight champion. 'I'm not getting bigheaded. Let's get Freitas on,' he says.

Hughes is determined to quell any talk of a match with the dangerous Brazilian. 'That was too hard,' he confides, making his way back to the dressing-room. 'He came to a peak too early for this fight. McLeod kept coming back at him.'

Gomez flops into a chair in the dressing-room and Hughes examines his eye. 'That hurts,' Gomez moans.

'What, after the 12 rounds you've been through?' Rhodes asks.

The doctor arrives and prepares to stitch up the wound. He injects Gomez, who is having difficulty coming to terms with his first cut. 'I can't believe it,' he says, shaking his head. 'He put everything into it because it was his last fight. How many stitches will it need, Doc?'

'I think it will be five.'

'Can you do it from the inside, Doc?' Hughes asks.

As the doctor goes to work with his needle and thread, Hughes finds a gold medallion on the floor. 'It's Michael's. Put it with his gum shield,' he tells Gomez's friend.

Gomez, who also has bruising under his eye, tells anyone listening: 'I'm going to sleep for two weeks.'

The doctor completes his work and says: 'Take them out on Saturday. The local practice will do.'

Hughes suggests a full week. 'Leave them till Monday, to make sure.'

Gomez has an ice pack on his head and still doesn't understand. 'I can't believe I got cut. First time.'

Referee Davies, a burly, gregarious character, enters the dressing-room and makes for the still-seated Gomez. 'You're a pleasure to work with,' he tells the boxer. 'I'm pleased for you. Have a good Christmas. You should see the blood next door. He's in agony. I think he's broken his hand. I was that close,' he says, indicating barely an inch with his thumb and index finger, 'from disqualifying him. It was the hardest fight I've had. I didn't want to stop it. It was a great fight.'

Davies departs and Gomez groans: 'I'm ill.'

Hughes is unsympathetic. 'You will be, throwing that City thing on me. Nice cold shower now for you.'

Gomez is still rooted to the chair. He spurts the words out like machine-gun fire: 'I don't want any more of those. It was all a clash of heads, and because I've got a reputation of being mean the ref was looking at me. I would have stopped him, but he wanted to leave on a high note. I'm made up about the belt. I've already got the cabinet for it. Cost me £609.95.

'I've got to get back to work. I've got to work on my defence and listen and learn more. I could have won on my jab but that's not my style. I took too many shots because I was thinking one fight ahead. He did rough me up, and hit me in the privates. He's a tough lad. I thought the ref could have disqualified him but he kept looking at me. He told me to keep it clean but he was dirtier. He tried to psyche me out but I'm too good a pro for that. The eye never worried me. Brian does an excellent job. I don't get tired – 12 rounds is too short for me. I'm good for 15. It's back to the drawing board – defence and boxing skills. I started to get stupid and silly. I need to calm down and not be too excited.'

A small group of reporters has squeezed into the room and they ask Gomez about his plans. Maybe a date with Paul Ingle?

'Let's get it on,' is the reflex response. No fighter wants to be known for ducking an opponent. 'I've only got two and a half years left in boxing. I want to go out at 26, so I've got to get some big money fights and give it everything. I don't want to be punch drunk. I always give good fights. Ingle would be a better fight. He's a world champion. Give him respect. I've got more desire. Naz is the long-term target. That's where the money is. I've got the chin, I've got the heart, I've got the punch. I'd go to Sheffield and take him now. I want to sit down with Brian and see what to do.'

The reporters seek Hughes' thoughts on his fighter's future. He is attracting interest from American TV. There is a suggestion Frank Warren, his promoter, wants to match him with Freitas.

Hughes' reaction is brusque: 'I decide who he fights, not Frank Warren. I'll have a talk with him.'

Half an hour on and Gomez is still in his shorts, but he is chirpier. He is on his feet. 'I won the stitches battle, as well. He had eight, I've had only five.'

He plants a kiss on Hughes and hugs him. 'Thanks for everything, Brian. Best cuts man in the business.' He shows his appreciation by giving his ailing boss a back massage. He is not so accommodating when Hughes tries to put the gloves Gomez wore tonight in his bag. Gomez wins that fight, too.

Hughes sits down and smiles the smile of the old sage. His son hands him a mobile phone so that he can speak to his wife. 'My back's not been too bad but those tablets seem to have worn off now. Can you do me eggs on toast when we get back? I'm just seeing to Michael. He's got five stitches. Yeah, five. Great fight. All four won.'

Gomez wanders out of the room muttering something about wanting to find a mirror to look at his eye. He beckons Hughes to follow him into the corridor and they put their heads together. Some things are private.

When they return Hughes issues instructions to Gomez and his friend: 'Cold shower, rub down, keep warm and lots of cold water. Plenty of ice. Stay with him. He might get giddy.'

The friend nods.

'Plenty of water and it will be right as rain,' Hughes emphasises. 'See you tomorrow, Mike. And don't be going in that smoky club!'

Before he leaves, Hughes pops into the dressing-room next door. 'I must just go and see the Scotch lad,' he explains. McLeod, who has indicated he now plans to retire, is badly marked but in no apparent distress. 'Well done,' Hughes says, offering his hand to those in the room. 'Great fight.'

He strolls out to the car and gingerly settles into the passenger seat. His back is giving him serious gyp, but the results tonight have more than compensated for his discomfort and, at 11.25 p.m., he is dropped off at his home, secure in the knowledge that Rosemary will have his eggs on toast ready.

'It's been a great end to the year,' he says. 'I've told them they can all go and enjoy their Christmases. But that Thomas – he'll be out jitterbugging now. I don't know what I'm going to do with him.'

4 ☆ BROTHERS IN ARMS

MARTIN JOLLEY'S LIFE OUTSIDE OF BOXING APPEARS TO HAVE THE solid foundations of normality. He lives in a normal, three-bed semi, in a normal street of Wingerworth, just outside the normal town of Chesterfield. He returns home from the early shift at the printing firm, pulls off his shoes, picks up his mail and switches on the answer phone. He passes through his newly equipped kitchen and into the lounge/dining area. The elegant, light-coloured parquet floor is his own handiwork. Other evidence of Jolley's resourcefulness, however, uncovers his previous life. The garage has been converted into a gym and a bedroom transformed into a library of boxing videos. His latest is ready to be shown on the wide-screen TV. The switch to normality may be a painful process.

'This was my last fight,' he says, aiming the remote control. 'Against Lee Molloy, in Liverpool. He's from Liverpool. Game kid, nothing special. I took the fight at a day's notice. I mean, I'm nothing special, but as you can see I'm well within myself and not being taken apart at all. He obviously got the verdict on points, the fight being in Liverpool.'

The video moves on to his Masters fight that never was. Mike Goodall announces Jolley's retirement and delivers his tribute. Second time around, those words, 'men die in this ring', are just as chilling. The video commentator cannot be accused of exaggeration or sensationalism. 'An emotional day for Martin Jolley,' he concludes, matter-of-factly. Also

44

second time around, it seems a pity that Jolley did not have the last word. 'I think maybe I did want to say something because I tend to find sometimes that MCs don't say it quite as well as you can say it,' he confides. 'But once I got in there my legs were shaking, which is very unusual for me entering the ring. I was very nervous. I would probably have messed it up because I was emotionally upset and didn't think I'd have been able to come out with it very clearly. I would have thanked all the people of Chesterfield for their support and said I was sorry I'd never won a title for them. I think I would have done that day. It was always within my capability to beat that guy.

'Every time I see the end there I feel myself filling up because it brings it home to me. Mentally I am very good at dealing with anything and everything, because I have been through the wars, not only in the ring but outside as well. You know me, Jolley by name, Jolley by nature. I'm a fool and play about and take the Mick out of myself to cheer up anybody who's down. People can see this coming out in my personality again. And normally it's when I've had a drink, because that's when you show your true personality. I am relaxed. It's different when you're in training and can't have a meal or even a cup of tea. You certainly can't have a night out. I don't think people realise the pressures a boxer has during the preparation for a fight, let alone when he's in there fighting. It's the everyday mental torture.

'I'm very disappointed, because I know what I could have done that day, but I have to admit I feel a different person. I feel better in myself. I feel as though I'm talking better, saying more words in sentences. They say that boxers can't string more than two words together but I know I can. I've put weight on, I feel healthier inside. I feel like the weight of the world has been taken off my shoulders.

'Don't forget that being in the limelight means you're under pressure all the time. When you go for a drink folk point their fingers at you, saying, "What's he doing out when he's got a fight coming up? He should be in bed." To my way of thinking you should do what suits you as an individual, whatever makes you tick.'

Jolley draws strength and inspiration from friends and family.

'I'm one of four kids, two boys and two girls. One of my sisters works with the mentally handicapped and she has a mentally handicapped boy. God must have put him there because He knew she'd look after him. My mother is very prim and proper. She hates swearing. She's pin-perfect in everything – her mannerisms, her dress code, the way she talks, the way she presents herself. I do get a lot of that from my mother. But then I get the chill-out side from my dad. He is a character. He's still working. He'll die up a ladder. He's 61, he has aches and pains, but he's a worker. If he won the lottery tomorrow he'd still work.

'When I was young we had everything. We were born with silver spoons in our mouths. My dad was a big industrial contractor, with 30 or 40 men working for him. Then it went from everything to nothing, basically because my dad wasn't business-minded or educated in that way. He went bust and the bank took the house, the cars, the caravan, money in the bank, everything. But he paid everybody off to keep his good name. It's taken him nearly 20 years to get back on his feet again. But he's a grafter and this is where I get my mental power. He will not be defeated, even though folk may have looked on him as a loser.

'Like me with boxing. Just because I've not got the verdict it doesn't mean I've lost. Ask the guy I've fought, not the referee. Trainers have come up to me and told me I should have had the decision. The father of one opponent came up to me, shoved 20 quid in my shorts and said that was the hardest fight his son had ever had. We know the referee gives it to the local fighter. That's why when I lost on points I didn't give a damn, because I know boxing is corrupt like that. I can't prove it, but I know it's working practice. So why be depressed? You either hang up your gloves or keep fighting. I've always loved boxing so I carried on.

'I've never been asked to throw a fight, probably because everybody knows I love boxing so much I wouldn't. My heart and soul are in it. I think it does happen. I've heard rumours that it does. But I'd fight for nothing. These up-and-coming champions are bound to be confident, but it goes to their heads a bit. They've got the swagger of bullies. That has always driven me on against them. They may be unbeaten, but I think to myself, "I can beat you."

'If I'd had the proper preparation, six weeks' notice for a fight, I'd have won every one. But it doesn't work like that, not for guys like me. If it wasn't for guys like me there wouldn't be boxing. Your secretaries, your referees, your inspectors, your trainers, your managers, your promoters – they wouldn't have jobs. Because if everybody relied on six weeks' notice for a fight, there wouldn't be any fights and there wouldn't be any champions. We're classed as cannon fodder and we are. At the end of the day they give the other guy every advantage and if he loses there's something up with him. He shouldn't be in there.'

Getting a fight at short notice can present a logistical as well as physical challenge for a part-time boxer.

'I've had a fight at, say, Bradford, gone back to work for half past nine and done a night shift. Or I've done a day shift, finished at two o'clock, driven down the motorway to London, got changed, got in the ring, had a punch-up, set off back home, gone to bed and been up at five o'clock for work the following morning.'

There have been the occasional perks, such as an all-expenses-paid trip to Duisburg, Germany. Alas for Jolley, it was not a five-star performance against Ahmed Oener.

'It was my last fight before I retired the first time and I went over with the impression this guy I was fighting was something really special. When you think you're going to get hurt it's funny how, even if they don't hit you hard, it does seem to hurt. So I was a bit hesitant to start with. He was big and strong and had a lot of support. But gradually I realised he wasn't so good after all. In fact he was rubbish. I was like a different fighter. I broke his nose; I had him all over the place. I was so excited I dived in carelessly and got caught in the fourth by this damn stupid shot, one of those punches you just don't see coming but has the effect on your legs that you just can't get up. Eventually I did get up and got back to my corner and didn't know whether to laugh or cry. I ended up doing both. I said to Glyn, "I can't believe it, he's rubbish." Then Glyn started laughing because he could hear the TV commentators saying something about me laughing, as though it was a set-up. But the referee took the first chance to stop it because I'd started to give him some stick back.

'We went to a party after and as well as his broken nose the other guy had both his eyes nearly shut – one was black as black could be – his lip was up and he looked a mess. I hadn't got a mark. I got showered, suit on, and the girls were all over me. Glyn couldn't believe it. He said, "Anybody would think you were the bloody winner." We had a great time. Five-star hotel, fantastic place, pool, sauna, jacuzzi, free drinks. We made a meal of it.'

Not that Jolley always came up smelling of roses. There was the infamous occasion when he tried to act as peacemaker and sparked a mass brawl. He was in the camp of Sheffield light-heavyweight Jason Barker, who lost a grudge match – stopped in the fifth – against Paul 'Silky' Jones. After the fight, Jolley approached Jones and proffered an olive branch.

'I told him "Well done," gave him a pat, a hug, kissed him on the cheek, the way you do, nowt queer like. I thought that was the perfect opportunity for him to make it up with Jason, so I said to Paul, "Come on, pal, bury the hatchet." He went very stern, a bit nasty and said, "No." His trainer, Ian Alcock, told me to get out. That made me a bit mad but I told myself to calm down. So I went back to the changing-room and started cutting Jason's bandages off.

'Ian Alcock decided to join in, cutting the bandages off the other hand, to try and make amends. He'd not spoken to me since he told me off in the ring. Now you're supposed to cut away from the main vein so that you don't risk going into it. But he was cutting down to the wrist so I pulled his arm away. Ian swore at me and that was like a red rag to a bull. He didn't have to say another word. He was horizontal. His mate decided to join in and everything went pear-shaped. Silky brought the doormen in, so then Glyn jumped in and it was just mayhem.'

Jolley's life has been a roller-coaster of laughter and tears. He will be eternally grateful for the influence of boxing on its course, yet would prefer his son to stay out of the ring.

'I would always let my son learn to box for self-defence and I couldn't stop him if he really wanted to box. But I would always advise him not to. You've seen what's happened to me. I've got the initial stage of a blood clot, a haemorrhage on the side of my head. It isn't through boxing entirely. They can prove, 90 per cent, it's down to when I got glassed in the face. However, I'll be totally honest, my speech has deteriorated. My memory was always good – now that has deteriorated. So that means something is happening inside my head. Now, although there can be risks in other sports, such as in football, heading the ball, in boxing you go out there intending to maim or hurt your opponent, so for that reason I would like him to stay away from it. It is dangerous.

'It's a very good sport and now there's no National Service I think boxing is a good way of disciplining these reckless young lads. I think they ought to do something, such as bringing back National Service, to get them off the streets. They walk around, taking drugs, nicking, breaking into homes and beating up old women for money. It's just a bad social climate, and that's why the streets are like they are now.'

Jolley is taking up the offer to become an inspector and plans to use the position to root out some of the game's ills.

'I'm not going to do it all on my own but I think I can give boxing the benefit of my knowledge and try to influence things. I'm a reader of anything important and that includes the rules in boxing. I'll spell out the rules as they are and any promoter or manager who tries to pull a fast one can get ready, because I'm not having it. I wouldn't have it when I was fighting and I won't have any of them do it to other fighters. I'll be open with all of them. I won't tell any lies.

'I see it as a form of policing, controlling boxing. As an inspector you weigh them in, ensure the contest is pretty even and, although the doctor checks them medically, you can pick up on any deterioration problems just by talking to a boxer. Being an ex-boxer now, I would be able to see the signs and pull the guy to one side so I didn't embarrass him, and say, "Hey up kid, your left hand looks a bit dodgy. Do you think you ought to be fighting tonight?" Let him give me a good, genuine answer and I'll know if he's all right to fight that night. If he carries on with the injury, or he starts slurring, or his balance goes and he starts wobbling a bit, I'll know he's not all right.

'Sometimes boxers are affected mentally. You hear stories about boxers getting a bit aggressive. They can't handle the pressures, they can't handle losing. If I know somebody who's going like that, getting fired up a bit, I'll go to him like a father figure, talk to him and calm him down. Hopefully he'll open up to me and then I can give him sound advice.'

Jolley would doubtless administer more paternal care in his role of trainer, but he has his reservations about pursuing this activity.

'I've got a trainer's licence but unless you've got a fighter to the level of British, European or Commonwealth champion, you don't earn anything from boxing. I'd say three-quarters of your money is thrown back into equipment, travelling, time off work and so on. I've been lucky with my firm, but some companies wouldn't have it – you'd either box or have a full-time job. I want to train but it's got to be done properly, got to have good backing. I'm not saying the biggest, poshest, fully equipped gyms are the best, but the new guys do tend to look at the mantelpiece. And if you've not got the weights, showers, saunas and jacuzzis, they're going somewhere else. They seem to want the luxury more than the quality.

'I can give them the quality; good, experienced advice. I'm not blowing my own trumpet. It's what I've been told. I'm brilliant on pads. I can push them to the limit. But hurting them physically is not enough. Mentally I can improve them, I can make them feel like a world champion. Some trainers are good but mentally they don't know how to hype a boxer up. Once a boxer is in there fighting it's too late. You can't turn the clock back. If he walks out of there having given up, thrown the towel in, to me he's lost face and that's the worst thing for a boxer.

'If he comes back after the first round and he's not been knocked down but I think the other kid is a bit good for my lad, and I know my lad can fight better, I'll lift him up. When you're up there it's like being in a cloud. You can't really see outside the ring. I'll tell him what a good combination he threw. He might have thrown only two shots, but believe you me, if you talk to him the right way you can make him believe he's caught his man with the best shot of the round. In truth that kid has knocked hell out of your man but if you can win him over mentally, you can talk him into anything. I guarantee, if you get to him properly, he'll go out there and fight like a different boxer.

'You've got to know your fighter inside out. That is vital to being a good trainer. If you know he can fight better, and you're not scared about sending him back out there for another round, then do so. But if you know your fighter has given his all, that the other guy is too good, then it's time to think of a way out. You shout to the referee, "He's twisted his ankle" or "He's broken his hand" or "He's choking, he's been sick twice." You've got to pull your man out. Always think about safety first. He'll fight another day then. If he goes back he might come out on a stretcher.'

Jolley's every word and sentiment conveys a fundamental morality. Even his base instincts encapsulate the virtues of simplicity and honesty. Fighting, like running, is an inherently natural human instinct. The ethical argument can never be won but Jolley, in common with so many of his ilk, has discovered purpose, mutual respect and dignity in boxing. They are brothers in arms and the bond will outlive their careers.

'It's really the ultimate, isn't it?' he reasons. 'There's no further to take it than hitting another man. You can't threaten them more than actually hitting them, so the physical contact is the end of the line. That's why you find boxers are quite close outside the ring and become very friendly. You have no reason to feel any bitterness. You've already expended all your aggression and nastiness towards each other, so what more is there to show?

'There was only one guy I ever felt a bit bitter towards. Win or lose, I'll always make a fuss of my opponent afterwards. This was a coloured guy – and I'm not prejudiced, because my girlfriend's got a half-caste kid. I gave this guy about a stone and a half and he decked me about four times and won. Afterwards I said, "Well done," and told him he'd boxed well and did nothing but compliment him. He shrugged his shoulders, pushed me away and didn't want to talk to me. However, two years later, when he'd packed in and I was still boxing, I fought one of his gym pals and I gave him a lesson in boxing. He came up to me, talking as sweet as anything. I think he must have been hyped up at the time. The camaraderie is brilliant.'

The memories and friendships will doubtless comfort him through his enforced retirement. So will the growing years of his children, Callum, six, and Geneva, five.

'My daughter is named after the Geneva Conference and Conventions,' he explains. 'I've always sorted out problems with my fists. The Geneva Conference and Conventions are about countries coming together, solving their problems without going to war and treating people in a humane way. I think that's a better way. Fighting is not the answer. I turned to boxing because I was getting in trouble with street-fighting, so at least it was legal. I could vent my aggression and anger and not get done for it. It is wrong, but unfortunately the way the social climate is, that was my answer.'

They are proud of their *Full Monty* in Sheffield, and another star-studded show at the city's Arena is duly promoted as *The Full Monty II*. Joe Calzaghe and Richie Woodhall top the bill, fighting for the WBO super-middleweight title. Acelino Freitas, the hard-punching Brazilian, defends his WBO super-featherweight title. For British fans, one of the main attractions is Paul Ingle's defence of the IBF featherweight title. Freitas concludes his business against Daniel Alicea in one destructive round and smiles broadly for the cameras.

Sky TV are enjoying their show and eagerly anticipate Ingle's match with South Africa's Mbulelo Botile, which precedes the Calzaghe–Woodhall fight. So are the BBC Radio Five Live commentary team. Soon, however, they are describing a gruesome struggle for the man from Scarborough. He is caught and shaken in the opening round and appears powerless to contain Botile. They paint the picture of a bleeding, pulverised face; a limp figure caught in a storm of unstoppable punches. It is no longer a contest but a slaughter. Towards the end of the 11th round Ingle goes down. The bell sounds before Botile can finish it but on-lookers suspect Ingle will be spared any further punishment by his corner. However, boxers and boxing folk are driven by a pride and courage that defy cold, objective calculation and Ingle stands for the final round. Twenty seconds later the fight is over. A left hook from Botile puts down the defenceless, hapless Ingle and the referee indicates the end.

The minutes, hours and days that follow are the constant dread of boxing. Ingle is fighting for his life and the sport is again in the dock. Ingle, given oxygen on the canvas, taken swiftly to Sheffield's Northern General Hospital and then to the Royal Hallamshire Hospital to have a blood clot removed from his brain, is benefiting from the lessons learned in previous serious incidents of this kind. The rapid response gives him the hope some never had. But the debate on the morality of boxing rages across the front and back pages of the national newspapers and at the top of TV and radio news bulletins.

Ingle's manager, Frank Maloney, and his trainer, Steve Pollard, are taken to task for allowing their boxer to confront that fateful 12th. They maintain they were satisfied he was fit to continue and that he was willing to do so. Pollard refutes any suggestion of undue coercion, or that Ingle had any problem of dehydration as a consequence of his making the weight. The subject of dehydration and staggered weight checks is taken up by boxing officials as well as the media. The wider, ethical question is inevitably aired by media and politicians. Calls for a total ban on boxing or at least an outlawing of blows to the head are countered by claims that the fight game would be driven underground. The argument that more men and women are killed or maimed in other sports, such as equestrianism, mountaineering and motor-racing, is no argument at all, since in boxing points are scored by hitting the opponent and victory assured by knock-out. It is more a matter of choice and the freedom to exercise that choice. The *Independent* newspaper carries a leader under the headline: 'Boxing is barbaric – but it should not be banned.'

Those in the game, men like Brian Hughes and Martin Jolley, will point to the positive aspects of boxing; the opportunities it presents to many who would otherwise self-destruct and worse. The grim scene at the Sheffield Arena and Ingle's desperate plight have, however, given Jolley a fresh perspective on his own case.

'It makes me realise I'm lucky,' he says. 'If I'd fought again, that might have been me. Maybe my retirement was a godsend. I've still got my life and the chance of seeing my kids. Paul shouldn't have come out for that last round. The corner should have pulled him out, because a boxer's instinct is to go on. It's up to a good trainer to take that decision. You think you're all right, but the brain is a computer, and highly sensitive. Weight should not have been a problem for Paul but he fought for 12 rounds, and that is a long fight when you are being hit as much as he was.'

Ingle is still in intensive care, his condition described as 'critical but stable', when the Court of Appeal rules in favour of the former boxer, Michael Watson, in his case against the British Boxing Board of Control (BBBC). The appeal judges uphold a verdict of the High Court, that the BBBC had owed Watson a duty of care on the night, in 1991, when he suffered injuries similar to those sustained by Ingle. Watson poses for pictures, smiling and dutifully giving the 'V' for victory sign on the pavement in the Strand. But Watson is still in a wheelchair and may never receive the £1 million damages. Representatives of the BBBC indicate such a settlement would bankrupt them.

5 ☆ HOME COMFORTS

BRIAN HUGHES ISSUES DIRECTIONS TO HIS HOME, AT CHADDERTON, Oldham, in the certain knowledge that the final landmark is unmissable.

'You'll see the van outside, a white one with "Collyhurst and Moston Lads' Club" on it.'

Christmas cards form a colourful collage in the front room. A crib in the corner and a crucifix on the wall confirm the family's religious conviction. A photograph of Hughes' beloved Busby Babes hangs in the back room. It is Manchester United's last line-up before the Munich air disaster, in 1958. Hughes finishes his tea and sits on the floor of the front room, straightening his troublesome back against a radiator.

The latest update on Paul Ingle's condition in Sheffield is encouraging. He is showing signs of improvement and boxing begins to breathe a collective sigh of relief. As a trainer, Hughes has been faced with that unenviable dilemma: does he pull a struggling boxer out of a fight, or let him carry on in the hope of turning it around?

'About five years ago we went to South Africa with a young coloured kid called Delroy Waul,' he says from his chosen seating position. 'He was fighting an unbeaten South African lad and I took Rosemary with us for the first time on a trip. The South African lad was really rough. We'd seen the tapes of him. Del was at the end of his career and we were told this lad marked up easily, so we told Del to have a go. First two or three rounds he absolutely hammered this fella, cut him to smithereens. If it had been any other country they would have stopped it, but it was South Africa, he was a white fighter, and he drew all the crowds. As the fight went on Del was like a light that was going out, getting dimmer and dimmer. Although he was badly cut, this fella was strong and he started to get to Del and I knew he was going to knock him out. When the bell rang I looked into Del's eyes and there was a vacant look, so I stopped the fight.

'I nearly got lynched, didn't I, Rosemary? Everybody was screaming, "What you stopped it for?" They wanted to see this Delroy Waul flattened. There was no police to protect us. We were lucky to get out alive. But it's safety first. Got to be. I thought of that on Saturday night with poor Paul Ingle.

'We've got a young heavyweight who I think is going to be exceptionally good and on Saturday morning we spent two and a half hours with him and another heavyweight, just practising defence. There was that much sweat in the ring at the end it was like a boating lake. They must have lost a stone each, going through all those manoeuvres. A lot's been said after the Paul Ingle fight, that it was a liberty and this, that and the other happened, but people don't see this other side to boxing. It's a game of chess with gloves on. It's moves and counter-moves.'

But it can also have horrifying consequences. Hughes is a family man. He has three sons and a daughter. He is transparently compassionate, caring and fair-minded. Surely he must examine himself and ask what he is doing in this business? He strokes his cropped grey beard and shuffles a little uneasily.

'I do. Very, very often. I did it last Monday when Michael Gomez won the Lonsdale Belt outright and I saw in that fight things that the referee should have stopped. There were low blows and it was a blatant butt that cut Michael's eye. I shouted to the referee that it was diabolical. After the fight Michael was really worried. He called me out of the dressing-room and said, "Look, I'm weeing blood. What shall I do?"'

So that was the private conversation at Widnes.

'I told him to just drink water, don't go any place where they were selling alcohol or where it was smoky, just go home and if it was like that the following morning I'd take him to hospital. When something like that happens you think, "What the hell am I doing? What's all this about?" The only thing I can say in defence is that there were 12 climbers killed last week, trying to rescue a dog, and no one has said they should stop. I know what they are going on about – it's blows to the head and so on.'

But isn't the object of the exercise in boxing to hurt the other man?

'No, it's not,' Hughes says adamantly. 'It's called the noble art of self-defence. The idea is to out-manoeuvre and out-think and, all right, out-punch the other fella. But there's no intention, not as far as I know, to cause damage to the other fella. I can swear on that. You'll get these trainers saying, "You've got to kill him," like Mike Tyson's lot, but that's the only thing they understand because it's absolutely brutal over there. They're at the top of the league, getting millions and millions, but down at our level, the British level, I've never heard any trainer tell his fella to go out and damage someone. You might get some needle with trainers and boxers, but after the fight it's all forgotten.'

Hughes cites the example of his club in the case for boxing's defence.

'God knows what would happen to a lot of the kids we've got in the gym if it wasn't for boxing. Like the lads who have been suspended from school. All the teachers are made up when they go back. They can't believe the change in their behaviour.'

Hughes can perhaps empathise with some of those youngsters. He would never claim to have been a model pupil. His was not an environment that nurtured academics.

'I never saw my dad till he died. I was brought up by my mother and older brother, who lived with our gran, further down the street. My mother re-married and had another five kids. Six of us are still alive. I was no good at school. I couldn't read or write, couldn't spell. I was hopeless. I didn't want to go into an apprenticeship. I worked on the market, Smithfield, just labouring, loading the lorries with bags of potatoes and veg. What really interested me was football and boxing.'

Among his chums at St Patrick's School in Collyhurst were two boys called Norbert Stiles and Brian Kidd, who grew up to play for Manchester United and England and were members of the club's 1968 European Cup-winning side. Stiles was also in the England team that won the World Cup in 1966. Hughes, too, developed associations with United. As a passionate fan he watched training sessions as well as those early, mesmerising European Cup performances. He was spell-bound by the coaching of Matt Busby's assistant, Jimmy Murphy, and became a friend of the Welshman and his family. Kidd and Stiles joined the youngsters at the Collyhurst Lads' Club.

Hughes recalls: 'Brian used to come training in the gym, Nobby would come down, we had loads down. We always had football teams as well as the boxing then. Len Cantello, who played for West Brom and Bolton, was with us. We had a lot of good players. Nobby's still a good pal.

'I started boxing as an amateur, first of all for the school and then different clubs, including Collyhurst Lads' Club. Then I went to Lily Lane, a famous amateur club in Moston, not far from where we are now. I ended up in hospital twice, so I know what it's like to get knocked out. Before we got married I had to go and get my nose straightened because I couldn't breathe. I wasn't a patch on the kids we've got now, but I was always with pros. I was with old Jack Bates, who trained Jock McAvoy, Johnny King and Jackie Brown, all great fighters. Because I had no father he used to advise me in any way he could. He said he was going to turn me pro and to this day I don't know whether he said that just to boost me up or whether he actually meant it. A lot of the old fighters said he did mean it, to get me a few quid, but I don't believe that. I knew I wasn't good enough.

'But although I wasn't good enough to become a pro, and anything about school and education bored me, I realised years later that I was good at analysing. I used to watch Bates and I was fascinated by the way he'd tell his fighters to get side on, and when the other fella threw punches to come up with their elbow and block them. It was brilliant to watch him. They all say he was a great trainer but not a good manager. They tell you that about Jimmy Murphy. He was a great coach but as a manager we don't know what he would have been like. Apart from running the Wales team he never did it.

'As we went on I got to know a lot of top-class fighters, and when we started the old Collyhurst Lads' Club I brought them in to do the training, thinking they were far superior to me and would be able to show the kids better than me. I was happy to run it and raise money. After a while I could see that these well-known fighters – I don't want to embarrass them by naming them – weren't teaching the kids anything. They were just telling them about prisons and that type of thing. I decided it would have to stop and told them so.

'I said what we wanted was to do the thing properly, buy them equipment – vests, shorts and socks. Go as a team. Have a bit of pride in what we were doing. It took us about three years to become affiliated to the Amateur Boxing Association (ABA). The first show we went to was at Middleton Baths, in 1964. It was organised by the police and they put two of our lads on. We took three busloads and the atmosphere was completely different from what they'd been used to. There was chanting, just like a football crowd. It was the United era of Law and Best, and they were all United supporters. It was the start of the big crowds. Every show was packed out. I got Denis Law to come down and present the trophies. Paddy Crerand, Nobby, all of them came down. We always had good fighters and people would always say, "This Collyhurst kid is good." People would leave the bar and watch them. We had loads of champions – schoolboys, juniors, seniors.'

When the landscape of Collyhurst changed, Hughes was persuaded to keep the club going and moved it to Moston. Eventually, however, the cost of hiring football pitches proved too great a burden and the club concentrated on boxing. Hughes is still responsible for the Lads' Club, although volunteers run the training sessions.

'We've got a couple of young fellas who've never boxed but are full of enthusiasm, and sometimes they're the best. You can't get ex-boxers to give their time. But like ex-footballers, they often try to teach the kids what they do naturally, which is not always the way. If the volunteers see any kid who's reasonable they'll tell me and I'll go down and have a look. We were going to close it down this year but the volunteers said there were so many kids who wanted to come and there was nothing else around the area.'

Hughes focuses his time and effort on those with recognised potential and makes no apologies for that.

'People like Nobby Nobbs and Martin Jolley are the backbone of boxing, but I couldn't do that. You need them but I couldn't be one of them. Don't get me wrong, that doesn't make me better than them. My philosophy on this is that to me my time is valuable and as I get older it becomes more valuable. So if I'm going to go down there and teach, then I expect the best. Training is now my living. You get loads of kids coming along and you know within an hour whether they're going to make anything.

'That doesn't mean you discard them. We've got a kid, we call him

"Steady Eddie", a nice kid, only 20, but he's already got a child and he'll never make a boxer. I've told him that. We encourage him, though. We say he can train with the lads, but he knows I won't get him a fight. He keeps coming in thinking I'm going to change my mind. Eventually you might give him an amateur fight, to let him see how hard it really is, but he'll never go pro, and there's a lot like that. He can be part of the team and he does create a bit of a laugh.

'We do let them have a bit of fun and I think we have a good atmosphere in our gym, but with the other lads we've also got to be really serious. You've got to study them. I have a book and I record everything about them – not only their physical attributes and condition but also their temperament and attitude. Like this young heavyweight we've got. I'll monitor him all the way through, to see what standard he's progressing to and whether he's ready for the next stage. As with a young footballer, you need to teach him good habits. They used to say George Best was just left to get on with it because he was so good, but believe you me, that wasn't entirely true. I remember seeing Jimmy Murphy go on to the training pitch in a brand new suit, getting himself splattered in mud, because he wanted to explain something to George. He was telling him where he should have made his runs, when he should have laid the ball off and so forth. He wasn't just left to his own devices, as the mythology would have us believe. He was coached.

'That is what you've got to do with these lads, because boxing is a dangerous game. It's only you and him and he's got dynamite. If you're not alert in your head and don't know how to stop it you're going to get hurt.'

Hughes exudes the kind of pride Murphy must have felt when he saw his young players develop into some of the finest footballers this country has ever produced.

'This current crop is as good as any I've had,' Hughes confirms. 'I was saying to Rosemary today, it would have been nice to get away for a couple of weeks in the New Year, somewhere warm, but I can't. We've got so many good young fighters and we're so busy. And the great thing about these kids is that they are all fantastic ticket sellers. They're very popular. And – I don't mean to be disrespectful and it's certainly not racist – most of them are white. Most of our good lads in the '60s and '70s were black. Pat Barrett was with us from a kid. Even the black lads in the gym will tell you we need the white lads because they sell tickets. They can get on the shows and start to make their way up. But generally you don't get black kids now, just as you don't have Jews in the game the way we used to.'

Those inside the game will tell you it is not only Hughes' coaching that is valued by boxers. Many reckon he is the best cuts man in the business, and many laud his hand-taping technique.

'I learned a lot from old Eddie Thomas. He used to train Ken Buchanan, Howard Winstone and lots more. I spent a long time with him in Wales and he taught me how to treat cuts and how to tape up the hands. It's a matter of experience. When you're in the corner you've got to keep nice and calm. Some fighters pay a lot of money to bring in cornermen. Our lads don't have that worry. They know we're there and can do everything for them. We're all a team, that's what makes the bond that we've got.'

No one who has ventured inside Hughes' gym would dispute that claim. Equally, they could not have failed to notice it scarcely fulfils the criteria stipulated by Martin Jolley for what today's boxers expect.

Hughes smiles and his wife laughs in the background. He acknowledges: 'It's the dirtiest, scruffiest place you could imagine. We've only just brought a speed-ball in this week. We've got showers, but if you see them . . . It's the old-fashioned type of gym, straight out of the '20s and '30s. The atmosphere is terrific and it produces champions. We've had lads come in from different places sparring, and they all say that about the atmosphere. Our lads help each other, they work with each other. Outside the gym they go with the locals and stay with the locals. They don't have fair-weather friends like a lot of these footballers. And I think when these lads finish they'll have the same friends.'

Gomez first turned up at the club as a young tearaway, only to wander off and seek his amusement elsewhere.

'He was about nine or ten, did some boxing, and then went missing,' Hughes says. 'But you get kids like that. They come and then just disappear and you never know what's happened to them. Anyway, months later, maybe a year later, this pal of mine who worked in a kids' home said they'd got an aggressive little kid there who'd make a belter for me. He said this kid liked football and asked if I could get him a game. It was young Michael. Well, you should have seen him. He was charging the goalkeeper into the back of the net, retaliating when anybody did anything – he was costing us a fortune in fines! After about four matches I said we couldn't afford to let him play any more, he'd be better off boxing, which he'd done before.

'From the little bit he'd done you couldn't tell if he was going to be any good, but when he started again there was no doubt. He was really good. We've got videos of him when he was 11, having his first fight. Watching them, you can see how good he was. The only thing was, he wouldn't go back to school. The other kids took the Mickey out of him because he couldn't read or write. He'd been away that much. So Pat Barrett, who I think was then undefeated European champion, and I took him to school and sat at the back of the class to make sure they didn't take the Mickey. After that we took him to a place where they taught kids with special needs. No big classes, just about ten of them. We took him one day, and the next day, and then suddenly he didn't turn up. I couldn't find him anywhere.

'Eventually, though, he came back to the club and took up boxing seriously. He was about 14. We put him in championships, but he had a lot of bad luck when he got to finals. Even though we knew he'd deserved to win, he never got the decisions because it was all political – he always boxed against Cockneys. That made him a bit bitter, and with his background as well he thought everything was against him. By the time he was seventeen he had two national titles, but he should have had six or seven. He was even more bitter and resentful when he beat this kid from London for a second time and the other kid got picked for the European Championships. He went off the rails a bit and one of the fellas helping us told me I'd better get hold of him or he'd end up in trouble. He said I should turn him professional and that way I'd be able to keep an eye on him all the time.

'So I went and got hold of Michael and asked him what was the matter. He said, "I'm never going to get any fair play, look what they've done." I told him these things are sent to try us, and went through all that. The outcome was that he was going to turn professional or finish altogether. I spoke to Frank Warren about him and told him that if we brought the kid on slowly he'd be all right. That's what happened. Officially he lost three of his early fights but two of those decisions were debatable. For me there was only one he really lost and that was because he wasn't physically or mentally tuned in to the professional game. He was too young.'

The incident outside a Manchester nightclub cast a tragic shadow over Gomez's career. He and two friends had already been involved in a skirmish with a group of older men inside the club. The older men were thrown out of the club but waited for Gomez and his friends to leave. They attacked one of his friends and the boxer tried to usher him to safety. However, Gomez again found himself confronting the other men and he threw a punch at one of them. The man fell, banging his head, and Gomez ran away. The men took their friend to hospital but he was sent home and later died. Gomez was watching television when a news bulletin reported the death and issued a description of the man they were seeking in connection with the incident. He went to the police station and gave himself up.

Hughes recalls: 'They had him in a cell for three days, charged him with murder at first, then it got reduced to manslaughter. Eventually, when it came to the court case, he was acquitted. I went as a character witness, although initially the barrister told me not to come near, because he didn't want to mention the boxing aspect. Then I got a phone call and was asked to go into the witness box. So I went and told them about Michael.'

Eye-witnesses confirmed that Gomez had acted in self-defence, but the memory of the dead man, Sam Powell, is rekindled every time the boxer climbs into the ring. Gomez wears a gold medallion around his ankle and crosses himself in a gesture of penitence and respect.

Hughes says: 'He always thinks of the lad, even when he goes in to fight. I don't really ask him about it. There are some things you don't want to pry into. There are some things that the kids don't want to discuss with the coaches. They'll discuss it with somebody younger, but they are very funny like that. They'll do everything you tell them, but you have to accept there is a generation gap. I find it hard at times. That's why I keep joking with them and they laugh at me something shocking. They take the Mickey out of me, but I can use that as a way of making them train harder.

'You've got to make the training enjoyable. I remember how many times I used to be bored rigid when I went to the gym. We try to make every day a learning experience for them. You've got to train the mind as well as the body. You see the circles we have in the gym, where we work on technique and footwork. We stand them in a box so they have to stand still and make the other fella miss. I can get through to them on things like that, but when it comes to modern life, I'm completely lost. I have to win their respect by being a good coach to them, and fighting to get the right type of money for them.

'It's lovely for Martin Jolley that he's been able to earn a few quid out of boxing over the years, but I honestly couldn't be with a lad like that. I don't think I'd have the courage to keep getting beaten. I'd have to be a winner. Nobby Nobbs is obviously making a living out of it because he has loads of fighters and he's busy all the time. They get more requests than fighters who are winning, because people want them on their shows.'

Hughes still has to work on Gomez but believes this protégé is applying himself to his potentially perilous trade. Would that he could be sure about the mercurial Thomas McDonagh.

'He could be a shining light in British boxing for the next ten years,' Hughes drools. 'He could be a sensation. It is getting through to him, very slowly. He's got a wonderful, kind-hearted nature and his skill is unbelievable. He can do everything that the others have got to work hard to achieve. He's phenomenal. He's like the George Best of boxing for me. He also got robbed a lot in his amateur days because the referees didn't like his showboating. I've told him he's got to punch correctly and not mess about with these pros because they'll take his head off. I think his father and mother are at their wits' end trying to tell him how important and dangerous this is.

'I think he does want it enough because he's certainly got no money. The higher up the ladder he goes, the better he'll become. I really hope and pray the penny drops, anyway, because by next year he could be a champion. Potentially he's as good as anything I've got and as good as anybody in the country has got. But how will he develop? This is the intriguing part of boxing.

'I've had other lads like him. A lad called Craig Dermody comes to mind. Everyone in boxing said he was a genius. Frank Warren was going to build him up before Prince Naseem. But he wouldn't train and he was so like Thomas in a lot of ways, although Thomas is more focused. I think he had 14 fights and lost one, to one of Nobby Nobbs' fighters. The referee was having his first professional fight. Dermody hadn't been at his best, but he'd well beaten this lad, five rounds out of six. But Nobby started shouting, "This is the winner, referee," and he got confused. Reg Gutteridge, the commentator, was at ringside and he shouted to the referee that he'd made a mistake. I don't think that referee had another fight after that, and neither did Dermody. He was so disgruntled he packed it in. Now he's sorry. He's heartbroken. He tells me he should have done as I said.'

Gomez says his ultimate target is Hamed, and Hughes contends that his man could achieve that objective.

'Somebody will get to Naz, eventually. It happens to 'em all. It could be Michael, it could be anybody, because the longer he goes on the more his reflexes will slow down, just like a goalscorer's. Denis Law wasn't a great goalscorer at the end of his career. I think Michael is serious about getting out at 26. They give up so much of their life, they sacrifice so much, and it comes to a stage where they realise they are missing out on their children. So I wouldn't try to talk him into staying on.

'I always say to them, "If you get a house out of it you've got something; you've used boxing, boxing's not used you." Michael's just bought his own house, which is absolutely fantastic from my point of view. We encourage pension funds and we tell all the kids to put their money away, let it gain interest – don't listen to all these people with businesses, let them use their money rather than yours.'

Hughes' paternal concern seemingly knows no bounds. He saw enough of Freitas the other evening to know he doesn't want him in the same ring as his fighter.

'I believe Michael can win a world title, but he's not ready yet. I wouldn't let him fight this Freitas. I'm going to give him a rest now. He's back in the gym already, but we've not let him spar or anything. We're working on his mind now. He's getting loads of interest in America because they like his exciting style, but we don't want him fighting toe-to-toe unless the chips are down. He fought in Atlantic City last year and Bill Cayton, who used to be Mike Tyson's manager, came up to me and said, "I've not seen anybody box like that since the '40s. Where's this kid from?" I said, "Manchester." He said, "Manchester, Massachusetts?" I said, "No, Manchester, England." He said, "I don't believe it – a Limey? I ain't never seen no Limey fight like that before."

Hughes relayed the story to a puzzled Gomez, who asked: 'What's a Limey?'

'A Limey's an Englishman,' Hughes replied.

'I'm not an Englishman,' an indignant Gomez came back. 'I'm an Irish-Mexican!'

Hughes returns to his point: 'I've told him, "Never mind going pleasing the crowd. Get back to boxing." He's got to do what's best for him, not what America or TV wants. To be honest, I don't watch all these TV shows. Yes, you can always learn and I will watch the big fights, but I'm bored with a lot of these English fights. If there's a fella who's going to be fighting one of my lads I'll get a tape and study it night after night. I wanted to see Freitas the other night and I saw enough. You don't want to be up against that kind of fighter. You plan and look after your fighter so he doesn't get hurt.

'I wouldn't bring Michael down a weight. That weakens them. There's a lot of talk about what happened to Paul Ingle, how he might have been dehydrated. I don't know. Eventually Michael could move up in weight and might have more success.'

Hughes balances his faith in his boxers with a father's protective embrace. He builds them up and tries to ensure they can't be knocked down. Reid may be back in business after a couple of setbacks, but he is approaching 30. Can he possibly have much of a future?

'These might be the best years of his life,' Hughes enthuses. 'If he takes into a fight what he shows in the gym he could be around for a long time. He's not intending to go on for a long time, maybe two years; he wants to go on to other things, possibly this modelling and what have you, and I don't blame him. But you never know.'

Mention of Anthony Farnell prompts another paean: 'He already excites the crowds like no one I've seen since Terry Downes. When you've got champions talking about wanting to fight a kid it tells you what an impact he's had already. They need him, he doesn't need them. But he's only 22 and again, I don't want him rushed, as too many British fighters have been. He's too tensed up at the moment. He's got to learn to relax. That will come. Don't judge them now, judge them when they're 25, 26. By all means knock them then if they're not delivering – knock me as well, because I'm responsible for them. I'm the one who has to teach them to box in a way that's safe; to keep the hands up, to bob and weave, slip and slide, and punch properly, turning the fist to hit with the three knuckles.

'All I want is to see them come out at the end of their careers so they can enjoy their families, their children, the money they've earned, the houses they've got because of their boxing, and settle down and become good citizens.'

The good citizen in Brian Hughes earned him an MBE and a sparring session with royalty. The big day was a family affair, so they piled into the Collyhurst and Moston Lads' Club van for the trip south. However, Rosemary dug in her heels when her husband suggested they drive into the grounds of Buckingham Palace. 'She said we'd look like the Clampetts!' Once inside the reception area, the pomp and grandeur proved too intimidating for the man from the fight game.

'There were all these paintings, as big as that wall,' he says, pointing to the wall where the crucifix hangs. And there's all these posh voices, "H-H-Hello, what's one doing here?" And I'm looking round and thinking, "What am I doing here? A scruffy kid from Collyhurst." So I did what I used to do at school, I went and hid in the toilet. And the toilets there, they've got these cushions on lovely seats. I could have sat there and read a book if I'd had one. There's throwaway toothbrushes, you can dab on this smelly stuff, all free. But I felt out of place in that big room. I must have been in the toilet for ages.

'Anyway, I eventually came out and Prince Charles' equerry or whatever they call him – he's got a uniform and spurs and everything – comes up and says, "W-h-h-here have you been?" Really posh. "We thought you'd taken orrff. Is your tummy upset or something?" I told him I was okay, so he went through the procedure again just for me. He told me that when I was called up to the Prince I should give a courtesy bow, take three steps forward, not hold my hand out and not speak unless he spoke to me. If he wanted to speak he'd instigate that. I wasn't to address him as "Charlie" or "Chas", but "Your Royal Highness" or "Sir".

'And then I thought, "Ah, let them talk posh, I'm as good as any of these," and I remembered what my mam used to say. She'd say, "Come on, put your Tommy on." There was an old Collyhurst trainer called Tommy Fynan and he used to walk down the road as though he was a rolling boat, with his shoulders going from side to side. He'd tell us to be proud we came from Collyhurst, throw back our shoulders and let them know what a great place it was. So if we came out of the pictures on a cold night we kids would "put our Tommy on" and swagger home.

'When I was called forward the Prince asked me how I was and talked about the Lads' Club. He wanted to know if any were going to the Olympic Games or the Commonwealth Games, in Manchester. He said, "Manchester's doing very well."

'I said, "Yeah, Manchester United's doing well."

'"Oh", he said, "don't mention that. There's a lot of Arsenal people here." And everybody started laughing.

'Then he said, "Tell me, Mr Hughes, do you still participate, put the gloves on with the youngsters and kick a ball about?"

'I just looked at my midriff and thought, "Is he taking the Mick?" But I just said, "No, I'm a bit past it now."

'He said, "Why, how old are you?"

'I said, "I'm in my 60s."

'He said, "I don't believe it." Just like Victor Meldrew.

'I said, "No, and that's why they call you Prince Charming."

'And everyone was laughing again. You can see them all on the video. So that was nice, and it was nicer still when me and Nobby Stiles, who also got an MBE – two lads from the same school, at the same time – had a presentation from our own people, from the area.'

Another of Hughes' treasured gifts is a gold medallion given him by Angelo Dundee, the former trainer of Muhammad Ali.

'It was from Zaire, and Ali gave it to him after he beat George Foreman in the "Rumble in the Jungle" to become world heavyweight champion for a third time. We'd mutual friends and whenever Angelo Dundee was in Manchester he'd come to the gym to see us. A couple of years ago he said, "Brian, I couldn't do what you're doing, teaching all these kids. The ones I get are all Golden Gloves champions or Olympic champions. I want you to have this." A lot of gyms in this country don't bring on their boxers from school kids, as we do.'

Hughes has come a long way since he was a 'hopeless' school kid. Not only has he learned to read and write, he has written several books about his heroes of the ring and football pitch. He tells the stories of the local triumvirate of McAvoy, Brown and King with a fan's homage and a coach's appreciation. His portrait of Tommy Taylor, one of the Busby Babes killed at Munich, is as touching as it is enlightening. He is currently working on a biography of another of his favourite Manchester United players, Dennis Viollet. His sporting connections, infectious enthusiasm and unpretentious demeanour make him a natural contributor to local programmes and newspaper columns.

He acknowledges he is approaching the stage where he could be regarded as 'an old fuddy-duddy' and may soon have to leave the corner to a younger man.

'I've already said I'll step aside if they want somebody else. I'll just do two or three days a week coaching or help any way I can. So far they've said they want me there, and I must say that as I get older I find I'm enjoying it more. It's giving me a boost again, because of the challenge. Like this heavyweight, it's a challenge to bring him on so we can say to the British public, "Look, this is a heavyweight born, bred and coached here." That's the real satisfaction for me. Like Jimmy Murphy used to say about Duncan Edwards: "When we got him he was a little seed that we planted in the garden. When the time was right we plucked him out and he blossomed, and he was getting better and more beautiful as time went on. And by the time he died, God rest his soul, at 21, he was already a colossus."

'I'm positive that's what gives Alex Ferguson his greatest pleasure about United's success now, the fact he's brought on so many young players. It's the same with us. We've got a couple of really good 16 year olds. We want to show the public that boxing's not ale-house brawlers but a scientific sport. If it's done correctly there's no danger. You can come out of it completely unmarked and make a living. It's better than being on the dole, out of work, or worse.'

Hughes has scrambled onto a chair, and insists his back pain has eased. He does not wish to dwell on the subject, any more than he is inclined to mention he has diabetes and a diseased kidney.

'I feel smashing, honest.'

He prefers to return to the therapeutic subject of his young charges: 'It's like getting a load of clay and moulding something out of it and people say, "That's brilliant".'

Much as he preaches the virtues of boxing and strives to minimise the dangers, he recognises fights do not always go to plan. That is when he suffers.

'It depresses me when they lose but especially when they get hurt. I can accept it if they are beaten on points but if they are hurt, and hurt badly, I am upset because I think I must have done something wrong.

I've not made them understand what we're doing. But all the way through my career, going on 40 years, we've always had good class lads. And we've never had anyone badly hurt. If I saw them getting hurt I'd throw the towel in. I normally wait till they come back to the corner and call the referee over and say, "He's hurt his shoulder."

'On five or six occasions I've told lads, "Pack it in," and they've got very bitter. I've always said to them, "Look, that's only my opinion. I think you're not going to get any further and you're going to get hurt if you carry on." I tell them they are welcome to train in the gym and help the other lads, but if they want to carry on boxing it won't be with us. Robbie Reid has said to me, "The time when you think that's it, I want you to tell me." I said, "Don't worry about that, I will." You've got to have that sort of relationship with them.

'I enjoy working with lads who listen and learn. That makes it worthwhile if I've given up my Saturday morning, when I like to have a rest and watch the Italian football programme on television. I think Italian defenders are brilliant and I use a lot of their psychology for boxing. I always say that if you don't give goals away the least you'll get is a 0–0 draw, and on the counter you can get a goal and take the three points. So we work on the technical side and train their brains.

'There are all types of trainers and people in the game now. Lennox Lewis has a fella who conditions his muscles. Now I'm not into that. There are people who work on diets and all sorts of things. It's all becoming more modern. But in the '40s, '50s and '60s you never heard of all these fatalities and serious injuries that we've had in recent years. I think that's down to dehydration. These kids are being forced to make weights, and they're all sticking to it. All sorts of things are being said about Paul Ingle and you do worry about the future of the game.'

The conversation has come full circle. Stories about Ingle are still making the national newspapers. Today's line from the boxer's beleaguered camp claims the 12th-round stoppage effectively saved his life because he received immediate attention from paramedics. Had he been pulled out earlier in the contest he may have walked away, only to collapse or slip into a fatal coma later. But would Hughes have pulled him out? He pauses and considers before replying.

'Me, personally, yes. But I'm not saying that Steve Pollard was wrong. I've just answered the question honestly. Yes, I would. I would have pulled him out in the seventh or eighth round. It's not as though it was a close fight. He'd lost every round. They know the lad better than I do. We don't know what went on leading up to the fight, whether he had to shed weight very quickly. So you're talking from a blind position. I would definitely have stopped it but that doesn't mean to say that I'm right.

'Having the weigh-in the day before the fight was supposed to help. They tell you that a boxer can dry out for a couple of days and it won't have a detrimental effect long term, but he definitely doesn't want to be doing it for every fight. It's a great concern. We weigh everybody at the start of the week and again at the end. We keep a record, and if they go more than half a stone over their weight we tell them they can't fight. Gomez doesn't know when he's fighting again, but if he puts on more than eight pounds it'll be a long time before his next fight.

'In fairness to Steve Pollard, he's not a medical man. I've done my first aid and all that, and I think all the cornermen will have done their first aid, but we're not specialists. We need the doctors on hand to look at boxers during fights. I think the game will survive this, but eventually something will happen. You just can't keep letting things carry on.'

6 ☆ IT'S SHOWTIME

THE TURN OF THE YEAR BRINGS ANOTHER TURN FOR THE BETTER IN
Paul Ingle's condition. He is still in Sheffield's Royal Hallamshire
Hospital but said to be 'improving'. A spokesman at the hospital goes on:
'He has tried to speak, which is a good sign.'

The bulletin cushions some of the verbal and emotional blows
pummelling Ingle's trainer, Steve Pollard, who is moved to respond in an
interview for the *Sunday Mirror* newspaper. He denies Ingle had to lose
three stones before the contest with Mbulelo Botile and that his fighter
asked to be pulled out several rounds before the ill-fated 12th. He
attributes these accusations to people with 'sick minds who take some
kind of warped pleasure in spreading rubbish'.

Another week on signals a further significant step forward for Ingle.
Literally. Consultant neurosurgeon Robert Battersby announces: 'Three
weeks down the line Paul is making remarkable progress. He is walking with
help.'

All of which enables the publicity machinery driving the build-up
to a televised show at the Wythenshawe Forum, Manchester, to move
a mite more smoothly for those concerned. Anthony Farnell tops the
bill, defending his WBO Inter-continental light-middleweight title
against Argentina's Sergio Acuna. The two men are paraded for the
media at Manchester United's Old Trafford stadium. The home
fighter exudes suitable self-belief for the reporters and cameras, but

away from the focus of attention and earshot, Brian Hughes is worried.

'It's going to be tough, and I mean tough,' says Hughes, the anxiety genuine rather than manufactured for TV consumption. 'I watched him train last night and he's good; if I'd known beforehand how good, I wouldn't have let Anthony fight him, not at this stage of his career. But it's too late now. There's nothing I can do about it. The trouble is you get mucked about. I speak to Frank Warren's office and they think I'm moaning, but you need to know who you're fighting. Manchester United wouldn't play in a European Cup-tie without having a scout watch their opponents first. That's the way it should be here. I like to see tapes of our boxers' opponents and know what we're up against. I now know Anthony is in for a harder fight than he needs.'

Thomas McDonagh v Michael 'Kid' Halls, from Walsall, is the other featured fight on Sky and Michael Gomez, still nursing his cut eye, is at ringside to lend vocal and visual support. McDonagh scarcely requires any assistance tonight. He out-manoeuvres Halls from the start and Gomez is on his feet, screeching his appreciation. By the third round Halls' right eye is closed and hideously swollen. The referee allows them to continue until the fourth, when he mercifully calls for the doctor to inspect the eye. The verdict is inevitable, despite Halls' pleas to go on, and McDonagh is declared the winner.

McDonagh perches on the edge of the ring to tell Sky's audience he is putting his days of fooling around behind him and getting serious about his work. 'New year, different fighter,' is his message. 'I've got to prove I am a prospect. Brian has told me I need to show the critics I'm not a clown.'

One local fighter leaves to a deafening ovation and another arrives to more of the same. It's standing room only as 'Arnie the Warrior' emerges from backstage to confront the umpteenth 'Bull of the Pampas'. Acuna has never been stopped in 27 fights, but is described as a 'blown-up' welterweight who should not present too many difficulties for Farnell. The referee brings them together and Acuna avoids the regulation eye contact by looking up to the ceiling. Or could it be somewhere higher still?

The evidence of the early rounds suggests Acuna may need guidance from above. Farnell is piling up the points as his opponent hustles with little success. However, by the sixth Acuna is managing to get to Farnell, who now realises he has a scrap on his hands. Hughes' words come to mind as the Argentine defies Farnell's much-vaunted aggression. Gomez is on his feet in the seventh, desperately calling instructions to his stable-mate.

Farnell finds his range again in the eighth and greets the bell with a laugh, but Acuna will not be repelled, much less put down. Farnell is forced back in the 10th and 11th by the Argentine's extraordinary strength and willpower. Farnell's expression betrays his bewilderment. The barrage continues during the final break – from Hughes.

'You're losing all your discipline,' Hughes tells his boxer. 'You're not going to knock him out so stop looking for it. You're throwing it away.'

Acuna is on his feet long before the bell for the final round. He is intent on exerting every psychological as well as physical pressure in his power. Farnell responds with a positive opening burst and revives the belief of his fans. But Acuna is equal to his determination in this gruelling fight of two halves. Farnell has a cadaverous look, clinging to Acuna's unsinkable frame as if it were a life raft. The bell is like dry land. Farnell gets the decision on all three cards but the points margins – two, two and three – fairly convey the closeness of the contest.

Farnell is steered to the now-familiar interview position with Gomez draped around his shoulders. 'He was the toughest fighter I've met,' Farnell concedes. 'I'm brilliant at that weight but it's just experience. Some fighters might be better skilled than me but nobody has more guts. I've maybe over-trained for this. I've got to calm down a bit.'

Ian Darke, Sky's commentator, tells Farnell that earlier in the day he received a call from the British champion, Wayne Alexander, who claimed the Manchester fighter was ducking him.

Farnell rises to the bait, replying to Alexander: 'I'll knock you spark out.'

Since both men are in the Frank Warren camp, a meeting at this stage seems unlikely. Hughes is irritated nonetheless.

'What a load of bull that was about Alexander phoning Ian Darke,' Hughes barks. 'I'm not rushing Anthony and he says he'll listen to me. His father's told me he's behind me as well. I said this was going to be a tough fight. We've got to learn from what has happened in the past.'

Martin Jolley is proving elusive. He cannot be contacted on his usual mobile number and the answer machine, as usual, is fielding calls to his home. The explanation, as usual, is not without its dramatic content.

'Oh, I got in a bit of trouble,' he begins, sheepishly. 'But honestly, it wasn't my fault at all. We'd broken up for Christmas and I went to the pub for a drink with some mates from work. But people are picking on me and no matter how hard I try not to get involved there are some who won't leave it alone. And would you believe it, it was the same pub where I got glassed last year. This gang of blokes came in and one of them pushed up against me. I told him, "Don't do that, I don't want any trouble." Anyway, one of them, a really tough guy, was waiting outside the pub, so I thought, "I'm not having this." He threw a punch but I ducked it and caught him with a great upper cut. Knocked him out. I didn't want to be around when the police came so I did a runner. Unfortunately, I lost my phone in the punch-up.

'I lay low for a few days over Christmas so that I could see the kids. I knew the police wanted to see me so I went to the police station after that. I told them my side of the story and they told me to stick to it. Apparently this guy is a bit of a hooligan, with a string of convictions. I got the impression I'd done the police a favour. Anyway, I've got a new phone . . .'

A covering of snow gives Moston an improbably engaging countenance but the stairwell leading to the gym above the Late Shop is as dingy as ever and it's business as usual in Hughes' camp. Sam Rawlinson, Hughes' great white hope, is being worked in the ring. Robin Reid is making good use of the speed-ball, while Michael Gomez and Michael Jennings are alternating in the box.

Sparring is a welcome if only temporary escape from the sorrow of family tragedy for Jennings. He pulled out of the Wythenshawe show after his 25-year-old brother, who boxed as an amateur, fell victim to the deadly allure of drugs.

Gomez is likely to fight again earlier than Hughes originally planned. His stock across the Atlantic is rising and *Showtime* want to introduce him to the American TV audience. Frank Warren is keen to make it happen and Hughes appreciates the potential of the US market. His priority, he maintains, is the long-term welfare of his boxer.

'As long as Michael is okay and I'm satisfied with his opponent we'll probably do it,' Hughes says. 'I've got to discuss one or two things with Frank. There's been a lot of flak over Anthony Farnell's fight, even on the Internet. They're saying I've been having a go at Frank Warren and all sorts of things. I've not had a go at Frank, I just said I wanted to know about my boxers' opponents first. We'll clear things up.'

Hughes moves around like a schoolteacher supervising class-work, all-seeing and all-hearing. He spins around to face two of his youngest pupils: 'What are you two talking about, women? Twenty press-ups.' They offer no resistance.

Hughes turns his attention to the action in the ring. 'Go side to side, like a windscreen wiper,' he urges.

The two youngest have resumed their sparring. 'See that lad there? He'll be another Nigel Benn,' the irrepressible Hughes predicts. 'The problem is these kids are like tigers on a leash. They want to be let go. But you can't get them fights. The amateur game is falling apart. Amateurs are actually being paid to stay on. Good kids are having to wait till the Championships to get fights. They can't turn professional till they're 18.'

Reid is the last boxer to finish work. 'He needs it,' someone whispers from a safe distance.

The muscular Reid smiles and confesses: 'Well, I am coming up to 30 so I suppose I am a bit of an old man now.'

He showers and wanders back into the gym, a towel wrapped around his waist. Only Gomez is left to acknowledge that the man from Runcorn still looks in his prime. 'That's what you call a six-pack,' Reid says, slapping his light-brown stomach.

The little 'Irish-Mexican' cannot argue. 'He's got an amazing physique. Look at me, skinny and white. It doesn't help when I've got a cold. Hopefully I'll be able to shake it off in a few days and get in shape for the next fight. I'm sure I will.'

Gomez is interrupted by a stream of calls on his mobile. He promises to ring back as soon as he can. He is equally confident his eye will stand up to another fight just two months after it was cut and required five stitches. The proposed next fight is scheduled for Widnes also, in three weeks' time. The opponent is yet to be named.

'My eye is healing okay so I don't think that will be a problem,' he says, sitting on the edge of the ring. 'I'll fight whoever Brian wants me to. He's been good to me; like a second dad, really. I'm lucky because I can turn to my own dad and Brian for advice. I've got the best of both worlds. I got into all sorts of trouble as a kid. Nicking stuff from shops, getting in fights, all that sort of thing. It was hard at school because I was dyslexic. My dad is almost blind with this hereditary eye problem and he went back to Ireland for a time. My mother ran off with another woman – can you imagine that? I've not seen her since. Eight years, it is. So the family got split up.'

He found a soul-mate in Alison, now the mother of his two children. Her mother had been killed by a drunken driver and she was cared for by an aunt. They shared their bitterness and frustration, each providing a pillar for the other. Alison was still a child when she became pregnant, yet her resolve gave strength to Michael, who confronted his own growing-up process in boxing. His reputation as a kid handy with his fists inevitably brought him trouble. He was only 13 when his nose was broken by two lads wielding Chinese fighting sticks. The boxing ring, he eventually realised, was the sensible answer.

'I remember boxing in Ireland when I was seven. When we came to Manchester I was always fighting lads older and bigger than me. I was cock of the school. Really evil. Then Brian got me boxing properly. He'd show me his videos of the old fighters. That's when I got into Wilfredo Gomez. He was brilliant. I loved that style and that's how I fight. Brian got me going with a few fights and I made a bit of money for me and Alison and little Michael. But then I got involved in that fight outside the nightclub and suddenly I'm on a murder charge.

'I knew it was self-defence and I didn't mean him to get hurt or anything, but when you're in a cell like that it's just the worst. I was thinking I'd go down and not be with Alison and Michael and . . . all that sort of stuff goes through your head. When they found me not guilty it was just an unbelievable feeling. The lad's parents have said they know what happened and don't blame me, and I thank them for that. I always think about him, though. That's why I wear the gold medallion on my left ankle. It was my nan's.

'It was such a waste of a life and I've been determined not to waste mine. I've got really serious about my boxing and I've put my money into buying our house. We talked about getting married but it was either a wedding or a house, and we decided to go for the house. We can maybe think about getting married in the future. I feel I'm lucky now. I'm 23, got a house, a car and a family. I love to spoil the kids. Brian tells me not to, so they'll appreciate the value of things. I know what he means, but I would have loved some of the toys I've bought Michael, and the look on his little face is just magic. The rest of my family is still close, apart from my mother. I have some real rows with my sisters but we always make it up and carry on as if nothing's happened. That's what families are like, aren't they?

'I'm still hungry for more in the ring, though, don't worry about that. My Lonsdale Belt is only the start. I'm going to make my world title dream come true in a year. Definitely. The money will come with that, and American TV. That's the target. It's up to me to show them what I can do in this next fight. That's if Brian says it's okay to fight.'

He heads for home, gripping a bag in one hand and punching numbers in his mobile phone with the other. 'See you, Robbie.'

Reid appears so self-assured and well-adjusted that it comes as a surprise to some when they learn he was placed into care at the age of six months because his father, a West Indian, and his English mother could no longer cope with him. He was born in Liverpool and raised on Merseyside, then in Runcorn, by foster parents.

'I've moved to Bolton now, but I go and see my foster mother regularly and call her mum, because that's what she's been to me,' he says. 'I did meet my proper father once and he called me "son" but I couldn't call him "dad". I did feel a bit better towards him because he wanted to give it a go with me, but my mother didn't.'

The reawakening of BBC Television's interest in boxing is widely welcomed inside the sport. Sky's zealous – some would say over-zealous – coverage may have set new standards, but its audience is limited and the boxing world is conscious that only a terrestrial service can restore it to a position of national prominence. Reid's fight, albeit short and one-sided, served to whet the appetite and Ingle's continued recovery has eased the political and public pressure. So it is with relish and undisguised satisfaction that the BBC announce a series of deals to put boxing back on their screens: the return of major amateur events; the launch of Olympic gold medallist Audley Harrison's professional career; and most significantly of all, Lennox Lewis' next defence of his world title.

The revival theme is sustained by the creation of a Kronk Club in London. The original Kronk, in Detroit, is the world's most famous gym and the new version, at the old St Pancras Club, aims to tap and train the raw talent of the capital. Emanuel Steward, who has schooled 29 champions in the 31 years since he first ventured down to the basement of the Kronk Community Centre, and Tommy Hearns, his most distinguished protégé, have teamed up again for the opening of Kronk-St Pancras. 'This is not about signing professional boxers,' Steward says, 'this is about finding Olympic champions.'

Michael Gomez will defend his WBO Inter-continental super-featherweight title against Hungary's Laszlo Bognar at the Kingsway Centre, Widnes. Three days before the fight, Hughes reveals no public sign of apprehension. 'I've had a good look at him on video,' Hughes says. 'He's tough, all East Europeans are, and he's a southpaw, which could make it difficult for Michael. But he should be okay.'

Thomas McDonagh is again in the supporting cast and Hughes again has a bone to pick with Sky. 'After his last fight they had a moan that Thomas wasn't mucking around. They want that. I've told him I want him boxing. Once the fight's over, all right. He can act the goat as much as he wants outside the ring. As long as it's not inside the ring.'

McDonagh and stable-mate Michael Jennings negotiate their latest tests with something to spare. Jennings makes it 11 professional wins from 11 by stopping Mark Haslam in 2 rounds, while McDonagh extends his run to 12 with a convincing points verdict over Harry Butler.

In the ring before Gomez and Bognar are the WBO light-middleweight champion Harry Simon, of Namibia, and a late substitute, Wayne Alexander, the undefeated British champion. The original challenger, Robbie Allen, struggled to make the weight and was taken to hospital with stomach cramps. Alexander describes the call-up as 'a dream come true'.

Simon is disinclined to perpetuate fantasy. 'It will be an easy and short fight,' he forecasts.

Jimmy Lennon Junior is this evening's MC, his excruciating, syrup-laden whine delivering his catchphrase: 'It's *Showtime*.' At least they have a spectacle worthy of the introduction. Alexander chooses to mix it with an acknowledged puncher and stuns the champion with a big right in the second. Simon responds with an extra gear and by the fourth the bombardment is becoming ominously one-sided. In the fifth, Alexander takes a pounding to the body and sinks to the canvas. He opts for a rest and a count of eight, but can delay the inevitable no longer. Simon moves in again and so does the referee. Simon's fourth defence is successful and Alexander has the consolation of a 'good pay day'. However, he has discovered the gulf between British and world class and knows he does not, at this stage, possess the means to bridge it.

No one anticipates anything other than a straightforward exercise for Gomez against the 32-year-old Hungarian. The sombrero ensemble are in typically boisterous form and greet Bognar with a volley of boos and jeers. He smiles the smile of an old pro who has heard it all before. Gomez's fans change their tune when he comes into view, to the usual Mexican Hat Dance routine. He pulls a mean face, hunches his shoulders and climbs into the ring, his blue and white top shimmering in the lights. He veers towards his opponent, aims a fierce glare and veers away again.

Our all-American MC welcomes viewers to Widnes, England, and, just in case they missed it the first time, reminds them 'It's *Showtime*.' He introduces Bognar, a man with a record of 30 fights, 25 wins, 3 defeats and 2 draws. And then the champion, 'Out of Manchester, England, by way of Dublin, Ireland.' Gomez, the hall is informed, weighed in at 9 stone 4 lb, the super-featherweight limit, Bognar half a pound lighter.

Gomez crosses himself, reaches down towards the medallion at his left ankle and goes through the motions of an uneventful first round. Hughes has seen enough to express his first concerns. 'You're giving him too much room,' he tells his boxer. Ian Darke, Sky's commentator, feels the evidence already warrants his revealing 'talk' of Gomez not having his usual conditioning, or 'cut'. The fight, Darke suggests, could have been made at lightweight.

The second round has the sound of alarm bells filling the Kingsway Leisure Centre. Bognar finds it inexplicably easy to get through to

Gomez. 'What's the matter with you?' an anxious Hughes asks back in the corner. 'Michael, slow down, slow down.' Gomez's vacant expression does nothing to reassure his trainer.

A few flickering signs of improvement briefly raise the spirits of his supporters, only for the southpaw to come back and score freely again. How much of a problem, Darke wonders aloud, did Gomez have getting down to 9 stone 4 lb? Questions must also be hammering the minds of Hughes and Warren as Gomez fumbles aimlessly through most of the fourth round.

Suddenly, in the fifth, Gomez summons the strength and accuracy to force back Bognar. In a few potentially decisive seconds both fighters are cut by a clash of heads – Bognar by the right eye, Gomez high on the brow – and a left to the body puts the challenger down. Bognar survives the round, but the momentum is with Gomez, who targets the body again in the sixth. By the end of the round, however, the Hungarian has recovered and more.

The seventh prompts a fresh inquisition from the commentator. Darke suggests Gomez's 'flat and jaded' look could indicate signs of decline, or that he needs a lay-off. Gomez is cautioned for a rabbit punch and resorts to schoolyard brawling.

Barry McGuigan joins the on-air inquest. 'I've never seen him as bad as this,' he says. 'He looks really tired and as if he's been hurt. He's in real trouble. He didn't look right in the dressing-room before the fight.'

Darke is in a state of near frenzy in the eighth. 'He looks like he's walking through treacle. He's got to be pulled out. He's all over the place. He's got nothing.'

Gomez makes it back to his corner and Hughes tells him: 'I'm going to stop it.'

The champion protests: 'No, Brian.'

His body language scarcely conveys defiance. He is shattered and says so, dropping his head on his chest. Hughes acknowledges he looks beaten but makes him lift his head and effectively issues an ultimatum: stop now or go for it.

Gomez rises from his stool for round nine but all strength has been drained from his body and legs. Worse still, his will is broken. The referee steps in and Gomez is stopped for the first time in a career of 57 amateur bouts and 27 as a professional. It is his first defeat in 20, a run stretching back 4 years. Far more disconcerting is the manner of his demise against a modest opponent and the doubts about his preparedness for the fight. Hughes' angst is transparent in a clash with Warren as Gomez is ushered back to his stool.

Hughes looks towards Warren, who is standing outside the ring, and says: 'Honestly, it's stupid this what you've done. You're going to get somebody killed here, I'm telling you.'

A flummoxed Warren turns away and says nothing.

Darke concludes that a lot of questions need answering and that the finger has to be pointed at Gomez's cornermen.

The new champion parades in the ring, rubbing salt into Gomez's wounded pride by donning a sombrero, as Warren is brought in front of the camera to confront some of those questions. 'I don't know what was wrong with him,' he says. 'Brian said he's had the flu. It's the first I've heard about that. With hindsight you can say he shouldn't have fought. He's been in the gym and I was told he was all right. I didn't know if he was playing a game with the guy.'

McGuigan, who saw Gomez in his dressing-room before the fight, says: 'He wasn't as focused or cocky as he usually is. From the start he looked only 40 to 50 per cent against a guy who wouldn't normally lace his boots. He shouldn't have been sent out for the ninth. Brian Hughes is a wonderful humanitarian and a great cornerman and trainer, but he shouldn't have put him in there.'

The inquisition continues in the dressing-room, where Hughes and Warren are standing uneasily, side by side. Hughes, looking shell-shocked, is asked how Gomez is.

'He's OK. He went down with flu this morning . . . The doctor examined him. He had him down just before . . . I would have pulled him out after another round if it had gone on like that.'

Sky's Adam Smith turns to Warren, who riles at the line of questioning. He accuses the reporter of trying to drive a wedge between manager and trainer.

The trainer adds: 'He needs a long rest. He should have had longer. He's heartbroken, but he will come back. He's a warrior.'

The warrior had no fighting talk for television, although he did confide in some of the press behind the scenes. The *Manchester Evening News* quote Gomez as saying: 'I started to feel ill after the weigh-in. I felt a bit tired and my legs were weak. I told a few of the Sports Network [Warren's organisation] people I didn't want to fight but they took no notice.'

Hughes is in turmoil all weekend. His family implore him to quit boxing and he turns up at the gym on Monday morning prepared to do so.

'I told Michael and all the others I would pack it in and let them go if they wanted, but they said no, they wanted me to stay. I feel terrible. I've hardly slept a wink since Saturday. Michael's fine, honestly. To look at him now you wouldn't think he was the same person. The doctor said it could have been a virus that worked through him in the fight. It happens a lot. Titles have been won by fighters with worse. Michael said if I'd pulled him out he wouldn't have spoken to me again. That doesn't bother me. I've retired people before and I'll do it again rather than risk one of my fighters. If Michael had told me before the fight he didn't want to fight there would have been no argument from me – I would have pulled him out. It was only after he lost that he told me he was ill and that he had told Sports Network officials. That was why I made that remark to Warren from the ring.'

Precisely what happened in the build-up to the fight has become the subject of debate, conjecture and perhaps mischievous rumour-mongering. The BBBC are expected to launch an inquiry, while Sky continue their analysis and dissection on *Ringside*. Ricky Hatton adds his voice to a now-familiar chorus. He says Gomez was not his usual bubbly self, but a shadow of the fighter everybody loves to see. He recognises that Hughes 'thinks the world' of his boxers but feels there were signs Gomez had given his all. Sky say Sports Network have told them Gomez was given sufficient notice of the fight. Sky also say they are assured Gomez is well, but that they have been unable to speak to him.

The following morning Hughes receives a number of calls about the programme. He did not see it, preferring to watch Manchester United's Champions League match in Valencia. No, thank you, he does not wish to see a tape of the programme. One of the calls is from a contrite Gomez.

'I've got you in trouble, haven't I?' Gomez says.

Hughes does not see it that way, but it is difficult even for those so close to this unpalatable affair to form a clear picture. However, the grapevine is yielding stories that might, if true, explain Gomez's condition and woeful performance at Widnes. There are reports he has been seen out drinking and brawling. He was even involved in a clash with another boxer booked on the Widnes bill, Tony Mulholland, and his brother, at a Liverpool hotel barely 24 hours before their scheduled fights. Confusion over the weigh-in raised further suspicion about Gomez. He did not step onto the scales when he was due to, although it is claimed he did so some time later and in mysterious circumstances. Inside sources believe that on the evening of the show he weighed as much as 10 stone 8 lb.

The very public hanging of this dirty linen served to compound Hughes' despair. He had negotiated a purse of £20,000 for Gomez, who was eager to order a new kitchen. The boxer's image has been tarnished, his association with Warren may well have been irrevocably jeopardised and the money could dry up. Those close to him fear he will go off the rails, much as he did in his youth.

Hughes is adamant he will not give up on Michael Gomez, but his fabled enthusiasm to find and nurture young boxing talent appears to have taken one blow too many.

'Rosemary and the kids are still telling me to jack it in because I don't need this. They're right there, I don't. But I can't leave it like this. I can't leave Michael like this. He needs a long rest, then we'll get him back in shape and get him another fight. When he's done that and got a win again I can go.'

Gomez's distress in the later stages of his fight against Bognar inevitably rekindled images of Paul Ingle's near-fatal beating in Sheffield, and this week the BBBC have announced new regulations intended to counter the dangers of excessive weight reduction and subsequent dehydration. Regular and random weight checks should dissuade trainers and boxers from entering inaccurate figures in diaries. Boxers will be allowed isotonic drinks between rounds and trainers will be required to have a proper grasp of health and dietary requirements.

The measures, like the motives behind them, are deemed laudable but the cynics – or maybe the realists – among the boxing fraternity fear they will be largely unenforceable. The full co-operation of boxers, trainers, managers and promoters, or a bullet-proof policing system is essential, and neither can be guaranteed.

Hughes says: 'If people think anything's been learnt from Paul Ingle they're living in cloud-cuckoo-land. Boxing is a dirty, rotten, stinking business, as I tell all my lads when they start. I tell them if they've got something better to do they should do it. But if they want to get into boxing they should know exactly what it's like.'

7 ☆ COMIC CUTS

THE RED-BRICK BLOCK ON THOMAS STREET, ASTON, IN THE SHADOW
of the expressway that links Birmingham city centre with the M6, is an
improbable haven of joy and opportunity. Security systems on the outside
doors and stark corridors are as welcoming as a punch below the belt. But
then, on the first floor, an incongruous, cheery face and a 'hello' message,
scrawled on the sign for the boxing gym, revive the soul like the star in the
East. Inside the square room of this single unit, the game's most celebrated
stand-up comic is about to perform.

'See here,' he says, nodding in the general direction of a slightly
embarrassed figure, who doubtless knows what's coming, 'best trainer in
this gym'. He points to his stooge's footwear and delivers his one-word
punch line: 'adidas.'

Before the giggles subside he follows up with another to test the solar
plexus: 'I had a kid here, hadn't won for a long time. Referee lifted his
arm up and a bat flew out.'

This is Norman 'Nobby' Nobbs, at 6ft 3in and with crooked teeth and
time-etched features, a Tommy Cooper of the knock-about game; the self-
styled guru of boxing for laughs. Or so his reputation would have us
believe. Behind the self-deprecating comedy lurks another trainer-
manager offering meal tickets for fighters and perhaps an escape from the
familiar snares of the inner city.

Like Brian Hughes, Nobbs went down to the market to find work.

Unlike Hughes, he is still going down to the market. He gets up at three o'clock in the morning to drive his lorryload to the traders and reports to his gym in the afternoon to try and make sure his boxers aren't turnips. Also unlike Hughes, he has far more black fighters than white and he is renowned for providing promoters with journeymen, boxers prepared to take defeat as long as the pay is good enough. And there is another difference. Nobby's gym makes Moston look like a palace.

The walls are plastered with posters featuring Nobbs' fighters down the years. His most successful protégé was Lloyd Hibbert, who broke with convention to win the British and Commonwealth light-middleweight titles in 1987. Half a dozen of Nobbs' current stable are training this afternoon, their clothes strewn across chairs. It's the nearest they get to a changing-room. A propped-up blackboard lists the names of fighters booked on forthcoming shows: at Wembley, Nottingham and Derby. Music blares from a portable stereo, competing with the sound of the boiling kettle.

Nobbs, dressed in black trousers and a black jumper, ticks off the rounds with chalk on a metal trolley as two of his men spar in the rickety ring. When their stint is over they are rewarded with a spray of water in the face from the boss's sponge and ordered to tackle the punch bags. Nobbs puts the squeeze on a tea bag, grabs his mug and browses through the display of posters and cuttings.

'We had a good 'un in Lloyd Hibbert. I've had about twenty-one Midlands champions, about five final eliminators, two title fights in one year,' he says, taking the obligatory seating position on the edge of the ring. 'The trouble is, when they fight for titles there's always the flying machine in the other corner. I can never get half a chance of winning some of 'em.'

In this corner of the gym the names on the posters include Martin Jolley and Paul Ingle.

Nobbs comes in with a sharp jab: 'Martin Jolley there, he's had more fights than John Wayne.'

At the risk of betraying his image, Nobbs interrupts the flow of jokes to join the serious debate over fitness and weight loss, and the concerns raised by the defeats inflicted on Ingle and Gomez. Just as Hughes maintains he would have pulled Ingle out of his fight in Sheffield, so Nobbs is now adamant he would have stopped Gomez long before the end in Widnes.

'After the fourth round you could see it wasn't Gomez fighting, it was somebody who looked like him. He wasn't right. All you do is pull him out with a bad hand and you live to fight another day. They took a bit of a risk and it didn't come off. They underestimated the other guy as well. These East Europeans, they're good amateurs and they know how to keep it together, and they're strong.

'I don't know about this business of the weigh-in with Gomez, I just think it was a bit of sour grapes. It wasn't his night. He could have pulled himself out but he knew American TV was there and he probably didn't want to, or they didn't want to pull him out. But he was going nowhere. I think at the end they were grasping at straws and it didn't come off. I think Brian, in hindsight, might be a bit mad with himself as well. I would have pulled out Gomez, and Ingle, but that's me with a cold view of it. When you're caught up in the action it's different, but I have pulled out kids many times. In the corner you live and breathe for the fighter, but when you see they're going nowhere you pull 'em out.

'That guy Ingle fought, he was still strong and still doing his thing. So pull him out and let him have another go. All the problems with some of these, Ingle and Spencer Oliver a few years ago, is because they're fighting two weights lower than they should be. I remember seeing Oliver at the Albert Hall and thinking he looked thin. That tells you a story. Ingle was reported to be weighing around 11 and a half stone 5 weeks before the fight. I always make my lads fight what they are. If they're 11 stone, fight 11 stone. Don't do the amateur game thing of losing half a stone to get down, because amateurs are doing only three or four rounds so you can get away with it. In the pros, with TV rights and everything, you're doing up to 12 rounds. You can't get away with it. It finds you out, end of story.

'It's better to be under-trained than over-trained because if you under train you've still got your strength, but if you over-train you haven't got that. And if you're struggling to make weight you're going to lose strength. I try to get my fighter a bit heavier and then he'll get through it. If they're the same weight as the flying machine you can't get 'em through it. There's never any danger I'll over-train my lads. The only time they run is when the policeman's after them.'

Nobbs' wit is as sharp as his instinct for survival. He was a nightclub doorman and a sparring boxer before establishing himself as a trainer and manager.

FIGHTING CHANCE

'I knew I wasn't no good as a fighter. I had three cuts men, one for me arse, one for me knees, one for me eyes. My cornermen used to have a red towel so it never showed the blood when I fought. It cost me nothing in transport; I always went home in an ambulance. I had 100 fights. I lost 99 and I was unlucky in the one I won, I thought I'd lost that one. There were 67,000 people at my last fight – when Villa played Man United I had a bottle over my head.

'I started an amateur club, the Rum Runner, in 1970 and had three internationals and an ABA champion. After about three years I turned pro. Over the years since then I've always supplied good opponents, kids who can look after themselves. It's a TV sport now. The TV fighters are in one corner and opponents in the other. We supply the opponents. I've had one or two upsets, though.'

An 'opponent' recently supplied by Nobbs for a TV show tore up the script, to the embarrassment of the promoters. A hard-nosed Nobbs told his boxer in the corner: 'If you don't win this you're walking home.'

For all the wisecracks, Nobbs takes pride in his care for those under his charge.

'We enjoy ourselves but we're professional. We know the score and when we get in the ring there's nobody more serious than us. Everybody knows that. My kids fight on the big shows, they walk in and, touch wood, they always walk out. Over nearly thirty years I've had three broken jaws, two broken noses, the odd cut eye and that's it. You tell me a rugby player or a horse-rider who hasn't had that. Boxing is as safe as you can make it.

'When two people fight there can only be one winner, but spare a thought for the loser. They've come second, but sometimes they come third, and that's what gets me annoyed. I hate getting kids stopped. Seeing my kids walk out, that's my game.'

Alas, Nobbs' kids rarely walk out as winners, which is why he and his gym will pass into boxing lore as 'Losers Limited'. It is a one-liner that has haunted him ever since he coined it.

'I shot myself in the foot a bit there,' he groans. 'I'd been on a Mickey Duff show. I had three fighters and two were hard done by, and it was just a quip. I said, "I'm going to start up a business, 'Losers Limited'." The week after I had a guy come over from America to interview me, a guy from the BBC Home Service, and the press just picked up on it. I went along with it and it stuck.

'People say they're losers and they'll always be losers, but listen, when you pay the rent they don't ask you how you got on. When you go to Tesco's for the shopping they don't ask you where you got the money. It pays for the extra luxuries for these guys, maybe a new TV or a better car, and they're earning the money the legal way. They ain't hurting or robbing anybody, or getting involved in drugs or anything like that. Boxing's given them the chance to earn that money.

'They go in to win but if it looks as if it's going to be hard we change down a gear and go into defensive mode. We just want to walk out, we don't want to be heroes. It's no use having ten cut eyes and losing on points. You're better off having no cut eyes and losing on points. Like when I used to do the doors – if I got beat up I got twenty quid, if I didn't get beat up I got twenty quid. So I earned the twenty quid the easy way. And that's what my fighters do. We earn as much as we can without getting hurt.'

Boxing's latest set of proposals for the protection of its participants makes Nobbs wince and blast the air with expletives.

'All they've done bringing all these rules out is make it even more expensive,' he protests. 'They're just being seen to be doing something about it. They'll just bow down to the BMA left, right and centre. They've screwed up the game by bringing in these weigh-ins the day before because the kid thinks, "Oh, I can do the weight now because I've got a day to put the weight back on."

'For 40 years, from 1929 to 1969, there were hardly any rules and regulations. They used to have a medical and that was it. They went 15 rounds and hardly a thing happened. Soon as they messed around with it, you got everything happening. Shouldn't mess around with it. If it ain't broke, don't fix it. They just listen to the BMA all the time. That Dr Shipman was a member of the BMA!

'We know the game. We're not going to get the kids hurt. The one thing that the Board have improved on is the medical care at ringside – the paramedics and all that, no one can argue about that, it's brilliant. But all the other things, like making the weigh-in the day before, it's encouraging kids to cheat, to get down a weight lower than they should be. They think they've got 24 hours to put the weight back on, but it don't work that way. Your strength needs more than a day. To get your strength up you need a good three days.

FIGHTING CHANCE

'I was on the Board of Control, Midlands Area Council, for 20 years, and I offered to do this staggered weigh-in for them, but nobody seemed that bothered so I thought, "Stuff it, then." It's up to a trainer to know what his fighter can do. It's hard to get a trainer's licence if you don't know what you're doing, especially now. So if the trainer knows what he's doing and the boxer knows what he's doing, and they don't kid each other, you've got half a chance. We're all our own men.'

Another of his men has finished for the day and departs with a trademark verbal cuff around the ear from Nobbs.

'See 'im? Takes 75 per cent of my earnings he does.'

The boxer laughs, shakes his head and waves wearily as he turns for the door. The chances are he will be back and keep coming back, because he reckons Nobbs' eccentric and irreverent style of training and management is worth the comic's 25 per cent cut.

Nobbs sips from his mug and resumes: 'All these started off with top managers, but they came to me in the end because they know there's no fairy stories. They know I'll look after 'em. They get rejuvenated. I treat people like I'd want to be treated. If you do that you can't go far wrong, can you? They all know it, and they all know I'll offer them fights. I say to them, "Do you want an easy one or a hard one?" They might go for the easy one or the hard one. Just as long as there's plenty of work.

'We're independent. We can box for anybody. A lot of boxers are tied down to certain managers and don't get many fights. We don't have contracts, we just have handshakes. I can look all of them straight in the face. I tell them if they've got a problem with me, tell me – I don't want to hear it from their mates. You know where you are then. Sometimes they say they think they deserve more money, but I explain to them why they didn't get more. If there's no TV you can't screw the promoter into the ground, because that's how you're going to kill the game. You need the small shows to keep the game going.

'We've got about 18 fighters here at the moment. Eight of them I can't take on the big shows because they're not quite good enough. But ten of them I can. These ten can fight anybody. You can run them in the Grand National, the Derby, anything, and you don't get the whip out.'

Perhaps their trainer could go on stage?

'People have said I should go on stage – sweeping it. Yeah, I play about, we have a laugh and a joke and that, but when that bell goes they're trying to bang my kids out and my kids are trying to bang their kids out, don't worry about that. And if we can't bang 'em out we try to stop 'em. I don't mess about. I show young lads how hard it is. After about a month I put 'em in with a pro and I tell the pro to give him a couple of stiff jabs. Make his eyes water. If they come back you know you've got something to work at. If they don't, at least you're not wasting your time. I'm a realist. At the end of the day they've got to fight. It's like having racehorses. It's no use having horses if they don't run. You shoot them. I don't shoot none of these, 'cos they fight.'

Nobbs considers himself to be of the old school. Like Hughes, he has scant respect for modern training methods. But then Hughes might not approve of Nobbs' more eccentric, personalised preparations for a fight.

'I say to them, "Do you want to warm up properly or do you want to put your hands on the radiator?"'

Another chorus of laughter fills the gym as Nobbs takes a long slurp.

'Naah, but some of these so-called top line trainers ain't really top line trainers. Many of them are fitness trainers and don't know that much about boxing. I learned the trade when I used to go down to London and go to all the gyms there. You could pick up things, looking at different fighters and styles and training.

'I don't believe in too many exercises, circuits and all that. As long as a fighter does his running he's okay, because you've got to have wind. If you've got a brand new yacht and don't have any wind, an old rowing boat'll overtake it, know what I mean? You've got to give them a bit of wind, then you teach them how to slip the right hand and block the left hook, and you're all right. But if you're tired you can't do anything. You're just reduced to a punch bag.

'The body's like a car. The more you use it, the quicker you knacker it up. That's why my kids have had so many fights. Two of them have had over 100 fights. All of them have had 50 fights plus. That's because we don't knacker ourselves. Why kill yourself?

'All decent trainers will tell you that if you've got a couple of good fighters in your gym the others will learn off 'em. If you've got crap fighters they're only going to end up crap. We've always had fighters who have fought world-class fighters. I put the kids in with them for a couple of rounds and they learn off them. And the good fighters will tell me if they're any good or not.'

Nobbs brackets Hughes with those 'decent' trainers, men who have served their time and learned their trade.

'Brian and I were in opposite corners as amateurs, when I was at the Rum Runner and he was with Collyhurst. We respect each other. Brian has got some real good kids and he's taught 'em well. When they fight they've always got the right opponent in the other corner, where mine have to fight the good fighters, like his kids. Many a time I've had kids fight his kids and they've lost on points, and he knows they give 'em a fight. Maybe not beat 'em, but he'll look at me and he'll think, "His kid knows the game." And they'll learn from it. We gave Jennings his hardest fight and he's come on a ton. Same with McDonagh. They've been taught well and they've learnt from going in the ring with fighters like mine.

'You haven't done boxing till you've been on your arse, you know what I mean? You've got to find out how hard it is. My fighters find that out quicker than others.'

Hughes admits he is finding some aspects of boxing too hard to take but Nobbs maintains the seamier side of the game is exaggerated.

'Brian ain't going to pack in. He ain't going to take up gardening, is he? It's in his blood, ain't it? Boxing ain't corrupt. Don't forget all these promoters – your Warrens, your Hearns, your Duffs – it's them that are putting the money down. They're paying the kids good wages. Before all these promoters came along kids were on three or four hundred quid a fight. You'd get the odd good pay day if you fought on a Harry Levene show, but you knew you was going down to get beat. Warren didn't start off a top-liner. He struggled at the start. If somebody wants to slag the promoter, let him try doing the job. See how easy it is.

'To put on a two-bob show now it costs you £6,000 – and you ain't going to get your money back. You think how many tickets you've got to sell to cover that and pay for everything – doctors, all the medical stuff, everything. I don't criticise promoters, because they pay their way. If Frank Warren offers me X amount to take a fight, I ain't got to take it, have I? And a promoter wouldn't go behind the trainer's back to a fighter – not with me he wouldn't.

'Boxing's saved Gomez. Probably stopped him serving time or something. Boxing's done a lot of good in Manchester. They've always had good fighters in Manchester. It's a great boxing town, better than Birmingham. This has never been a good fight town. You can put a show on in the Black Country and the place will be full. Put the same show on in Birmingham and it'll be half empty. It's drugs here. All these inner cities, they're all drugs, ain't they? Either kids want to box or they want to take drugs. Round here they mostly want to take drugs, unfortunately. You can't beat it. It's eaten in so much now.'

Nobbs was raised by his grandparents in Kingstanding, an area of Birmingham that evidently stockpiles material for his comedy routine.

'Even the dogs walk round in twos where I live . . . The window cleaner uses a Black and Decker . . . Kate Adie's the newspaper girl . . . My house used to be a four-star hotel. You can see four stars through the roof.'

Nobbs was in no mood for jokes one morning when he walked out of his house and opened the door of his car.

'I don't bother locking me car. No point. This particular morning I got in me car and someone had nicked me radio. So I went to the snooker hall and said, "Somebody's nicked me radio." Next morning I got up, got in the car, and there's a brand new radio. True story.

'I help a lot of kids, as Brian does. When kids go inside I sort them out. I send them money and that. I visit one or two and help them out. Write references for them, tell one or two little white lies. We're all social workers, really. Brendan Ingle is. He does a lot for Sheffield. He's had some stick lately but he's done a lot, like Brian Hughes. People who criticise them could never do what they're doing. I don't mind people criticising me. If anybody says anything against them or me I'd say, "That building over there's empty, get in there and let's see you do what we do and last 30 years." They wouldn't last a fortnight.'

Boxing has given Nobbs a purpose in life, a niche and a kind of fame but, he insists, it has scarcely earned him a fortune.

'If I could earn a living out of it I wouldn't be going down to the market six days a week. You try getting up at three o'clock in the morning at 52 years of age. I'm down there till midday, then go home and get on the phone, or try to get half-hour's kip. Then I come up here from about three to half-six or seven. I've got a good trainer now, so he's taken a bit of weight off me. You get a couple of good months and then nothing happens, especially if a boxer gets stopped. He can't fight for a month. I've got only the ten who can fight anybody and once they've fought 'em you struggle to get fights.

'I never go away or leave it. I don't bother with holidays. You've got to keep at it. If you're going to take money off 'em, you've got to earn it. None of these have to pay anything to come here, though. No subs or anything. I pay all their medicals for them and all this – four bags, speed-ball, trainer, petrol. I wear my car out every two years. They don't have to pay a penny more. To turn a kid out now costs about 400 quid, and they've got to have about four fights before you get your money back.

'All they gotta do is fight. And it's up to them who they fight. If somebody comes to me and asks if one of my kids will fight Naseem Hamed I'll ask the kid first. In the old days they'd just take it without asking the fighter. I don't do that. I have had kids fight Naseem Hamed. I've got the only English fighter who went the distance with him, Peter Buckley. He would have gone the distance a second time, only the referee stepped in when Peter was making him look a bit stupid.

'I'm like a broker and an agent as well as a trainer and a manager. I book them a fight, X amount of pounds. If they want it they usually ask me if I can get a bit more. If I can't they'll probably give the fight to somebody else. They've done that before.

'When I have kids come here I want to know what they're doing. I hate to see kids get their heads knocked about. I don't like kids boxing at 12, 13, 14. When they're 15, 16, 17, OK. But we don't have many of them. I've got 8 boxers over 30. They're all MOT'd, mine are. When they walk in the ring you don't get to worry about 'em. When kids walk in the ring you worry about 'em. They've got to learn. That's the trouble with the amateur game. You go to an amateur club, there's a hundred doing exercises and skipping and two sparring. It should be a hundred sparring and two skipping. That's why we've got no top amateurs.

'That "Ordinary" Harrison, as we call him [Audley] up here, he's no Lennox Lewis, is he? When Lewis was an amateur he fought the likes of Bowe and that. Harrison did all right in the Olympics, but listen, there were 16 heavyweights there and 10 of them were crap. The kid he beat in the final was no better than a six-rounder – that's how you have to look at it in the cold light of day. People like Wayne Alexander, bloody good fighter, them are the ones you want. Brian has done a great job with Gomez and Farnell. Ingle's done a great job with Nelson. He ain't that good to watch but I tell you something, he'll take some bloody beating. Same with that Damaen Kelly. It's like watching paint dry watching him, but it'll take a good 'un to beat him. So if you've got a good 'un, you put him in.'

Nobbs is intent on continuing as long as he has good 'uns, or even not so good 'uns, to put in, and is convinced the game will go on as long as man has the impulse to trade blows.

'The game has changed. It is a TV sport now. But it will survive. If they don't do it legally they'll do it illegally, won't they? If somebody wants to do something it's freedom of choice. You can get killed just driving away from here. A man's a man. Look at the 1914 war. They all wanted to join up, didn't they? They must have been crackers. If you didn't go over the top they shot you, but they still wanted to do it, and it's the same here. The kids can express themselves. Boxing gets them in front of the TV cameras and all of a sudden they're somebody. From nobody they're somebody. You know the song, "You're Nobody Till Somebody Loves You".

'Life's a struggle. The only way you beat it is if you win something. To win something you've got to have something in the first place to put down to win. I tell all these kids here that life's like Snakes and Ladders, but there's more snakes than ladders. Now and then you find the ladder and you've got to hope it's a big one. Boxing's a ladder.

'I'll go on till I drop down dead. Just my luck, I'll probably have a kid win the world title and drop down dead. I'll keep in the game forever and ever. You have your good times and your bad times. I had a gym for six months with no fighters. Then all of a sudden you get one or two come in. I'm going to be in trouble in a couple of years' time because, as I say, all these are over 30, so what am I going to do then? I'm going to be struggling. There might be one or two more, but you just hope you do get them. Otherwise I'm finished, ain't I? I'll have to be a bucket man for Brian Hughes. Or a lollipop man.'

He could always train women boxers . . .? Another volley of expletives.

'Forget about it. Women should be in the kitchen or the bedroom. I don't even watch it, I don't even talk about it. It's not taken off and it never will. All this with the Ali/Frazier daughters – gimmick, just a gimmick. If you watch 'em they're crap, anyway. No way I'll have anything to do with it.

'I don't advertise for fighters. Somebody asked me to put an advertisement in the papers. I said the day I've got to advertise is the day

I'll pack it up. All these fighters talk to each other at shows and ask each other, "What's so and so like?" It is a small world, ain't it? They'll go, "He's okay". I mean, I'm no angel, like. But I'm all right. I look after them.

'Sometimes I can be hard. I had a kid – I knew he couldn't win – and he's come back to the corner, got on the stool, and I've shouted to him, "You see them things on the end of your arms? Try throwing 'em!" And he went out and knocked the kid out. I might tell a kid after four rounds of a six-rounder, "Well done, you've lost five rounds." They know what I mean. Or I might give them a good hard slap or something and I'll say, "Don't feel sorry for yourself, I don't want excuses, the time is now."

'But when we go home, we stop at the services and I get them meals and drinks. Even if you don't get the result – like last week, all three lost – in a way, you're winning. You're winning because they haven't got hurt and they've earned half-decent money. So when they go home they give their wives some money and they take their kids to the pictures and McDonald's, and they've got mustard and ketchup down their cheeks, all laughing. You've won then, ain't you? If the kids are starving you ain't won.'

And yet no one who steps into the competitive arena can be immune to the naked thrill of victory. Even Nobby Nobbs must get a buzz when one of his boxers registers a rare win.

'No,' he responds with a deadpan expression. 'Only when somebody rings the door bell.'

He gives cursory instructions to two fighters exercising – none too strenuously, it should be recorded – and adopts a genuinely solemn countenance.

'I've been around a long time. If they win, or they lose, or they knock somebody out, life still goes on. There's a lot more to life. All these earthquakes, loads of people being killed. All these diseases, all this drug-taking. I've had kids come round to my place crying their eyes out. Tough kids, on to drugs and that. I'll take them to the clinic. That's when you've got to take life a bit more seriously.'

He reverts to jocular mode as he delivers his parting shot, but even now it is a black humour spawned by the reality he and the rest here confront daily in the inner cities.

'Be careful you don't get mugged out there. Mind you, if you do, give us a call – we'll come down and join in!'

FIGHTING CHANCE

Gales of laughter provide a fair wind all the way along the corridor, down the stairs and out into Thomas Street. One of Nobbs' boxers, his training finished, puts his bag in the boot of his car. So what is that man like to work for? The boxer sniggers and then, in an instant, is straight-faced. It seems to be a trait of the gym.

'He gets me good money, that's why I come here,' the boxer says. 'You don't need no better reason that that. Yeah, there's all that joking and messing about, but he's not afraid to slap you in the corner if he thinks he has to. There's no messing then. You know you've got to be serious and do the job. He knows the game, he's been around a long time. You know where you stand with him. That's what you want. That's what anybody wants.'

Martin Jolley's career prospects appear to be improving, despite an apparent difference of opinion with the boxing authorities and another turn of events in his private life. His plan to become an inspector appears to have been scuppered and he has split from his girlfriend, but he is evidently assuming a responsible role with at least one of Chesterfield's licensed premises.

'I've knocked that inspector's job on the head,' he says. 'I had a big fall out with the Board. I'm owed £3,295 for the fights where I got messed around and what have you, but they are trying to make out I'm not entitled to it. Apparently, it's something to do with the Michael Watson case and they say they can't do anything about it. They just keep fobbing me off so I told them they can stuff the inspector's job. I've also finished with my girlfriend. After 15 months I had to decide whether I wanted a permanent relationship and I couldn't do that. I felt it was going nowhere. Anyway, I've got a new girlfriend now.

'To be honest everything's looking good because I'm effectively running Bar 69 now and I could be like the manager there. And the training is going well. I've even got a kick-boxer, an English title winner. I got offered the chance to try it, but I wouldn't. I couldn't risk it. You wouldn't guess the latest, though. I got a call from a woman boxer, Caroline, from Stoke. I didn't catch her surname. But she asked me if I'd train her. Some of these women boxers are, well, butch, to be perfectly honest. But she's not, she's lovely. She's a British champion, eight and a half stone. So she's coming over to my place, to train in my garage. We'll see how it goes and take it from there.'

Jolley should not hold his breath for Nobbs' approval. But then wasn't John Wayne's real name Marion?

8 ☆ IN THE DOGHOUSE

ANOTHER OF THOSE TV SHOWS NOBBY NOBBS TALKS ABOUT IS coming up at Wythenshawe, Manchester, and familiar names from Moston feature on the bill. Brian Hughes, emotionally scarred by the controversy surrounding Michael Gomez's defeat to Laszlo Bognar, is comforted by the expressions of faith and loyalty from his fighters during the build-up. The gym's senior pro, Robin Reid, is not in action but willingly appears as spokesman for 'Team Collyhurst and Moston'.

Reid, who has the eloquence to match his looks, addresses 'all the critics out there' with a stirring defence of his colleagues and, in particular, Gomez. 'We help the lads who have had a loss,' Reid says. 'They'll bounce back. It's a better fighter who can come back from a loss. That's what the atmosphere is like in the Collyhurst and Moston Club now. I've got 100 per cent belief that Michael can beat any of them out there. I see him every day in the gym. I know what he's doing. He's maturing all the time and I'd back him 100 per cent. But he doesn't want to be rushed. It's better for him to fight for the world title when he's ready.'

Gomez begins his public rehabilitation with an exhibition fight against stable-mate Michael Jennings, whose opponent has pulled out at the 11th hour. The hastily arranged match helps Gomez's personal cause and eases Jennings' discomfiture. He has sold 200 tickets and his fans have to be assuaged. Anthony Farnell and Thomas McDonagh add wins to their

CVs so the evening would appear to have been a professional and PR success for the Moston gym.

However, things do not run smoothly throughout the show for Gomez, who is conspicuous by his absence from ringside as Farnell retains his WBO Inter-continental light-middleweight title. The whisper in the hall is that he took what he considered to be his usual place, only to be asked to move. Suddenly, it seems, he is no longer wanted on camera and stories of a rift with the Warren organisation are given added credence. Those closest to the boxer are concerned that a sense of rejection could undermine his fragile self-discipline.

A fresh, spring morning outside; routine toil, sweat and laddish larking inside. Reid, Farnell and Jennings are among those punching, skipping and stretching their way through another session at Moston. Two Welsh amateurs are exercising Reid, who gives them a stinging close-up of the professional game. Farnell takes over from Reid in the ring and is as uncompromising as the message on his T-shirt: 'Absolutely, positively, most definitely, without a doubt, NO FEAR'. His face tightens with savage intent and his sparring partner doubles up under the ferocity of a low punch. Farnell apologises yet quickly resumes his venomous attack.

Missing from the regular line-up is Gomez. He has not been seen for several days. The word on the street is that he is in trouble with the law. He is said to be implicated in underworld skirmishes and facing possible charges. There is talk of family connections with a drug dealer, of a stabbing, of retribution. The knowing nods challenge the much-vaunted bond with colleague and friend.

Hughes has tried harder than most to protect Gomez and cover his wandering tracks. But now the years of anxiety are becoming evident in his wearied countenance. He can no longer contain his dismay.

'I've heard nothing from him and Anthony says he's heard nothing from him,' Hughes sighs. 'What I do hear from people is that he's in trouble. But I don't know what's happening or where he is. I won't go chasing him. I used to, but not any more. I'll try to phone him but that's all. He's not a kid any more. He's a grown man with family responsibilities and professional responsibilities. He's got to stand on his own two feet.'

Jennings presents no such problem. He mostly keeps his feelings to himself. He has none of Gomez's cockiness, none of Farnell's bravado and much less of Reid's presence. He is 23, dark haired, pale skinned, slim and unassuming. He goes about his work with the diligence of a young man on a mission. He is not one of the stars so he must work at his game and make the most of every opportunity.

'I suppose it's harder for me to get the publicity because all these lads are at a higher level,' Jennings accepts. 'But with our lads up there already it helps me get fights. I can go on the undercard, get the experience and hopefully one day I'll be topping the bill. I don't get the Manchester publicity that Tom, Mike and Anthony get but I get a lot back home in Chorley. I always sell a lot of tickets, to friends and people I've known for years. I'm looking forward to a British title fight. Brian says it's up to me now. I need a few more fights under my belt and I'll be ready.'

Commitment and dedication to that cause come with little difficulty to Jennings. For a start he simply cannot afford too many damaging distractions.

'I don't drink, I don't smoke and I don't spend much when I go out. A weekend outing for me is going to the pictures with my girlfriend. She's all right. She knows I can't go out a lot. I live at home so I don't have bills to pay. I manage to make a living out of boxing. I've got a car and three of us share, take it in turns to drive down here.'

Jennings has no doubt that the lure of the boxing gym has steered him away from a course of self-destruction. One of his brothers, Raymond, boxed as an amateur but was diverted into a downward spiral of drugs and crime. He was killed by a heroin overdose at the age of 25. Another brother, Stephen, died of leukaemia at 19. Jennings has one other brother and two sisters.

'If I'd taken the same way as all my mates I'd probably have been on drugs,' he says in a chillingly matter-of-fact way. 'They're all either locked up in prison or drug addicts. It was the same with our Raymond. He was about 16 when he started going off the rails with his mates. My mum and dad tried to help him, putting him on the straight and narrow, but he was always playing truant from school and going glue-sniffing with his mates. One thing led to another. He started getting into drugs and through drugs he lost his job. Because he lost his job he had no money so he started thieving and got sent to prison. Then he came out, straight back on thieving and drugs, and back into prison.

'I tried to talk to Raymond and help him but he was with a different group of mates. He didn't like it when I tried to keep him with me. He'd been boxing before me and he seemed to love it when I took him training again, at a gym in Chorley. But something just pulled him back to the drugs. It was too strong. My mum could never stop worrying about him. If he didn't come home she'd think he'd been locked up or killed by drug dealers.

'He died just before Christmas. I pulled out of my next fight. I couldn't fight. I couldn't train. The verdict at the inquest was accidental death. Heroin is the worst. It's like an epidemic around Chorley. It's only a little place but there's that many people on it you wouldn't believe it. You see the drug dealing that goes on and I don't understand why the police don't get involved. They know who sold my brother the drugs but they don't do anything. I never got tempted by drugs. Even as a kid I was determined to be dedicated. All my mates were going out boozing and that at 16 but it didn't bother me. I don't know why, but something in my head just made me go running.'

That sporting instinct steered him towards a gym in his home town but it was only after his younger brother, David, gave it a try that Michael summoned the nerve to look inside. It was the start of a career that brought him titles through the amateur age groups and carried him into the professional ranks.

'There were a few times I walked past that boxing club in Chorley and wanted to go in but didn't have the guts to go in. I was a bit wary. Raymond had already done a bit but then my little brother went down there and, a week later, I went. That was it. I've never looked back. I was 13. I think it has saved me. I'd probably have gone the same way as the others. It's not like you want to, but if everyone else is doing that sort of thing, it's just natural to follow your mates.

'Dave was a good amateur. He's been up here a few times, sparring with Anthony when he's been boxing southpaws. He's working now and he's a good worker, but he still does the training because he loves it. Both my sisters are working and I'm always at the gym, so at least my mum's got some peace of mind now.'

Jennings acknowledges the potential perils of his addiction, but he maintains he at least has a fighting chance. He is on a high every time he climbs into the ring. And, by the time he retires, he hopes to have the means to make him secure for the rest of his life.

'This is my chance,' he says. 'I wouldn't mind a bit of money. As long as I get something out of it. Enough to maybe set up some sort of business. Maybe a house. You expect to get something out of it after all the years of hard work you've put into it. There are dangers in boxing, but not like my brother had. Every time they have heroin it could kill them, and they have it five or six times a day. They're playing Russian Roulette.

'You don't think of the risk when you get into the ring. All you think about is winning. That's all I think about, anyway. I suppose it's my drug. There's nothing better than when you've got all your supporters behind you. When you're walking up and everyone's shouting for you it gives you such an adrenaline rush. And when you've won, it's just the best feeling.

'I don't know how far I can go. I'll just keep trying my hardest and go as far as I can. Even as an amateur I didn't set myself any goals. I just took it as it came and I won more or less all I could. As a pro I hope to do the same. I'd never be a journeyman boxer. I'm not just doing it for a living. If I had the choice of winning and not getting paid, or losing and getting paid, I'd win and not get paid. I'd pack it up tomorrow rather than be a journeyman.

'Hopefully, I'll have a long career. I don't see why not. I never really have a weight problem. I'm always within a few pounds of my boxing weight. I'm used to the work. I look forward to roadwork. Our house backs on to the West Pennine Moors, so I go running on the hills. I don't eat junk food, but I can eat more or less anything without really putting weight on. When I've got a fight coming up I start dieting and get my weight down to what I need it to be.'

There was a time when Jennings' tormented mother could not bear to watch her son in the ring. Those worries, too, are behind her now.

'Mum never used to come when I was an amateur because she got too nervous, but when I turned pro, she bucked up the courage to come. Now, she comes to all my fights. My dad has always come to my fights. My girlfriend does, as well. And my brother is mad on it. All the family come. I suppose it kind of helps us all.'

FIGHTING CHANCE

A couple of weeks on and Gomez is back in the gym. He is his usual impish and mischievous self. He has plenty to say and works feverishly. He playfully wrestles a young sparring partner to the grubby canvas. The dark stains on his top bear testimony to his physical effort. And yet something is different. Hughes is discernibly cool towards the protégé he treated like a son. Gomez is conscious that the man he regarded as a second father is keeping his distance. Those brooding eyes flash glances at Hughes, but the trainer has no intention of returning the look. Gomez, his face seized with concentration, pushes himself through another round of exercises as, one by one, his colleagues change and leave the gym. Hughes, too, is gone before Gomez calls it a day. Only Reid remains to keep him company.

The gym is eerily still and tranquil. Even the mandatory blare of the radio has been silenced. Reid is showering. Gomez slumps on to the edge of the ring and stretches out his legs. He rubs his face and neck with a towel and cannot get the words out fast enough.

'I'm back and it's just going to be awesome this time. Like I was before. The whole lot wasn't right for the last fight. I said I didn't want to fight. I was pushed into it. I was offered more money, that's why I ended up taking it. Now they are denying it, coming up smelling of roses. I wasn't myself. I'd done two and a half weeks of training. To do it properly you need six weeks. I need that to get in perfect condition, which I'd been getting for my previous fights. But all of a sudden they pulled this out. I was well overweight. I was ill with flu.

'I went off the rails after the fight. Before the fight, I was going out, but not too naughty, really. It was far from the real Michael Gomez in there, even mentally. I didn't want it as much. I've always got my hunger but I didn't feel the same desire and incentive. It was my pride that was hurt. I've fought not fully fit before, when I was a junior and was brought in as an opponent and you get through it. But this time was different. My arms were aching, my legs were aching, through the flu. I had a viral infection. I was really bad.

'As soon as I walked into the venue I said, "I don't want to fight, can I have a hot chocolate?" I know when I'm ready to fight and I wasn't that night. I'm a grown man and I should have stood up and said, "Listen, I'm not fighting." And I shouldn't have been worried about what they might think or other people might say. I wasn't standing up for myself.

I'm a father. I've got two kids. I've got to start being a man. That's what I'm doing now. Standing up for myself and starting to do things right.'

Gomez's private life has already been a parallel drama of emotional turmoil and sometimes violent conflict. In the aftermath of that traumatic defeat in the ring he had to contend with more of the family ferment that few could ever comprehend, let alone encounter.

'There was a murder in Moston, this lad got stabbed. My sister got arrested because her boyfriend was involved. He's a no-good, washed-up kid who's been dealing in weed and all that. He thinks he's a drug dealer, a gangster, and he's not. That's what set me off. I'm very protective of my sisters, so I gave him a few cracks and got arrested for it. It's probably what any other brother would have done. I did it for the right reason but the wrong way. I accept that. I was just looking after my family, my sisters, as I always have. That's how I got into boxing, through fighting for my sisters.'

Gomez then reveals how this sibling obligation has landed him in further trouble with the police. Another of his sisters, aged 19, 'has just got pregnant to some waste-of-time lad and I crashed my car chasing him. I'm on an affray charge. I'm on bail, banned from Manchester city centre.

'I've been through a bad patch, a bad experience. I've been in pubs and clubs, fighting and doing stuff, messing about with women, things I shouldn't be doing. People don't pick fights with me – it's the other way round. I've been a bit of a bully, to tell the truth. That's nothing I'm proud about. I'm heartbroken. Now the rumours are going about that I'm finished and washed up. Maybe it's good because it's made me sit up and think, "Right, now I'm going to show you all." I got beat, I drowned in my sorrows, I got into a bit of trouble with my family. But I've been down this path before. I've been in worse trouble than this. I got charged with murder and came back. I'll come back again. I'll learn from this bad experience. I shall come back stronger.'

He has also made these promises before. He knows he will be judged on deeds rather than words by the sceptics and those who harbour a sense of betrayal.

'I think I've really let Brian down,' he confesses with a humility that belies his reputation. 'I think he's a bit disappointed in me now and I can tell he's a bit stand-offish and thinking, "What's this kid going to do now?" I want to prove myself to him more than anybody. I love Brian.

Brian's been good to me. I want it to get back to the relationship we used to have. But you have to take the rough with the smooth. It's just a bad patch, that's all. I just hope Brian doesn't cut me off, which I don't think he will. I think I can get things back to where we were after a couple of wins. It's just a matter of time.

'With Brian back on my side it's half the battle won. We was a team. It's hard to explain, but with Brian there in the corner, reminding me of the little tricks I've got, I could take on anybody in the world and give them a top fight, even now when I'm not at my best. Hopefully, we're working back to that, slowly but surely.'

It would appear Gomez ought also to patch up his relationship with Warren's organisation if he is to put his career back on track.

'That exhibition fight with Michael Jennings was another job Brian got me,' he acknowledges. 'It was a few quid for the family. He's always trying to help me out. And that's why it really hurts me, really upsets me. So I was there and I sat down for Anthony's fight. Then one of Warren's people said, "That's someone's seat, Mike." There was two ways I could have reacted. I could have cracked him or I could have walked away. I thought if I crack him that will get me nowhere, so I got up and walked away. But, as I did, I had a lump in my throat and I was thinking that if I'd won that last fight they'd have sent that person somewhere else, like they used to.

'They phoned me for the first time since then a couple of weeks ago. They wanted me to do a photo shoot with Anthony and Ricky Hatton. They said they wanted to get me back in the limelight, but it wasn't about me. They needed me to sell tickets for the next big show, because Ricky Hatton can't sell tickets like me and Anthony Farnell can. I told them I couldn't be bothered. They promised me a re-match with Bognar, but he's fighting for a world title. Now they say I'll get a re-match in the summer.

'It's when you're down that you start to think you're nothing and you wonder whether you have any friends. I've got one real friend, who was there from day one, who still comes round, still speaks to me. When I was going through a bad patch he turned up with a bowl of pasta and said, "Come on, let's have some of this together." He's my one real friend. All the others cling on. Brian's seen it all before and warned me. But I'm young enough to get away from them and carry on without them.

'The most important thing to me is my kids, and they are the ones I'll start looking after now. To look after them, I've got to look after myself. I've got to look after my body and live the right life, as I have done in the past. I'll get my head down and get back into serious training. I've had to take it on the chin and now it's time to get back and stop all these rumours.

'The next fight will get me back in it. I'm going to look sparkling, sharp and in good shape. I want to be spectacular. I want to tell them, all the people who have written me off, I'm still No. 1 in Britain, I'm still No. 1 in the Commonwealth. I'm 23 years of age and I've been a pro six years. How many can say that? I've got to use my experience and start coming back to my best. I will be world champion. I know I will.'

The reappearance of a freshly spruced Reid changes the mood and the subject. They are reminded of a previous occasion when they were the only two boxers in the gym.

Gomez: 'We'd stayed in late one night. Robbie was fighting for the world title. It was about eight, half past eight, middle of winter, so it was pitch black outside.'

Reid: 'It was just prior to my first WBC fight. It was a weekend.'

Gomez: 'We were in the changing-room, talking as you do about the sparring, and laughing and joking, and we heard a noise. We thought it was downstairs in the Co-op and carried on talking. The noise got louder and Robbie said, "The Co-op's closed, isn't it?" So we came out of the changing-room and could see stuff falling from the ceiling.'

Reid: 'It was a scraping noise. We looked up and there's some guy's leg banging through the roof.'

Gomez: 'Yeah, there's somebody's leg knocking through it. So we got a couple of mop handles that we use in training and moved over to the side.'

Reid: 'I grabbed one of the mop handles, stood at the side of the door and said to Mike, "When I give you the wink, go." But before I could, the guy's dropped down and Mike's put the head on him. Then I come in and whack him with the pole.'

Gomez illustrates his heading technique and giggles, out of control.

Reid contains his laughter to resume: 'The police come and say, "What happened to him?" We said, "He fell." They just gave us that "Oh yeah" look. Apparently the guy was a druggie, trying to get down to the Co-op.

But we didn't know who it was. He could have had a gun, anything. So anyway, the police just sort of winked. I think there was another one, who ran off. He wasn't as stupid as his mate.'

Hughes has a postscript to the story of the bungled burglary. He recalls that the two men involved subsequently appeared in court on a number of charges, including robbing old ladies. The defendant who was unfortunate enough to fall into the hands of Gomez and Reid told the judge: 'We would have been better off falling into a pit of Dobermanns!'

Gomez's re-match with Bognar has been confirmed. His chance to avenge that devastating defeat against the Hungarian comes on a 'Mad 4 It' bill at Manchester's Velodrome. His relationship with Hughes has evidently improved and he is training hard, perhaps too hard. 'Slow down, slow down, Michael,' Hughes pleads. Gomez is then instructed to step on the scales and Hughes expresses his satisfaction. 'No drinking,' is the final warning.

The boxer is adamant he has returned to the straight and narrow, and that nothing can divert him from it, yet trouble seems to be an unshakeable travelling companion. Another violent incident in his eventful young life left him in hospital with stab wounds, fighting for survival. Gomez relates his latest escapade:

'I was doing some extra training at Fitness First, with Mike Jennings and his brother, on the treadmill and stuff, getting a sweat on, having a laugh and a joke, but still working hard. We decided to go for something to eat in China Town. So we did and then walked up past Yates's, eyeing the birds, having a bit of a chit-chat. We didn't drink. I told Brian I wouldn't. I'm on curfew from town but we weren't looking for trouble. As we were talking to a few birds these two black guys came over on their bikes and asked us what we were saying to them. I said "What?" but they rode off and that was it.

'We walked on up to Oldham Road and were by the Post Office when all of a sudden the two lads came running out of the entry. Michael was stabbed in the back, his brother got whacked over the head with a truncheon. I turned round to see what's going on and the lad turned and sliced me right down my left arm. We didn't hit them or anything. We phoned the police; they came, the ambulance came. We went to hospital, Mike got six stitches in his back, David had a bit of a cut on his head and some stitches, and I had 26 stitches on the outside of my arm, seven on the inside of my muscle, seven on the outside of my muscle, and a plastic plate in my arm.

'I'd never had an operation before, and I know I'm a boxer, but I was pretty scared. The other lads there laughed and called me a soft git. Told me to say hello to Elvis and all that. So I'm going for the operation and I ask the nurse if I'll be all right. She said I'd be absolutely fine, one in a million chance of anything going wrong. I wake up two days later in intensive care, machines and tubes everywhere, even a tube in my willy to wee. I'd had an allergic reaction to the anaesthetic. I actually stopped breathing for four minutes. They told my family that because I was fit I should be all right, but they didn't know. My dad fainted, my sisters were crying.

'When I came round, the police tried to speak to me, but I was just rambling. I've been to see them since and given a statement, but they were never going to catch the lads. There's always different ways of dealing with it yourself, you know what I mean? I just happened to pull up at some traffic lights one day and I saw the two lads who'd stabbed me with a third lad outside a pub. They saw me and started laughing and joking and pointing at me. That just wound me up, so I stopped and followed them into the pub. I wanted to fight the two who'd done it, or let them fight Mike Jennings, but they wouldn't.

'I had a few beers and just got mad. When they left, I went looking for them. I chased them in my car, across fields and all that. I got the two of them, one after the other, and gave them a good walloping. I got my own back and at least I've got my pride back. But the police stopped me and got me for drink-driving. I'm banned and I've got to go back to court for that. I'm hopefully just looking at a fine and maybe a five-year ban. I just want to get all this court business out of the way, hopefully without going to prison, and start again.

'I've got a lot of making up to do with my girlfriend. She's stood by me for ten years, but now she's fallen out with me and I've moved out of the house. I'm living round the corner with a mate. I'm trying to get back with her. I want to convince her that I've changed. She wants proof. She's seen how I used to play with the kids, but since I got beat, I've not been playing with the kids. I've been doing all the wrong things. I've promised my girlfriend that if Bognar beats me again, I'll retire, that's how convinced I am that I'll win this fight.

'All this has started me thinking. I've got my family, a lovely house, with a massive garden – why do I want to blow it? There's no way in the world I'm going to do that. It's unbelievable how far I've come. When I was a kid I had nothing. Holes in my trainers. Tell you what me and my brother did once. We were at my sister's flat, seven or eight of us, playing cards. I was about 16. Next thing, we heard this smack. We looked out of the window. Somebody had jumped.

'So me and our kid flies down the stairs. We thought it was a man but when we got close we could see a woman's chest sticking out. We could see by the state of her she was definitely brown bread, so we covered her with a blanket. Somebody called the ambulance and police. Someone else said she had a wheelchair. So we went up to her floor and there's her wheelchair. She'd parked it there and climbed over the balcony. Then we saw her purse was there. So I kept watch and my brother opened it. There was more than twenty quid in it. It was no good to her where she was going, and she had no family, so we took it. It was going to be put to good use. We couldn't believe it. When I first fought I got £1,250, but this twenty–odd quid meant more to me at the time. We used to save up and get pot noodles. Me and my brother went to the chippy and bought bags of chips for everybody. We also got some pieces of chicken, but we scoffed them on the way back so we wouldn't have to share them. We was made up.

'The other day, I went to the Criminal Injuries to put a claim in. They asked me for my National Insurance number. I said I hadn't got one, so I had to go on the dole. I hadn't signed on for years. They asked me for my address. They'd got an address I'd forgotten all about. It was one room. I rented it on my own for 40 quid a week. I didn't have a telly till my dad gave me a black and white that he'd got off the flea market. Some people don't believe half the stories I tell them. I'm only 24 but I've lived the life of a man of 50.'

There are those who suspect the ravages of that concentrated life are taking a heavy and irreversible toll. The boxing ring has probably been Gomez's salvation, but if he loses his next fight, the professional and personal consequences could be catastrophic.

'A lot of people think Gomez is finished, a lot of them round here,' he says, lowering his voice to a whisper. 'For the first time, I've struggled selling tickets. I've done 350. People think I'm washed up. I don't blame them. If I'd seen a sportsman acting like I have I'd think, "Oh, he's just a piss-head." The way I was in that last fight I was a shot fighter. It wasn't me, it was only 40 per cent of me in there. When I win – not if – I'll win them all back. My girlfriend will probably be a bit harder work, but she's worth it. She's been through a hell of a lot. She's only 23 and she's got little Mike and Jade to look after. When I was going out and that she was trying to keep me under control. You push too many buttons. She can take only so much. Hopefully, I'll win her over and after this fight we'll go on a nice family holiday. It's a big chance I've been given, and I'm going to take it.'

And off he saunters, bag over his shoulder. He pops into the Late Shop and comes back out, swigging from a bottle of orange juice. It could have been the young scally, scoffing chicken and chips, all those years ago.

9 ☆ CYCLE OF CHANGE

THE BUILD-UP IS THE USUAL MIX OF PRIVATE RITUAL AND PUBLIC bluster. Brian Hughes goes through his time-honoured routine of trimming his hair and beard four days before the show, and cutting his finger and toe nails two days before. Michael Gomez has been fined for affray but spared a custodial sentence, so he is free to take his re-match with Laszlo Bognar and put on a little rumpus for the cameras at the press conference. A snarling Gomez fails in his attempt to goad Bognar and has to be pulled away from the inscrutable Hungarian.

The self-proclaimed Irish–Mexican declares: 'I've got a blood-red 666 shaved on my head. It feels like I've got the devil in me and he'll feel like he's in the ring with Satan.'

This just might be more than staged-managed hostility. There are those who wonder aloud whether Gomez really is possessed. Even away from the glare of the media, back at the gym, Gomez has been confrontational, butting a new stable-mate, David Barnes, in sparring. Hughes has six boxers on the Velodrome bill, yet Gomez remains his deepest concern, the loose canon in his formidable arsenal.

'I think Michael psyches himself up,' Hughes says. 'He sees the others getting the attention and he feels ignored. He doesn't like that. He's been really aggressive in training. Too aggressive. He's been going at it like a bull at a gate. I think he should be okay, but I don't really know. He's got to work on the mental side. He seems to be all right with Warren's people now, but everything depends on this fight and he knows that. It's up to him.'

Anthony Farnell's main pre-fight publicity is altogether more genteel, and a source of unconfined mirth in the gym. The 'Warrior' has been taking dancing lessons at a ballroom in Oldham to improve his footwork and he practises his movement to music in the ring at Moston. Sniggering colleagues wrap towels around their waists and waltz out of the changing-room to accompany Twinkle Toes.

'I thought Brian was joking when he said I was going dancing,' Farnell says. 'The lads are taking the Mickey all the time now, but I don't care. If it helps me become the best, it'll be worth it. They can laugh as much as they like.'

Some shows need gimmicks and fabricated stories. This show doesn't. It is a 5,500 sell-out, confirming Manchester's status as a hotbed of boxing and sport in general. United and City football fans will overlook their differences and join forces to put their weight behind this Mancunian cause. The red and light-blue club shirts brighten up the bustling approach roads as rain patters a familiar local accompaniment on this summer's evening. The regulation sombreros worn by Gomez's supporters are still more illuminating, if somewhat incongruous. At least they provide shelter.

The Velodrome is a symbol of Manchester's ever-developing sphere of influence in sport. This is the region's cycling centre and will be one of the principal venues for the Commonwealth Games. A javelin throw away from here, the City of Manchester Stadium, centrepiece of the 2002 Games, is taking imposing shape. From the start of the 2003–04 football season, it will be the home of Manchester City.

It is tea-time when the boxers emerge for the first of the 12 contests and, unsurprisingly, the Velodrome is barely half full. Frank Warren is occupied in the reception area and his sidekick Frank Maloney has hands to shake as Thomas McDonagh outboxes Birmingham's Paul Denton, in a six-rounder. Michael Jennings, too, is early to work. Hughes' instructions in the corner have to compete with the orchestrated blast of klaxon horns. His man is comfortably in control against David Kirk, from Sutton-in-Ashfield, until he is cut by a clash of heads and has to adopt a more judicious strategy. Jennings secures a points verdict over the six rounds to make it 12 wins from 12.

FIGHTING CHANCE

Blocks of seats are still empty as the contestants for the first title fight on the bill are introduced. Salford's undefeated Jamie Moore faces the seasoned Scott Dixon, from Hamilton, for the vacant WBO Intercontinental light-middleweight championship and the volume rises as the local man climbs into the ring. Chants of 'Mooresy' echo the message on the back of his black trunks. His head is shaven, his look cool. He exudes confidence.

This self-belief is reinforced by the younger man's ability to breach the Scot's defences. Dixon returns to his corner at the end of the opening round with a nosebleed and is out-punched again in the second. Moore is warned for a low punch in the third, but responds by launching a still-more frenzied attack. A left to the body forces Dixon down for a count of eight and the gallery roar Moore on to finish the job. Dixon's survival instincts steer him through the round and, in the fourth, he summons a counter-offensive. The baying of the mob gives way to a murmur of apprehension. 'Wake up, Jamie,' someone implores. Moore does not heed the warning. He is pummelled to the floor in round five. He tries desperately to get back to his feet, but is counted out, a veil of bewilderment falling over his face. Dixon, scarcely able to take in what he has achieved, is on his knees, in praise and thanksgiving to his god.

The abrupt ending of that fight means Hughes, in a change of garb, is on duty again, this time ushering Darren Rhodes to the ring. He anticipates few problems against Birmingham's Wayne Elcock in a four-round bout and Sky's commentary duo, Ian Darke and Glenn McCrory, decide this is a good time to go through their to-camera spiel. They stand with their backs on the action, much to the ire of a spectator whose view of the boxing is suddenly obscured. An apologetic Sky minion begs his patience. The commentators sit down before the end of the first round but pay scant attention to events in the ring.

Hughes would rather not see what is unfolding before him. Elcock is getting through to Rhodes with ominous regularity and the fighter from Leeds cannot hide his discomfort. Hughes gives his final instructions to Rhodes and hands over the reins of responsibility to Steve Goodwin. Hughes palpably feels he has to be with Gomez in the final minutes before his fight. Rhodes, he doubtless reasons, should be able to handle Elcock. However, this fight is veering out of Rhodes' control. He rocks Elcock in the last round and looks towards the referee at the bell. Instead,

Elcock gets the decision. Rhodes screws up his face in dismay and protests: 'No way, no way.' He rushes away from the ring, still shaking his head as if it will rid his mind of the truth.

Just about every seat is occupied now. Alan Minter, one of the British boxing greats from another era, takes his place at ringside. Further back, hard-looking lads of all ages mingle with brassy-looking women of all ages. Youngsters in Hatton T-shirts shriek excitedly. The sense of anticipation rises with the temperature. Programmes come in handy as makeshift fans. Nicky Piper, another member of the Sky team, removes his jacket and uses his notes to waft air. A water bottle positioned in the VIP and media seating area has already run dry. A security man with arms like logs and a chest bursting out of his green polo shirt wipes his brow. The lights go down, bringing a cooling respite. A replacement water bottle is rigged up and instantly a queue forms. In the elevated goldfish bowl that serves as the TV studio, Barry McGuigan is helped on with his jacket for the start of the live transmission. Another water bottle has been brought to replace the empty one. Somebody then points out that the bottle could be an obstruction for the paramedics and their equipment so it is moved back, out of harm's way, by staff.

The stage is ready for Gomez and he receives a rousing reception. The blue and white top, the Mexican Hat Dance and the confident strut seem to be saying the defeat by Bognar was simply a bad dream; it didn't really happen. Gomez holds his arms aloft and the lights gleam off his yellow gloves. His expression is mean and intense. He appears to leer in the direction of Warren, who is now sitting at ringside. Hughes gathers Gomez in his embrace and shepherds him to his corner. Warren applauds Bognar into the ring and again the challenger throws him a contemptuous stare. Hughes delivers more orders and his boxer nods attentively. The MC introduces Gomez, who beats his chest in defiance. The champion is unruffled.

Bognar just might be the coolest customer in the house. A ringside cameraman is sweating profusely before either fighter has mustered a meaningful punch. Gomez, characteristically, tries to force the pace and go for the body, but Bognar defends and counters effectively. A right gives Gomez food for thought, yet still he presses forward and is caught by a left, which dumps him on the floor. He is quickly back on his feet and stands for the rest of the referee's count to eight. He wipes blood from around his left eye as the bell sounds. 'He's been found out,' a veteran in the press corps concludes.

Gomez sticks to his policy of aggression in the second round and again walks into trouble. The Hungarian puts him down with a right-left combination. Gomez takes another count of eight and Hughes urges him to move from side to side as Bognar seeks to end proceedings. Gomez delves deep into his stores of resilience to fend off the measured blows and somehow launch his own assault. The barrage of shots bends Bognar double and sinks him to the canvas. The bell can scarcely be heard above the din, but it saves the champion.

It gives Bognar only brief respite. A rampant Gomez seizes his moment, resuming his attack in the third. Bognar is trapped in a corner, unable to resist the savage onslaught. He goes down again and, although he is up at seven, the referee decides he cannot continue. The fight is stopped and Bognar has no complaints.

Gomez's emotions are released in his moment of redemption. All the pent-up hurt and humiliation is unleashed. The shackles of shame and injustice are cast aside. He is exultant, leaping in the middle of the ring and then jumping on to the ropes to bask in the acclaim of his supporters. He tosses his gum shield to the reaching hands, but he also snarls and writhes to wring every drop of satisfaction from this act of retribution. It is vindication, vengeance and so much more. He told them, didn't he? Now do they believe him? Bognar evidently does, and nods his acknowledgement. Hughes puts a restraining, as well as congratulatory, arm around his boxer. Warren quickly appears in the ring, joining the celebrations. You do not go as far as he has without being an opportunist. He even wipes Gomez with a towel. The champion holds aloft his re-claimed WBO Inter-continental super-featherweight belt and tells the world: 'Gomez is back.'

Gomez re-enacts his fight all the way back to the dressing-room: the downs, the ups, the misery, the joy. It is a microcosm of his life. A young man tries to catch up with Gomez, but is held back by two minders. 'He knows me, honest,' the young man pleads. 'Michael, tell them,' he calls. Gomez doesn't hear. He is already walking through the dressing-room door and the stony-faced minders are unmoved.

Robin Reid, a spectator and club supporter this evening, greets Gomez with a firm clasp. 'You've got your act together,' Reid tells him. Gomez likes that.

Someone is evidently less convinced. 'If you'd listened, you wouldn't have got hit,' Hughes says. Gomez may not like that so much, but he does not contradict the sagacious trainer.

Anthony Farnell has his own fight to think about. His head is shaved, he has a fixed, stern expression on his face and Roy Keane's Manchester United shirt on his back.

Reid helps Gomez remove his gloves and tapes, and offers more words of encouragement: 'I know it wasn't a proper drop. You were off balance.'

Gomez cradles the gloves. 'I want these,' he says. 'I'll pay for them.'

He looks up at a scribbled prophesy on the wall, 'Win Gomez 666'. He smirks contentedly.

Reid's massaging flow is interrupted by Hughes' rhetorical enquiry, 'Are you swearing?' Reid grins and Gomez giggles.

The mood in the camp is buoyant. The relief is tangible. Yet Gomez feels the need to explain: 'One of his shots was a good one. The other I was off balance. So I thought right, I'm going to finish him.'

Reid recognises it is time to switch the team's attention and support to Farnell. 'Come on Arnie, you're going to do the business,' he assures him. Farnell grunts affirmation of his intent.

'Who Let The Dogs Out?' announces the arrival of Farnell's opponent for the vacant WBU light-middleweight crown to the ring. Takaloo – real name Mehrdud Takalobigashi – shakes his limbs as if to ward off the volley of boos. Gomez sits at ringside and this time no one asks him to move. The atmosphere changes with the music. Farnell walks out to 'We Are The Champions' and then has to muscle his way through a scrum of over-exuberant fans. Hughes is anxious and implores stewards to clear the path. Farnell is as delirious as his followers. He climbs into the ring, singing along with Queen, and makes straight for the Iranian-born fighter. Farnell, as menacing as Keane on a revenge mission, confronts Takaloo head to head and has to be pulled away by Hughes. Takaloo, seemingly a mite bemused, is reassured by his trainer, Jim McDonnell, if not the crowd. The formal introduction of Takaloo is virtually drowned by a storm of derision. The roar for Farnell rattles the Velodrome to its foundations. Takaloo is reminded that the Mancunian has a perfect record of 26 wins from 26, 17 by knock-out or stoppage. Farnell has to be cajoled by the referee in to touching gloves and the man from Margate smiles. It may be a nervous smile; it may be that he knows something Farnell doesn't.

FIGHTING CHANCE

Farnell is still scowling as the bell goes and he homes in on Takaloo. The crescendo of noise is at its peak. Within seconds it begins to subside, raucous conviction giving way to apprehension and then a shudder of disbelief. Takaloo stuns Farnell and supporters alike with his aggression and the precision of his punching. Farnell vainly attempts to assert himself, but Takaloo is as elusive as he is dangerous. As Farnell recklessly lunges in again, Takaloo directs an uppercut towards his jaw. Farnell tumbles to the floor. He clambers back to his feet, but the vacant expression on his face betrays his distress. When he tries to repel the inevitable barrage his legs begin to buckle. The referee decides Farnell is no longer in a position to defend himself and steps in. It is all over in 123 seconds.

Farnell, his mind scrambling to make sense of what has happened, appeals to the official to let him continue. He turns his gaze of bewilderment this way and that, as if in search of help or perhaps a way out of this bad dream. But, even now, his legs are like plasticine and the scene before him is painfully real. Takaloo is hoisted off his feet by his cornermen, a contemptuous grin splitting his face. 'Now who's the tough guy?' he seems to be taunting the vanquished Farnell. His fate re-affirmed, Farnell is shepherded back to his corner. What he would really like now is to be a million miles from here. He does not wish to face anyone, least of all Takaloo, who saunters across the ring to proffer a conciliatory kiss and hug. An inconsolably distraught Farnell is hurriedly led to the sanctuary of the dressing-room by Pat Barrett, a former camp member and still-loyal aide.

Farnell is not alone in his anguish. A spectator, unable to contain his fury, rushes towards the ring and is hustled away by security men. Suddenly, the volcanic tension is on the point of eruption. Farnell's defeat, and more especially the manner of his defeat, has triggered fighting in the crowd. A huge man lumbers onto the banked cycling track and hurls himself into a potential brawl. Security staff eventually manage to overpower him, but they are now at full stretch and struggling to restore order. Those in the VIP seats shuffle uneasily in the shadow of the spitting volcano. However, security reinforcements arrive from other parts of the arena and root out the principal troublemakers. The unscheduled fights are over almost as quickly as Farnell's.

A couple of little men from the undercard are sent on to help the crowd settle and draw breath before the main event. Another local fighter, flyweight Darren Cleary, takes on one of Nobby Nobbs' charges, Marty Kayes, who doesn't even look the 8 stone 1½ lb pounds he apparently weighed in at. 'There was more meat on that chicken leg I had earlier,' someone at ringside mutters. Others barely notice. Many are stretching their legs, and those who are still in their seats have opened the inquest on Farnell.

One by one, the rounds go to Cleary, but Nobbs smiles through it all. He sends out his boy for the fourth and last round with a pat on the face and a fatherly push, but the verdict is beyond dispute. Cleary has won every round and Nobbs congratulates him with an extra-large, gap-toothed smile. Cleary persuades a lone and indifferent ringside photographer to take his picture, gloves cocked in traditional pose.

That interlude over, the build-up to the top-of-the-bill contest begins with an introduction of famous faces. With Alan Minter, the former world middleweight champion, is his son, Ross, an aspiring boxer. Over there is Earnie Shavers, one of the hardest-punching heavyweights of all time. Reid receives a warm ovation, but perhaps the biggest cheer is reserved for the eternally popular McGuigan, who was WBA featherweight champion in 1985 and 1986.

Due respect paid, it is time for the main business of the evening. Jason Rowland, the Londoner challenging for the WBU light-welterweight title, defiantly parades the claret and blue of West Ham United on a night of raw passion to rival almost any football occasion. The inevitable symphony of whistles and jeers ends abruptly with the entrance of the champion. The boom of approval competes for air space with the rendition of 'Blue Moon', the theme tune Hatton, a City fan, has brought with him from Maine Road. The fervour raises the temperature another couple of notches from hot and steamy to sweltering and unbearable. But Hatton, fair-haired and still fairer-skinned, remains cool and composed.

The contrast with Farnell is stark: no snarling, no overt aggression, no hysteria. Hatton, 22, looks like a boy you would be happy to have next door. His expression and demeanour border on the angelic. The illusion only blurs when he has Vaseline applied to his face and then punches his cheek as if to click a schizoid switch. The reception for the referee, Mickey Vann, of Leeds, is suitably hostile. Venom flows freely between the cross-Pennine cities, whatever the sport. Rowland becomes the main target of abuse again as the formal introductions are made and the faithful reaffirm their commitment to the 'Hitman' with another thunderclap of an ovation.

Rowland is finally exposed to the devil within. Hatton, small, chunky, ever-hustling, lands a stinging right and then a left. A large black man runs around the ring to a neutral corner and yells instructions to Rowland. A minder diplomatically – and cautiously – persuades him to return to his seat. Rowland begins to make use of his height and reach advantage to jab the eager Hatton at bay. The champion gets in close, a little too close for his camp's liking, in the second. Hatton has been susceptible to cuts in recent fights and an agitated fan screams: 'Watch his head.' Hatton directs his next attack downstairs, to the approval of his followers. 'Come on Rick, his body's knackered,' one bellows. The referee, glistening with perspiration, reaches for a towel at the end of the round and wipes his face.

Hatton's yellow glove thuds against the side of Rowland's head in the third, sending a spray of sweat across the canvas. Rowland responds smartly, and again prompts Hatton's fans to warn him about the challenger's head. However, it is Rowland who goes back to his corner marked, under the right eye.

Undaunted, he scores confidently and regularly early in the fourth, and Hatton is content to back off for a moment's respite. But he is also gathering himself to launch his most powerful offensive so far. Hatton moves in with purpose and conviction. Three lefts propel Rowland into a corner and on to the floor. He is up at seven but must realise he is about to be engulfed in an unstoppable whirlwind. Hatton, as voracious as the mob yet clinical in the execution of his task, buckles Rowland's ribcage with a left and the challenger goes down again. He makes a token effort to beat the count but, even before Vann can reach ten, Rowland's trainer, Jimmy Tibbs, is in the ring, acknowledging his man's fate.

Hatton leaps on to the ropes and his gum shield flies several rows back into the ecstatic throng. Hatton soon has his feet on the ground again, willingly sharing the limelight with a young fan, James Bowes, who has a much bigger fight on his hands, against life-threatening illness. The boy next door reappears and Hatton describes Rowland as 'a credit to the game'. He signs off with a word of appreciation to the people: 'Manchester, thank you.' They jig like City fans in the Kippax stand at

Maine Road as he departs with an unblemished record now stretching to 24 fights. Giddy in the after-glow of Hatton's latest success, they even seek out and shake hands with Warren and Maloney.

The rest of the show is played out to a rapidly dwindling audience. Anthony Hughes, from Salford, requires just 35 seconds to win a bizarre bantamweight match. His opponent, Peterborough's Daniel Ring, complains of a dead leg and cannot go on.

Wayne Pinder, the middleweight Martin Jolley had been scheduled to meet on that ill-starred bill at a Manchester hotel, has turned up tonight and the man in the opposite corner, Ian Toby, from Newcastle, probably wishes he hadn't. The Geordie goes down in the first, to the delight of Pinder's fan club, whose cheers echo around an arena that is three-quarters empty. Pinder is cut above the left eye in the second but catches Toby at the end of the round, and the bell saves him. The action is evidently not, alas, making an impression on Sky. Technicians are dismantling the television equipment and Darke is idly chatting. Toby earns his corn by prolonging the unequal contest to the fifth round, but that proves to be the last. He is out of the ring before the official announcement confirms that he has retired.

It is eleven o'clock when Hughes brings the last of his six boxers into the ring. David Barnes, who was known as David Smith when he fought, with distinction, as an amateur, has spared the remaining on-lookers some confusion by changing his name ahead of his professional debut. His opponent at welterweight is Trevor Smith, a member of Nobbs' camp. Smith or Barnes, the new boy has evidently not got round to organising personalised kit, so Hughes is wearing Reid's black and red 'Grim Reaper' gear. Reid is still at ringside, although he seems preoccupied with his mobile phone.

Gomez joins him and they watch in admiration as Barnes, bearing an uncanny resemblance to Floyd Patterson, the former world heavyweight champion, with a modern version of that trademark quiff, goes to work with total self-belief. His small yet voluble band of supporters urge him to sustain the flow of powerful punches through an impressive maiden round. Nobbs observes in silence from a neutral corner, leaving the work to a colleague. There is nothing Smith or his seconds can do to restrain Barnes, who lands with increasing ferocity in the second. Smith is trapped on the ropes and the referee has seen enough. It has taken Barnes just 3 minutes and 50 seconds to put down his marker in the professional game. He is hugged by Hughes and then milks the applause of his rapt fans.

Hughes' long shift is over. 'It's been a pretty good night, overall,' he says, reflecting on four wins from six, but the obvious setbacks cannot be brushed off. 'It's a pity about Anthony. I don't know what was wrong with him tonight. He's gone home, I think. He's disappointed. I'm okay. Just tired, that's all.'

Nobbs' working day isn't quite finished. He ambles out to the ring with Jason Nesbitt for the final contest, against Liverpool's Colin Toohey. Barely a handful of spectators have stayed the course. Even the majority of the security staff have gone. Some are loitering outside, having a smoke. Those still inside the arena can take their pick of the posh seats and watch Toohey outclass Nesbitt over four rounds of lightweight boxing. If the lack of attention is discouraging it doesn't show. This, too, is part of the game.

It is difficult to imagine that, not so long ago, this was a scene of pandemonium and mass hysteria; a pit of seething, heaving, breathless humanity. Now it is barren, soulless, abandoned; a place fit only for the rubble of shattered dreams. The rain has stopped, the car parks are all but emptied. The calm beyond the storm is a poignant re-acquaintance with reality.

10 ☆ A DIRTY, ROTTEN, STINKING BUSINESS

BRIAN HUGHES IS BUSINESS-LIKE, ORGANISED, MUCH THE SAME AS usual. He is coaxing and cajoling, calling on his time-honed psychology as well as his coaching skills to harness the talent at his disposal. Outwardly, at least, all is well at Team Collyhurst and Moston, and yet there is a sub-text here that is threatening the main plot. Hughes, for all his wiles, is struggling to suppress it.

Here, as in every gym, club, pub and workplace where boxing people meet, the Velodrome show has been analysed and dissected. It would appear the evening was not considered a total success after all and that the over-heated cycling centre is unlikely to become an established home for boxing.

'I thought the atmosphere was superb,' Hughes enthuses. 'You know what it reminded me of? It reminded me of the United v Bilbao European Cup-tie, back in 1957, when they had to play at Maine Road because they had no floodlights at Old Trafford. The noise was just unbelievable. And it was like that at the Velodrome. Brilliant. But there were lots of complaints about the place and the way people were messed about. They say it was disorganised and nobody seemed to know what was happening. People turned up and were left outside in the rain. All that kind of thing.'

Hughes, of course, was concerned with developments inside the Velodrome. Four of his fighters won, but the expectations here were for a clean sweep and the two defeats cannot be dismissed as mere blips.

FIGHTING CHANCE

Anthony Farnell's first round stoppage, especially, is the talk of the fight game. Just as a fighter's success reflects on his gym, so does his failure. Hughes is conscious of that and it hurts. There are suggestions that Farnell was not properly prepared for a dangerous opponent, that Takaloo was underestimated. The Manchester grapevine is speculating that Farnell is seriously considering his future. That hurts even more.

'Anthony's gone to Spain for a break,' Hughes says. 'He just wanted to get away from it all and have a rest. He doesn't know what happened in his fight. I told him he would be drained if he got himself too hyped up and that's what it did to him. The crowd can do that. All that emotion is great for the atmosphere and every fighter wants the crowd behind him, but you mustn't let it affect you in the wrong way. We didn't underestimate Takaloo, not at all. But Anthony never got to work on him. He just wasn't himself.'

Michael Gomez told the world he was back after his victory at the Velodrome and he is in the gym already, seemingly intent on proving he meant it. He is his familiar, bumptious self, enjoying the craic and the training, and already promising to show in his next fight that he is here to stay. Hughes is aware that Gomez teetered on the brink before over-powering Laszlo Bognar and is relieved to have averted another catastrophe.

'Michael was too hyped up at the start of his fight as well,' Hughes says. 'I had to calm him down and tell him to go about his job in the right way. He got caught, but it wasn't a real bombardment. Then he showed something like his real self and finished the job well. He called me at eight o'clock the following morning and said he'd do anything I told him from now on. He said it would be just like before. And he's back in the gym straightaway. He looks all right. So does Thomas McDonagh. I don't think he got as much credit as he should have. He did well to win every round against a dangerous guy.'

The Frank Warren cast are not due on show again for a couple of months but Robin Reid, who split from the promoter to find another route, is now fine-tuning preparations for his next fight. So, too, must Hughes. 'I suppose I'll have to cut my hair and nails again this week!'

Reid comes through his contest but, back at base, all is not well. Farnell announces that he has jumped the Collyhurst ship and climbed on board with Ricky Hatton at Billy Graham's Phoenix Camp, across

Greater Manchester, in Hyde. Hughes, a proud and sensitive man, is wounded by the defection and its obvious implication.

'I've never even spoken to him about it, that's what really hurts,' Hughes sighs. 'But, after 40 years in this business, nothing surprises me. I don't deal in contracts. If somebody doesn't want to work with me then that's it. Before I accepted the Takaloo fight, I went to Anthony's house and begged him and his father not to take the fight. I said, "Wait 12 months, gain more experience," but they both insisted they wanted the fight. I knew Anthony would have to blame somebody when he went away and thought it over. I've worked with him for nine years. He had 26 wins from 26 fights and when he loses one he takes his ball home. That's life.'

Hughes' morale is scarcely bolstered by more word on the street that Gomez is lurching back into his old self-destructive ways. 'People keep telling me this and that about Michael, that he's getting himself involved in more trouble,' the harassed trainer says. 'Michael assures me he's got it all sorted out, but I'm not so sure. The sooner I get out of this the better. As I keep telling all of them, this is a dirty, rotten, stinking business. In fact, when I write my book, that's what I'm going to call it.'

Writing has given Hughes a means of retreat from the deepening angst of his boxing life. He is putting the finishing touches to his biography of Jimmy Murphy, the man who helped Matt Busby nurture his Babes at Manchester United, and is already planning a tribute to Denis Law, another of the club's legends.

'I know I'm no great writer, or anything like. Professional writers are different again. But I enjoy it. It's therapeutic. It takes my mind off everything else. I couldn't write at all when I was a kid. Now I lock myself away and write about the people I admire, in boxing and football. People tell me they like reading my books and if they make a few quid for the club then so much the better. It's a lot of effort, but it's worth while.'

The next big show at the MEN Arena, 'Mad 4 It 2', is only eight days away. Gomez is still featured on the publicity bills, but he will not be fighting. Hughes' suspicions have been confirmed: Gomez has been in more trouble, with more family strife and stories of involvement with gangsters and the underworld. Consequently, Gomez is in no physical or mental condition to go through with his scheduled contest. The plan now is for him to return to the ring later in the autumn.

Hughes calls Gomez into his 'Rest Room' to be weighed. The boxer steps onto the scales under the gaze of Hughes' sepia heroes, hanging on the wall. They include, naturally, the local triumvirate of McAvoy, Brown and King, but pride of place goes to Hughes' idol, Willie Pep, perhaps the greatest featherweight of all time. Gomez is a stone overweight, yet evidently unperturbed. 'It won't be a problem, I'm telling you,' he says.

Hughes smiles a resigned smile and goes about his other business as Gomez heads for the changing-room.

Gomez, dressed and scrubbed, promises: 'There are seven weeks to my next fight and I'll get fit. I want to be fit and I will be. I didn't want to fight next week. I told them I had chicken pox. I just wasn't fit. It was all because of trouble with one of my sisters again. Worse than before. I've been banned for three years and fined £250. And I was already banned. All my troubles come from my family. Now I've washed my hands of my sisters. I've told them to look after themselves. I want to clear the decks. I'm back with my girlfriend and kids and now I've just got to win over Brian.

'I've been asked to go to Billy Graham's gym, like Anthony, but this is where I've been since I was a kid. Brian's been like a dad to me. I've not really spoken to Anthony. He wanted to try something different. It's up to him. Brian thinks I'm not going to win my next fight. I'm sure he thinks I won't be back to my best. But nothing's going to stop me now – no family, no clubs, no women, no charge sheets. It's just boxing, Alison, the kids and my dad. I owe it to Alison.'

He pauses for a moment in thought, chuckles and then offers further insight into his eventful past.

'I got Alison through shoplifting, you know. Yeah. I used to bring her chocolates and spot cream that I nicked. My mother taught me how to shoplift in Ireland. We used to nick chocolate, anything, then go round the houses and sell the stuff to people. When I came to Manchester, I went bigger. I started breaking into cars. Somebody would say they wanted a stereo for an Escort. Easy. Twenty-five pounds – a lot of money then. I always had money because of that. But I've had hard times, as well. Nobody was hungrier than me, and now I've got five houses in Moston that I let to friends and relatives. Terraces, they are. I want to sell our house in Crumpsall and move to Rossendale, out in the country. It'll be good for the kids and for me. Good for running. I'm lucky. If it hadn't been for boxing I'd probably have been a gangster or something and be banged up, serving a long sentence.'

Gomez skips down the steps and avoids the light drizzle by ducking into a conveniently parked car. Alison and his daughter are waiting to take him home.

Hughes, too, is ready to go. His faith in Gomez is threadbare and he feels he is weighed down by the excess baggage as much as his boxer is.

'You can't go on like Michael is,' Hughes says. 'You can't keep taking that much weight off. Something has to give. He's using the seven weeks to get fit instead of preparing for the fight. The good thing is that he knows he'll get a good opponent. I think he's frightened. But Michael isn't the only one with problems. Pat Barrett's told them they shouldn't come in if they're not going to do it properly. A lot of them have problems.'

To compound Hughes' disillusionment, his great white heavyweight hope has also departed, not for another gym but for another trade.

'He's retired after two amateur wins, both knock-outs,' says a rueful Hughes. 'He called me to say he was setting up his own business, laying pipes. He's 21 and could have been something special, but I couldn't stop him. I just hope he's gone away a better person. He said he was grateful for the way we looked after him.

'You're going to get this sort of thing and you have to take the rough with the smooth. Things are looking good for Robbie, Michael Jennings gets on with his work, no trouble at all, and Thomas is coming on by leaps and bounds. In fact, Thomas has been blossoming since Farnell left. I think it's because I spent so much time teaching Farnell that Thomas possibly thought I was neglecting him and the rest.'

Gomez does keep his next date, a month on and also at the MEN Arena, although it is a British rather than a global title at stake. His opponent is Craig Docherty, a Glaswegian with a growing reputation and a record of

12 wins and a draw from 13 contests to back it up. Gomez has shed the unwanted weight and claims he is sharp, but the pundits patently have their doubts. This, they contend, could be the perfect opportunity for the young and ambitious Docherty to make his mark.

A tingling atmosphere and boisterous entrance by Gomez leaves Docherty unfazed. He turns his back on the Mancunian to show the message on his T-shirt: 'New British Champion'. He smiles as Gomez glares and growls. Gomez, who has the shape of a shamrock restored to the back of his head, shuffles back to his corner for final instructions and draws breath. Indignation pumps up the adrenaline flow. Who does this kid think he is? We'll see who's champion. The thoughts whir inside his head and reveal themselves in his concentrated expression.

At the bell, Gomez goes to work in characteristic, bustling style. Slugging is his game and Docherty, against the best advice of his corner, willingly engages the local man centre ring. Docherty's bravado and Gomez's Latino–like aggression makes for rich entertainment and the volume in the Arena registers the crowd's approval. The more accurate and punishing shots are coming from Gomez, who targets mainly the body but is alert to the opportunity to deliver a shuddering uppercut. Docherty returns to his corner at the end of the round with signs of damage beneath the right eye.

Gomez comes out for the second intent on inflicting more of the same. He resumes his attack and, with every succeeding delivery, intensifies the pressure. Docherty defiantly, and perhaps unwisely, tries to stand his ground but the bombardment is irresistible. Blood gushes from his cheek and his nose as the merciless Gomez senses the end. Docherty appears disorientated as the champion finds yet another gear. The challenger's resistance is broken and the referee, Terry O'Connor, steps in to spare him further torture.

It has taken Gomez just 4 minutes and 42 seconds. An emphatic win is precisely what was needed and he is more conciliatory than triumphal. He wants to thank Frank Warren and Brian Hughes for getting him back on track and having the faith to persevere with him.

'Frank is the best promoter in the world,' Gomez is at pains to declare. 'Frank and Brian have sorted my life out of the ring. They sat me down and talked to me.'

Warren is as relieved as he is appreciative and picks up the team baton.

'Another couple of fights and he'll be ready for a world title fight,' Warren maintains.

Other seasoned observers are less convinced. Barry McGuigan articulates the reservations of several old pros when he contends there are still doubts about Gomez's ability to take a punch. Docherty may have courage and potential, but he mustered scant examination of the champion's capability. Tougher, more meaningful challenges have to be negotiated if that dream of a world title is to be realised.

Ricky Hatton has eclipsed the rest of Manchester's much-vaunted tiros and his top-of-the-bill status cannot be disputed. The Arena again reverberates with its welcome for this apparently unassuming young man. In front of him this time is the gnarled but still potent Freddie Pendleton. The American seems disbelieving that this here white kid with the funny long trunks is the one who's supposed to be the new big deal, the one they want to promote in the States and even pitch for the real championship of the world. Many have made the same mistake.

Hatton bounces out of his corner, yet adopts a measured, respectful approach. Pendleton may be 38, he may have been a replacement and he may have shed weight in a hurry to make the light-welterweight limit, but he has been in there with some of the best and dispatched some of the best, and Hatton prudently engages in a little reconnaissance. He avoids a hopeful right from Pendleton and gradually weaves his way beneath the jab to work on the ageing black body. A dismissive Pendleton pats his ribs, making out that Hatton can hit him there as much as he likes. A blinkered Hatton ignores the taunt and carries on doing what he knows he has to do. The power and persistence of Hatton's punching bulldoze Pendleton back onto the ropes and only at the bell does the challenger throw a retaliatory right.

Pendleton is soon under pressure again in the second, abandoning any positive plans to try and cover up against the indefatigable younger man. Now he is searching the memory bank to figure a way out of this whirlwind. Briefly, his wit keeps him afloat and defies Hatton, but the champion comes back and pummels him to the verge of submission. Hatton aims another left hook to the body and Pendleton can take no more. He falls backward, onto the ropes, and then down onto the canvas, rolling away from his tormentor. He stays down for the count as Hatton turns away, roaring his self-satisfaction. It is another immaculate and clinical display by Hatton, whose vision of the ultimate prize becomes clearer by the fight.

Farnell, having safely negotiated his first fight for the Pheonix Camp, defeating Lee Blundell in 2 rounds to win the vacant WBO Inter-continental light–middleweight title, has to toil for all but 10 seconds of his scheduled 12-round defence to stop the durable Russian, Pavel Melnikov. Farnell yells and celebrates wildly, as much in relief as self-glorification, when the referee calls a halt to the late barrage. Farnell's controversial defection has brought him under particularly critical scrutiny and Collyhurst's sympathisers claim he has sacrificed some of his venom in the quest for a makeover. The jury may be out for some time.

Brian Hughes takes little time reaching the conclusion that one of the latest young hopefuls to walk through the door of his gym is not going to make it. 'You get a lot of lads coming in here wanting a chance and I'll try to give them that chance,' Hughes says. 'But if I don't think they're going to do it, I have to tell them. It wouldn't be fair on them to kid them on, and it wouldn't be fair on the others to spend time on them. I think, possibly, young Curtis picked up too many bad habits at other places.'

Young Curtis is the son of a former boxer and something of a legend in these parts. Des Gargano was a journeyman, a hod-carrier by day and a fighter on as many nights as he could get the bookings. He was a bantamweight but regularly confronted bigger men if the money was right and the contest did not come between him and his No. 1 passion – fishing. Outside the ring he was, and is, known as Des Southern. He reverted to his father's name when he boxed.

'I didn't see my father till I was 35,' he says, sitting in the front room of his home in Middleton, Manchester. 'Augustus, he's called. His father was Italian. He told me 19 brothers came over in the nineteenth century and most of them settled in the South. I didn't know anything about my sisters, Gina and Nicky, but they knew about me and they traced me after reading an article about me in the paper. They contacted the BBBC, who got in touch with Nat Basso, who had me at the time, and he told me. He was like Cilla Black. I just wanted to use "Gargano" for boxing. I love my stepfather as if he's my real father. He's been like a real father to me. He took me fishing and brought me up.'

Gargano has no intention of losing contact with own sons, Curtis, 18, and Spencer, 12. He encourages them to box and makes no apologies for doing so. All about him he sees the perilous options for youngsters and he is determined to ensure his boys will not succumb to them. He feels boxing can keep them away from those snares and offer the chance of something better. Perhaps it also holds out the prospect of satisfying some of his own unfulfilled aspirations.

'I'd encourage any young person to box, especially on an estate where there's kids smoking drugs and drinking beer outside shops,' Gargano says. 'I'd want my kids in a gym, not wanting to do them things, wanting to do other things, and Spencer's going to do this. He's completely different from Curtis. Spencer will do anything I tell him. If Curtis had that asset he could be a world champion. He's got all the skill. He's definitely more naturally gifted than most fighters. He's 11 stone. Has been since he was 14. Spencer is 5 ft 6 in. Probably more now. I don't know what happened with Curtis at Brian's gym. I go away a lot and I'm not sure what the problem was. But he's coming back to boxing now and goes with his brother to the gym at Oldham Boys.'

Gargano is a small, wiry figure who, at 41, is still proud of his 'natural fitness'. It appears to hurt him to recall that the fights dried up and effectively forced him to retire a couple of years ago. The pain was compounded by an apparent lack of recognition in the trade press. He rolls a cigarette and airs his festering grievance:

'The only thing in boxing that's made me, personally, sad is *Boxing News* not putting in that Des Gargano retired. I hate it. I had 122 fights. I was never knocked out. Nobody went the distance with more champions. Now somebody does ten fights and he gets a little picture in. Not a thing for me, and that kills me.'

Des Southern earned a reputation as a fighter when he was a youngster on the streets of Middleton.

'I was always in trouble as a young lad,' he says, suddenly lowering the tone and tempo of his voice. 'I was a completely different person to what I am now. I was wild. I was small, I came from a rough area and people always wanted to have a go at me. When you're small you've got gangs of lads who think they can just knock you out. They had a problem with me. I got into trouble with my fighting and went to certain places. I was in care, I was in assessment centres and detention centres. But, apart from my aggressive side, I was a good lad. I'd work, I'd wash the pots for my mum, I'd do whatever my dad told me. But I just had a problem there and a social worker took me to a gym, to control my aggression if you like. That's what boxing is, controlled aggression.'

He turned professional not so much to pursue a dream in boxing as to fund his ambitions in fishing.

'The sport I loved more than boxing at that time was match angling,' he says. 'I wanted the money for a carbon pole. I got £150 for that first fight and I think that paid for it. Until I retired I didn't realise how much boxing meant to me. But I do miss it now. I was always fighting people one or two divisions heavier than me. I'd be way out of my depth. Because I was working, I didn't have the chance to train as much as my opponents. Most of them trained three times a day, seven days a week. They just wanted to be a champion. They are fanatical about it, the good 'uns. I'd be fighting these people as they were on their way up. They'd be putting people away and I was always dragged in to take them the distance. I didn't care whether I won or lost a lot of them.

'I was in it for the money. My wages were crap. When you are boxing at the level I was boxing, you don't exactly get astronomical money, you get five or six hundred quid. But that was three weeks' wages all at once to me at that time. The one thing I did care about was never being knocked out, and I did manage to do that. They'd put me in with somebody they were expecting to do big things and the kid knows that if he knocks me out, he'll be the first person to do so, and that's going to catapult him up the rankings. If they wanted to put me in a fight like that and pay me twice as much as normal I was happy to do it because they still didn't knock me out. They'd wind up their shots bigger, trying to knock me out, and I could see 'em coming. I got a buzz out of taking all these champions the distance. I won 32 of my fights and had a few draws. I know I could have won so many more. The politics of boxing kept me away from bigger things.

'I was with Nat Basso for a long time, seven years, at the peak of my career, and I beat a lot of Central Area champions, including Kevin Taylor. That was one of only three times that I got six weeks' notice for a fight. He was two weight divisions heavier than me and I'd seen him fight and believed he could knock me out, but I wasn't going to allow that to happen. Fatigue would have been the only thing, but that notice made the difference. That's always the problem when you can't train properly. But, for this one, I trained so hard, and got on the road. It was like a *Rocky* film. I beat him easily. But then the next fight I'd go and lose against somebody crap because I'd been out all week and not in the gym, and I never got as far as a title. Nat was money-inclined. He never really looked to get me wins, he just wanted me in the ring every week, bringing money back.'

The nearest he came to a title was a challenge to Central Area super-featherweight champion Gary Thornhill, of Liverpool. Gargano was stopped in the second round. He was the classic journeyman boxer, yet even a bumper pay-night could not necessarily compensate for missing a major angling match.

'There was an occasion when Barry Hearn wanted me to fight on a Chris Eubank bill in Glasgow, and he was really big then. It was on TV and they showed all the fights. It was on a Saturday night and I had a match that day. Barry offered me really good money. I said I could jump on a plane after the match and get straight in the ring, but he said he needed me there in the afternoon for the TV weigh-in, so I didn't take the fight.

'I'd never commit myself and capitalise on my ability. I didn't care. I had my kids and I was living with a woman who worked evenings. I just couldn't be a professional boxer to the extent of those who are more inclined to want to be champions. Even if I'd had the time, I couldn't have done the training you need to do, and I wouldn't spar. I wanted to save myself. Being called a journeyman didn't really bother me, perhaps because I don't even understand what they mean by journeyman. I'm dead logical. I look at it this way: I know that if I'd just taken the fights I could win, I could have had an unbeaten 50-fight record – easily – but I would have earned exactly half as much money.'

Gargano's willingness to take a fight at a few days' or even hours' notice made him useful to promoters and matchmakers, while he was content to use the system for his own ends. Promoters, too, have had to fight their way up and he sees in men such as Hearn and Frank Maloney kindred spirits.

'They changed boxing. Barry Hearn really kicked boxing off with a full card on cable television. He's a pioneer. He even got fishing on TV. Frank Maloney is a great guy and he's done great things for boxing as well. He's a guy off the streets. He started those boxing shows from four o' clock through to midnight. Any boxing nut is going to love that. And because he's got that many fighters, he manages to get them all a fight. I say "good luck" to guys like them.

'There are some good guys in the game. If I'd lived in the Midlands I would have boxed for Nobby Nobbs. I had a laugh with him one night. I was at Grimsby, or Cleethorpes, or somewhere miles out of the way. I used to go with my mate, but this night Nobby jumped in my corner, looking after me. Then, halfway through the fight, I go back to my stool and I'm thinking, "Where is he?" I'm sitting there on my own and he's back in the dressing-room, clowning around. He shouts, "You don't need me, you're beating him easy." Course, he was seeing to his next fighter, but he was right, I did beat this lad dead easy. He's a character, Nobby. He'd brag that he'd been a heavyweight and he used to shadow box and show how he did it, just for a laugh.

'Jack Doughty is another trainer I boxed for in this area and he gave me something that nobody else could – respect. He took me in this big gym – and he had a lot of famous fighters – but he put his arm around me. He liked me, and he treated me like a true professional. He had these photos taken and put them up on the wall, and in the papers, me in my 100th fight, here at Middleton. He always found a bit of time for me.

'Jack took me on the pads and he'd say, "Des, I don't understand. You punch hard, but you don't knock them out." That was because I wouldn't commit myself. If you knock someone out, you're in a position to be knocked out, and I just wanted to fight every week. They didn't all like me. Some of them thought I ripped 'em off because I'd showboat and have a good time.

'After I'd had 70 or 80 fights, I had a rib broken for the first time but I got fights straight after, loads of them. I just carried on. After I'd had 100 fights, I wasn't quite the same person. I really did have glass ribs. All the injuries I had from boxing were pain from my ribs and a torn cartilage in my chest. That was the worst I ever had. It just wouldn't heal up for a long time.

'I gave up in the end because I'd reached an age where I was starting to slow down. I couldn't get a chance against anybody. I wouldn't get any notice for a fight. I'd been stopped by somebody . . . the ref didn't need to stop it. It was just ridiculous, but I got stopped by somebody who was crap and that had never happened to me before, so they were protecting me. I couldn't hardly get a fight and I couldn't keep myself going to box just two or three times a year. I think I had seven fights in the last two years of my career. It wasn't worth carrying on.

'I never worried for myself in the ring, and I don't worry for my boys. You see Curtis in the ring, he's brilliant. He can look after himself. He's got a very good brain. It's these 12-round fights where they end up in a wheelchair, or dead. It's at the end of a championship fight. These days, as in any other sport, boxers are far superior to what they were. Records are broken every year. You watch the old fights, when they fought for 20 rounds, they just held each other. I don't care what anyone says, it looks crap and it was. They just get straight into it now because there's more at stake.

'The problem is dehydration more than anything. They're physically drained. It's fatigue. It went from 20 rounds to 15, then 12, and now it's time to make it 10. I boxed Paul Ingle, I boxed Bradley Stone. McGuigan used to walk around at 10 stone 8 lb and weigh in the same day as he boxed. Now they weigh the day before so they've all dropped down a division. That was one of the reasons I came to the end of my boxing, because I was fighting people a stone heavier then me.'

Gargano believes most of the concerns in boxing can be eradicated and remains fervently convinced that the sport provides a solution to the deeper problems within society.

'All these "ban the boxing" brigades, these women who don't know what they are talking about, they want to invite them to go to the outdoors and off-licences that sell booze, and look at the packs of kids, aged from 9 to 15, asking adults to buy them beer. They're drinking outside the shops, they're smoking spliffs, and these kids don't care about themselves or their future. Take these same kids – and they're on every housing estate – to a boxing gym and they'll see kids of the same age, but they're in the gyms every night because they don't want to drink, they don't want to smoke, they want to be champions. Let them see what harm boxing has done to the likes of me, and other people what have come from the same place as them, and you might be able to show them something that they just can't see.'

11 ☆ COUNT ME OUT

THE MICHAEL GOMEZ ROLLER-COASTER HAS SPED ON, INEXORABLY,
through another winter, wrenching the emotions of all those obliged to take
the ride with him. His girlfriend, Alison, is pregnant with their third child
and his trainer and promoter would like to plot his future. But Brian
Hughes, for one, is reluctant to make long-term plans for his errant
protégé. The regular bulletins relayed to his gym tell of more turmoil, more
brawling, more boozing. Just the mention of Gomez's name draws a veil of
dismay across Hughes' face.

'I honestly fear for him,' Hughes confides. 'I'm still hoping he'll be all
right for his next fight, but you can't be sure of anything with Michael
any more. You don't want to see anybody wasting their life, but I can't
afford to keep on worrying about him. I've got these other lads to think
about and I can't neglect them.'

Gomez's response is a re-run of old apologies and pledges. He admits
he has slewed off course again and that having to shed a stone of excess
weight has been the least of his problems. But he is back in training and
adamant that he will be fit enough and focused enough to see off his next
opponent.

'I know what everyone's saying about me and yeah, I have been doing
everything I shouldn't have been doing,' he acknowledges. 'But it's not
just been about crashes and fighting and birds and booze. I was genuinely
ill, with pneumonia and pleurisy. That cost me a lot of time. I couldn't

train or anything. Last year was a bad year, I know that better than anyone, but all I can do is write that off and look forward. I'm going to get back on top, I know I am. I'm still young enough.'

The immediate test of that resolve comes in the shape of Kevin Lear, a 25-year-old Londoner who is unbeaten in 12 contests yet has, by general consensus, the flimsiest of credentials to warrant a shot at the vacant WBU title. More significantly, from Gomez's perspective, he should not represent a serious threat. It ought to be the perfect opportunity to show that the fire still burns and that he remains one of the most exciting and potent forces in British boxing. Gomez still has a colourful, vociferous hard core of support inside the MEN, but the noise level and sense of expectation throughout the Arena are markedly down a notch or two compared with some of his previous fight nights. Many of the seats in the VIP section are empty.

That loyal band of followers gasp and then fall silent as Lear's jab confounds Gomez and opens a gash close to the local man's left eye. Instinct tells Gomez to assert himself, but he is reduced to desperate lunges and the composed Lear counters with ease. Gomez again comes forward with positive intent in the second, only to be picked off by the boxer deemed a 9-2 underdog. The confused expression on Gomez's face is as ominous as Lear's accuracy. The cumulative effect becomes more obvious in the third as blood appears around nose and mouth. Gomez gamely attempts to retaliate, but the punches carry no weight.

In the fourth, Gomez has more success, burrowing his way inside and reviving the hopes of his anxious fans. He pursues his head-down style – the only style he knows – in the fifth. Perhaps all is not lost after all. But, even now, Lear is scoring intelligently and, by the sixth, the Gomez revival is waning. He is taking heavy shots and shedding more blood. Somehow, Gomez summons the will and energy to launch an offensive in the seventh. Lear's right eye is damaged and he rocks on unsteady legs, but he regains his balance and responds with more stinging deliveries.

Gomez trudges forward again in the eighth, only for Lear to fend him off with a seemingly contemptuous air. The man who terrorised so many opponents with the intensity of his attacks is now on the wrong end of a grotesque beating. Lear's searing shots penetrate the remnants of Gomez's resistance and the Mancunian is reduced to a static, unmissable target. His face is a contorted, bloodied mess. He cuts a hapless, pitiful figure as he shakes his head and seeks the refuge of his corner at the end of the round.

Hughes has seen and endured too much. He calls over the referee.

'I'm stopping it,' he tells his boxer.

'Don't stop it, Brian,' Gomez beseeches.

Hughes restrains the writhing, protesting Gomez, who is so distraught and confused he tries to climb out of the ring.

'I will not let you take any more punishment,' says Hughes. It is an act of mercy that requires no explanation.

The night becomes a long and torrid ordeal for the local heroes. Anthony Farnell is embroiled in a messy, ill-tempered and contentious fight with a South African, Ruben Groenewald, for the vacant WBU middleweight title. Groenewald sustains two cut eyes and goes down twice, but Farnell is docked three points for punching low and that carelessness tilts the decision. Groenewald is declared champion with a unanimous win. A tearful and almost speechless Farnell manages to convey his conviction that he is the victim of a gross miscarriage of justice. An agitated, indignant and more articulate Frank Warren immediately announces a re-match.

Ricky Hatton is also taken the distance, by Northern Ireland's Eamonn Magee, in the sixth defence of his WBU light-welterweight belt. Both fighters are hoisted shoulder high at the end, claiming victory, but Hatton is given the verdict by all three judges. However, the champion has absorbed the kind of punishment he usually inflicts on others and recognises that it is a salutary lesson. Some opponents will be capable of taking those much-vaunted body punches and some will be good enough to hit back. Magee is durable and dangerous, as he has proved by putting Hatton down in the opening minute, the first time he has been on the canvas in his professional career. By the end Hatton is cut, but he still has his title and will be wiser for this experience. He now knows he cannot always blow away his challenger.

Hughes and a meagre representation of his full squad are standing outside the Collyhurst and Moston gym in the cool and damp of a June morning. Matthew Hall, his latest tiro, takes the blame for forgetting the keys and is despatched to find a set. Among the missing is David Barnes, who has been otherwise engaged of late. It transpires he went AWOL from the army. Hughes drove the deserter back to Aldershot to face the music. He was given six weeks' detention at Colchester. Another absentee is Gomez, but that comes as no surprise to Hughes. The trainer grins wryly and says: 'He won't be coming now.'

Gomez, supported by Hughes, has come to an arrangement with the courts that, following his latest drink-driving conviction, he will serve 250 hours' community service by training the amateurs at the Collyhurst and Moston Club. However, the fall-out from the boxer's latest defeat is patently contaminating the atmosphere in the camp and Hughes can take no more. He has told Gomez he should quit the ring.

'That last fight could have been fatal for Michael,' Hughes says, at last leading his troops into the gym. 'I mean it. I hope he packs it in, because of the way he is living his life. He says he wants to work as a second and I've told him I'll help him. But now he's fallen out with me. Like Farnell, slagging me off in the *Evening News*. He'd gone in that fight. He was like an old man. I could see it in his eyes. His face was like a mask. He was battered. He had three cuts, a nosebleed. He threw good punches, but there was nothing there. Twelve months ago, he would have taken that lad out, no trouble. Now, I've had to save him from being taken out in a coffin. He claims the stress of not getting a world title fight has affected him. He's a ticking time bomb. I'm fed up with it all.'

Gomez is affronted by the suggestion that he is all washed up as a fighter. The old forces of defiance stir up inside and, yet again, he declares his determination to come back. But he agrees it is time for an end of sorts – an end to his association with Hughes. He has decided to follow Farnell's lead and switch to Billy Graham's camp.

Hughes confides: 'He came to collect some money I kept for him in a building society and told me he was leaving. What do I keep saying about this business? He said I was too old. He said I didn't go running with him any more. There aren't many trainers who ever went running with their boxers. I might not do the pads any more because of my kidneys and diabetes, but I'm sharp. I know what I'm doing in the gym and corner. I've got lads who do the rest. He talked about getting a second's licence but, as everyone keeps telling me, you wouldn't want him in your corner.

'Those who get hurt are those who help him. You can only help them so far and to be honest I'm glad to be relieved of him. You can't keep making excuses for him. We all come from rough backgrounds, but we have to make something better of ourselves. He wants to fight on, but he's one of those fighters who get old very quickly. I've seen this coming. A lot of people have. I've still got good lads. Better one good one than half a dozen bad ones. I've got another heavyweight who looks better than I thought he was. He tries. He trains well and he listens. If they do that, they've got a chance.'

The following evening Gomez is said to be training. He returns home late that night and is more than willing to give his side of the story:

'I need a fresh start. Brian's lost his spark. He wants to retire. For skill, Brian's is the best gym, but I need to work on my fitness. I can't be taught any more. Brian talked about me retiring and getting a second's licence, but I want to go on. I didn't agree with him pulling me out of that fight. I was only two rounds behind. I could have done it. I wasn't at my best, I know that. I'd not done any sparring. I had a shoulder injury, ligaments. Then there's all the trouble I've had: four drink-drives, road rage with some blokes – that's what did my shoulder. There was a problem over my community service and I had to get a sick note, otherwise it was 28 days in jail. It was like jumping bail.

'I've never slagged Brian, or said things behind his back. I went to see him and told him. No one talked me into going to Billy Graham's gym. He's younger. Brian is not the trainer he was five years ago. It was hard for me to leave. I'd been with him for 15 years, he was like a big brother, but I don't think I let him down. I never ripped him off and I've told him if there's anything I owe him I'll pay it. I'll sort everything with Warren. I'm a free agent now.

'I've come back before and I'll do it again. I'm just 25. I know I can get a world title. I have to start at the bottom and show them. Brian thinks I should retire and, if I get hammered in my next fight, I'll admit he was right. But that won't happen. I could have gone to a number of gyms. I wanted to go to Ireland, to Steve Collins, but Alison didn't fancy that. She doesn't know anybody over there and the baby's due next week, so that wasn't on. I enjoy it at Billy's. Hatton's there, young Steve Foster, Anthony. It's a good gym, but I'll never forget Brian and his gym, no matter what. I also think I deserve respect, from Brian and everyone else.'

Back at Moston, the sapient Robin Reid peels off his tapes after a rigorous session in the ring and offers words of sympathy to his trainer and his former colleague:

'I've spoken to Michael and I've told him I'm not falling out with him. I hope it works out for the best for everyone. I feel sorry for Brian. He's brought me and a lot of others on, and made them champions. If Michael wants to be fitter he should lay off the booze. I've told him. I drink red wine and lemonade if I want a drink. Three of them and I'm gone because I don't drink much, and red wine is good for the heart, anyway. I'm always telling them here that I'm the old man, but I'm fitter than anyone because I've looked after myself.'

When Reid is in training for a fight he eats one meal a day and runs after midnight, relishing the stillness and solitude.

He goes on:

'We'll see what happens to Michael, but Farnell has gone backwards since he went over there. Michael listens, but then it goes out of his head again. He's one of them. I like him – you can't help liking him – but he's got to look after himself. Brian's tried and he thinks he shouldn't go on. If Michael thinks he should, and proves himself, then great. Good luck to him.'

Reid, a man with a taste for sporty cars and personalised registration plates, has kept his career running against the advice and expectations of many, yet acknowledges time is not on his side as he endeavours to drive back to the top of his trade. His frustration is compounded by the global success and acclaim currently being enjoyed by his nemesis, Joe Calzaghe. Reid is due to appear again next week, in a supporting act on the much-derided Audley Harrison roadshow.

'I don't know who he's fighting,' Reid says. 'Probably his auntie. Mind you, Calzaghe's not exactly putting his career on the line with his next fight. He's shouting his mouth off one minute saying he wants to fight Roy Jones, and the next he's lined up somebody who's way down the rankings. I'm not saying the rest of us don't like to take an easy one, but you shouldn't go making out it's a difficult one when it obviously isn't.'

Reid's pride and care in self-preservation have helped extend and widen the range of his extra-curricular activities, as he is happy to reveal:

'I'm still doing the modelling, but I've also been doing stuff for porno mags. Well, I tried the clean-cut image and that didn't work, so when I was asked if I fancied doing this, I thought, "Why not?" People don't worry about that sort of thing as much as they did years ago, do they? The fellas look at you and go, "Jammy sod," and the women say, "Hey, isn't that him, you know? Phew!" So you've won both ways. Great. If it sells tickets, that's the main thing. It's all about bums on seats.'

There will be another bum to seat in the Gomez household from now on. Alison has given birth to their third child, a girl. They have called her Louise, after the little sister Michael lost when he was a boy.

Jack Doughty, the mentor recalled fondly, almost reverentially, by Des Gargano, is still operating, on the north-eastern edge of Greater Manchester. He has had several gyms and many more pursuits in his active life. He is a trainer and manager, but also a promoter of small-town shows, held on Sunday afternoons, at the Tara Sports and Leisure Centre, in Shaw, a suitably small town lodged between Rochdale, Oldham and the Pennines. Doughty's current gym is on the other side of town, a light-grey building with bright-green paintwork. Unsurprisingly, he is of Irish stock. He is another elder statesman of the boxing community, a distinguished-looking figure with a head of white hair like whipped ice cream. He is deliberate in every word and deed.

Doughty's gym is huge. It would house those of Hughes, Graham and Nobbs, and still have room for circuit training. It is also clean, tidy and airy. The distinct smell is of floor polish rather than sweat. It has two large, solid-looking rings. Beyond them are weights and other equipment. At the front end of the gym is the main floor space. Along the wall a row of bags hang in anticipation. They seem in remarkably good fettle. Pictures of boxers from the dim and more recent past bear silent witness to the evening's workout. An uncompromising sign on the wall cautions: 'No swearing in this gym.'

Does Doughty really mean it?

'Of course I mean it,' he says, as uncompromisingly as the sign on the wall.

It is early evening, a convenient time to train for most of the regulars here. Amateurs, hopefuls, dreamers, or those simply intent on retrieving their fitness, will soon arrive to be put through their paces by one of

Doughty's aides. The pros – a mixed bag of championship material and journeymen – have the benefit of Doughty's personal attention.

'These days, in every other sport, I think they expect wonderful facilities,' Doughty says, retreating to his small office. 'But with boxing, because it's a rough and ready thing, I don't think they mind, whatever it is. I do believe, though, that it should be clean and the fact that we've got space here is a big plus.

'I'm interested in all boxers. I've got the greatest of respect for journeymen. Years ago there were fighters who fought for a few bob. They were, in effect, the journeymen of their time. Most of them were never going to reach the top. I've got one now, Wayne Shepherd. He's lost a lot more than he's won. He's not a clever boxer and really he's not a puncher, but he's got such guts. He doesn't just do it for the money. He loves the scrap. Most of these journeymen really want to win and they're elated when they do, but when they don't, they will tell you how they were robbed. All boxers are tremendously self-centred.

'Des Gargano came to me when he got to the end of his contract with Nat Basso, who was a famous old character in these parts, a manager and MC. He just sent his boxers out. There was no build-up, ever. I told Des he was with the right manager for the kind of fights he was taking on, but he said, "No, I want to win." It definitely wasn't just money for him. I helped him in a way. I put him on as the home fighter, which was a great luxury for him. He was normally the opponent, but we put him on at Middleton, his home town, and for the first time in a long time he won. And then he won again. I had a belt made for him, commemorating his 100th contest, and he won that fight, too. I can just see him now, leaping up onto the lower ring ropes and proudly holding the belt aloft. That was his world title.

'Generally, it's very difficult to get them to admit they are journeymen. I was at a press conference and one of the boxers there was Wayne Rigby. I'd had Wayne before he went to Jack Trickett, another character in Manchester, and I said I really admired boxers like him because he'd been a kind of journeyman, the type who had to battle his way from the bottom and never got any favours. I said he'd done it through his own toughness, determination and dedication, and the help of his trainer. But he took offence and after the press conference he told me he didn't like what I'd said about him.'

FIGHTING CHANCE

An affinity with boxing is in the Doughty family genes, although he has also the old woman who lived next door to thank for his indoctrination.

'It was the late '30s and I was only a young lad,' he remembers with a childlike glint in his eye. 'We didn't have a wireless, but the lady next door did and she was a boxing fan. She also happened to be deaf, so she would always turn up the volume. When the big fights were on, my dad and me would have our ears to the wall, listening to the commentary. So, from an early age, I was interested in boxing. I did a bit of boxing at school and in the Army, but never fought as a pro.'

Despite that interest in boxing, the young Doughty found another outlet for his sporting passion and energy.

'I went into rugby league because this area is a hotbed of the sport. I played for local teams and then signed for Oldham. I was a pro for two or three years and made progress, but then I got a bad injury. Although I tried to come back, it was very difficult and I had other interests, anyway. I was into the theatre and acting. I started in amateur productions, then did Oldham Rep and some television. I was also interested in music hall and dance. My wife runs a dance school.'

Doughty has extended his artistic portfolio by writing books, but he never lost his infatuation with the noble art and, in 1986, he was finally lured back by his old flame. He went to the local boxing shows and, through a network of associates and contacts, became involved in the running of gyms. He and an old trainer, Paddy Lyons, opened a gym over a pub in Bacup, another small-town stepping-stone between Greater Manchester and the moors. Doughty then joined forces with a trainer called Dave Fraser, to set up a gym in Rochdale, before establishing his camp at the Tara Sports and Leisure Centre. That venture lost too much money, so Doughty moved to more economical premises in the town, although he still promotes his shows at the Centre.

'I usually do four shows a year, which is a lot now,' he says. 'I've done as many as seven or eight a year. It was tough when I first came into it, but it's got worse and worse. Times have changed in boxing. In the '50s and '60s there'd be shows most nights of the week and there would be boxers outside, with their gear, waiting in case somebody dropped out. Now we're ringing round the night before, saying, "So and so's dropped out, can you come?" There are quite a few managers who also promote in a small way. I have promoted in a big way. I've done shows, a while back, with Barry Hearn, in Bury, as the local, smaller man.'

As a promoter, as well as a trainer and manager, Doughty has another perspective on Nobby Nobbs' way of doing business.

He explains: 'If my matchmaker rings up Nobby and asks for somebody for our show the following month, there's no chance of getting him because Nobby will always say, "Ring me a bit later." He's hanging on to see if any of the big shows want them, so I have to hang on till the last few days. It's hard on us and that way of dealing is detrimental to all small shows. It's not good for any boxer who might be trying to sell tickets and can't tell his friends or his local newspaper who he's fighting. There used to be a bigger walk-up in the old days, but as the years have gone by, it's got to the situation where you can't put a boxer on your show if he doesn't sell tickets.

'I do this because I'm nuts. You've got to be in this game. There's another thing – ego. We like to be seen on TV, just like anybody else. And not just on TV. People get to know that you're the man in your area that does the boxing, and it is a fact that if I hadn't been a promoter in the last few years, there wouldn't be any boxing in north Manchester. So I think I've done a little bit of good.

'I certainly don't make money out of it. People don't believe me when I tell them that, so I suggest to them, "Come in with me and I'll split the profits with you – providing you share the losses." What happens is that you get somebody coming along who's willing to put money into a show because they're interested in boxing and want to help – and again, it's the ego thing – but they lose money and drop out. Then somebody else steps in and gets involved. There's always some mug who comes along and just about keeps it afloat.

'The way I look at it is that, if we expect boxers to get up when they've been knocked down, then I guess we have to take the knocks and carry on. Boxing is like a woman that you love and hate as well. One day you've had enough and want to strangle her; the next you love her again. It's not a case of my wife being tolerant – she has no idea how much money I've lost through boxing. But she would think I'm the biggest mug in the world if she knew the full story.'

Doughty's income from his shareholding in a family business, manufacturing and wholesaling dancewear, funds his enduring love affair with boxing. Novices' subs and hire fees charged to Oldham Athletic Football Club help pay for the gym, but any profit depends on the success of the professional boxers Doughty trains and manages. Ambitiously, and exotically, he has taken on two Mongolians, Choi Tseveenpurev and Shinny Bayaar. They have brought colour, charm and an unlikely fan club of their countrymen to these parts, but since neither can fight for British, European or Commonwealth titles, their sporting and commercial scope is restricted.

'They're both talented and very tough, but I don't know where this will take us,' Doughty concedes. 'Choi is 30, a featherweight who could fight at super-bantam. He's been here two years and lived most of the time with me and my wife. He's won nine of his ten fights and done quite a bit of sparring in the north-east and in Denmark. He also wins over everyone he meets with his warmth. Shinny is based in Carlisle. He's 24, still youngish, but he's had only 3 fights – won 2, lost 1. The problem is that very few people want to fight them.'

Wayne Shepherd, also based in Carlisle, is regularly employed, though scarcely championship material. His claim to fame is that, at 43, he is Britain's oldest professional boxer. His younger brother, Charles, is a more gifted boxer. He won IBO world, British and Commonwealth championships and Doughty is hopeful he will make a productive comeback after retiring from the ring. However, the potential golden boy and big money-earner is the enigmatic Bobby Vanzie, who has his own trainer and does most of his work in his home city of Bradford, but travels over the Pennines to Doughty's gym to spar when a fight is imminent. He has recently left Tommy Gilmour to join the Frank Warren stable, with the promise of a WBO lightweight title eliminator.

'I think Bobby has a chance to win a world title,' Doughty says without a semblance of affected enthusiasm. 'It's true he doesn't shine in every fight. He's erratic, but he comes up with the goods, especially when he's up against it. He's different; he's awkward and confident.

'I like to work with boxers. If I had to promote and manage but not train, I wouldn't do it. This is the part I'm really interested in. It's getting harder because there is a dearth of boxers. They come and go. I have 10 or 12 at the moment, but they are never all active at the same time. The old thing about hungry fighters doesn't apply now. I don't think poverty is an issue so much as it used to be. When somebody is badly knocked out and hurt I say to myself, "What are you doing in this?" But then people get killed and hurt in other sports. If you banned boxing, it would go underground. There's already unlicensed boxing and this free-for-all stuff.

'Wayne, like many boxers, works as a doorman. They're tough guys. The odd ones may get into trouble on the street or in pubs, but very seldom. The reason for that is they don't have to prove they are tough guys because they *are* tough guys. Most of these people out there get a bit of drink in them and want to fight, but if you said to them, "Right, come in here," they wouldn't want to know.'

Doughty politely explains he has to go to work now, although he offers a parting thought on this irresistible dangerous liaison: 'A belt is precious to the boxer because, to him, it represents the achievement. That's the word, that's what motivates me. Achievement.'

12 ☆ PREACHING TO THE CONVERTED

ANTHONY FARNELL IS SITTING IN HIS CAR, JABBING AT A MOBILE phone. He is amusing himself as he waits for the gym to be opened up. It is an ugly building, a construction of prefabricated pebble-dashed concrete slabs, perched on land behind the library, just off Hyde's bustling town centre. This, as the various signs inside and outside the building inform, is Billy 'Preacher' Graham's Phoenix Camp; in association with Frank Warren's Sports Network; home to Ricky 'Hitman' Hatton; Nichols Police Amateur Boxing Club, sponsored by North Cheshire Security Services Ltd. It is also the place where Farnell and Michael Gomez now work.

Farnell is evidently eager to start his afternoon training session. It is more than a year since he left Brian Hughes' gym and during that period he has had mixed fortunes. His promised re-match with Ruben Groenewald, for the WBU middleweight title, is barely three weeks away and he dare not get it wrong this time.

He still seems ill at ease talking of his split, fumbling for the words to convey his reasons and emotions. 'Brian took it the wrong way when I left,' he says. 'He took it bad. I didn't mean him to. It was hard for me, really hard, but I felt it was the best thing for me. I knew I had to come here. These things happen. It's like footballers switching clubs. Like Rio Ferdinand going from Leeds to United. Sometimes you have to make these decisions. I don't want to sound bigheaded and I don't want to say

I'd outgrown the other place, but after so long you can reach the stage where you feel you have to find something different. That's all I've done. I'm enjoying it here. It's a good gym and they're good lads.'

It is past 12.30 and Farnell is quickly out of his car as the door of the gym is opened. Stairs lead up to a tiny changing area. Straight ahead is the shower and toilet. In a room to the left is a ring. On the walls hang obligatory photographs of boxing luminaries, many of them signed and dedicated to the Phoenix Camp. A room to the right is bisected by a metal bar that looks like a length of railway line, balanced on two trestles. Heavy punch bags await the day's first encounters with gloved fists.

This has been Graham's base since he moved from Salford, a couple of years ago. Apart from anything else, it is more convenient for Hatton, who lives just up the road, and he is the main man. Graham started training boxers 12 years ago, at the Champs Camp, in Manchester's Moss Side. Three years later, he decided to branch out on his own.

'Since I started on my own I'm smoking twice as many as I used to,' he says, stepping outside and gazing contemptuously at the cigarette he is about to light. 'I love working with boxers, I love my job, but it does your head in, you know what I mean?'

You can take the lad out of Salford, but you cannot take the harsh Salford accent out of the lad. This lad is 47 and has the craggy features of an ageing rock star or a supporting actor in a spaghetti western. Like many highly successful trainers, coaches and managers in sport, Graham had an unspectacular career as a competitor. He concedes he wasted much of his earlier life, but has now found his niche, honing some of British boxing's finest talent.

'I was an amateur, had only 3 junior fights, then turned pro at 18 or 19,' he says. 'I won 12 out of the 14 fights I had. I lost two on points. One of them I lost to I knocked out in a return and I was due to fight the other for an area title, but the fight got called off. That's when I walked away. I actually fought in the last fight at Belle Vue. I didn't mean to walk away, but I was dead pissed off with it all, lost my temper and stormed off. I thought I'd come back one day, but I never did. With hindsight, I realise I was too young.

'I messed it up, just as I messed up most things in my life before I got into this. I've got a dodgy past, I admit it. Not too dodgy, though! I've done bricklaying, plastering, bar work, all sorts. I've been on the dole, just picking up enough to get by. I didn't care. Nothing . . . excited me. Like when you're a kid. You need something to excite you, something to give you butterflies in your stomach. I couldn't find anything that gave me that feeling. The only thing I could think of was boxing, but this happened by accident.

'I decided I was going to try and come back and have a fight. I was 35, I had nothing and just wanted to do it once, or something, I don't know. It would have been a mistake, but it didn't happen anyway because they wouldn't let me. Then Phil Martin asked me if I'd like to start training with him at Champs. I'd known him since he was a kid. We'd been stable-mates in amateurs and pros. He was doing great, training all these up-and-coming guys and causing upsets. I didn't think I'd get the excitement out of it, but I became addicted to it, I suppose, and that was it.

'I am a better trainer than I was a fighter, but then I don't know how good I could have been because I stopped before I really started. If I knew then what I know now it might have been different. What's helped me as a trainer is that as a boxer I had good balance and rhythm. I also teach them to throw punches correctly, to get the leverage. People say punchers are born, not made. I think that's nonsense. Some punchers are born, but as long as you've got reasonable balance and co-ordination, you can be taught punching power because punching power is simple mechanics.

'The difference between me as a trainer and as a fighter is that I've applied myself as a trainer. As a fighter, I was very dedicated early on, then after a few pro fights I was just out on the piss all the time. Same old story. But it means I didn't have what it takes, and that's not an excuse, it's a fact. It was a weakness in my character, as a person. I've got loads of drive and determination, and once I'd got the bug that was it. The only thing better than being a champion trainer is being a champion boxer. Second best is better than doing anything else for a living.'

Graham takes pride in practising what he preaches. He is renowned for his work in the ring, coaching, sparring and taking punches to a heavy, padded contraption, which he straps to his body for protection. In the build-up to big fights he will pad up and subject himself to 15 rounds of torso-jolting sparring. He is wearing joggers and a vest and has his hands strapped in readiness for today's workout.

'It's the closest thing you get to fighting,' he enthuses. 'People are amazed when they see how tough it is. It wasn't as tough when I was young, but now it's getting hard. I enjoy the technical side more than the hard slog. It isn't really fun for me any more because I've got too many injuries. You have to hold your breath when you take the body shots, but you've also got to move around and your body wants to pant. But you can't because you get winded, so you've got to keep stealing sharp breaths. It's just age. Mind you, the smoking doesn't help.'

The defection of Farnell and Gomez to Graham's gym has brought him the kind of criticism he has grown accustomed to through his training career. He rejects the current accusations of poaching as he has rejected others in the past.

'There are quite a lot of people in the area who are not keen on me,' Graham admits. 'Maybe they are a little envious. I think I treat everybody with respect. I never badmouth anybody in the press. I take an awful lot of stick from, I think, bogus people who write and say things about this and that. With the public, the fans, the press and TV, I get treated fantastic. The people I'm talking about, who aren't too keen on me, are the so-called rivals from other gyms.'

Graham appears to be pointing the finger at Hughes, but he contends: 'One thing I'm not going to do is take a pop at anybody. They can all have a pop at me, I don't care. Because, to be honest, I don't feel any threat whatsoever. That's not to be arrogant. They'll always have a pop at me. I know what they say about me. Sometimes it gets on my nerves because the things they say about me are untrue. Like the letters people have been writing in *Boxing News*, saying I'm taking fighters, and stuff on the Internet, slagging me off. I just put it down to people who are envious. They're jealous. I'm not jealous of anyone.

'I got it when I left Phil and some of the fighters came with me. But the fighters we're talking about weren't spring chickens. They were all 30-odd and not expected to win titles, but they all did. Yet my rivals tend to give all the credit to Phil for that. I did all the pad work with Phil, and for the first 18 months, I did it for free. For the next 18 months I was with him, he gave me £50 a week. I always knew I wanted my own fighters so I just left.

'Another thing I get thrown at me is that anybody could have trained Ricky Hatton, because he has so much talent. I've even heard it said he was the finished article when he walked into my gym. But he was 17 years old, and I've spent the last 6 or 7 years working with him. When people say things like that, it hurts.

'I have worked really hard, physically and mentally, for everything I've got, everything I've achieved in boxing. When I think back now . . . you could wring my clothes out every day after training, they were so soaked in sweat. I wouldn't have missed it for the world. It was great. I've got absolutely no regrets. But if I thought I had to go through all that again and wait all this time to get any financial reward, no way. I couldn't do it. I'm doing okay now, but because people see you on telly, they think you've got it made.

'Before Ricky came, I'd trained loads of champions. I'd trained a fighter to get every title you can get, except for an area title, and Ricky got the area title. So when people have a pop at me, which they always are, I just . . . I've been too consistent. My record speaks for itself, if you check it out statistically. So I don't bother with it. I'd rather get on with everybody, but this business is real bitchy. People think I'm arrogant and bigheaded, but I don't get involved in cliques and things like that. I'm not interested. If they think that's being arrogant or bigheaded I don't care. I'll never get the MBE, and I don't want it. I just like what I'm doing and I'm past caring what anybody else is up to.

'In boxing, like anything else, show business and that, there's only a very few people who make anything out of it, so the stakes are high. If you're not at the top, you're just scratching a living. The only way you can make a living then is by having loads of fighters, journeymen fighters, working regularly. That's not what I do. I work on a kid knowing I'm not going to get any money to start with, but if he wins a title, then maybe. It's a gamble. I'm not knocking journeymen, and especially not people like Nobby Nobbs, because when fighters go with Nobby they know what they're going to be. Nobby doesn't tell them any lies; he gets them plenty of work, gets them good money and looks after them. Without those guys there's no chance. It's just that it's not what I like about boxing. I like to win titles. I don't want to sound like I'm moaning about people having a pop at me, but they are always doing it.'

Even the best and most dedicated require a break or two along the way, regardless of their profession, and any trainer would bless the day a boxer of Ricky Hatton's calibre came into the fold.

Graham acknowledges: 'The first day Ricky walked into the gym you could see something special. Obviously he looked nothing like he does now, not physically, but I had some really good light-welterweights and I put him in with them, and he shouldn't have been able to do what he could do. I saw his balance and anticipation and everything else, so I knew from day one . . . I've got tapes of me on television, when Ricky was doing four-rounders, and I said then that I thought he would be one of the best fighters ever to come out of this country.

'Everyone's waiting for the day when someone's going to come in their gym and maybe get a British title. I was used to that by the time Ricky came along. I'd had British and Commonwealth champions. I was used to working with good kids. But then he comes in and you couldn't ask for better. He's the best I've ever had. I suppose it's like . . . I don't know much about football, but I suppose it's like how Manchester United felt when George Best appeared. We want to go against the best in the world, but we want to be paid the proper money for it. I'd rather he had somebody really good in the other corner. It's better for me.'

The addition of Farnell and Gomez to the Phoenix ranks has increased Graham's capacity for professional satisfaction and financial reward, yet he is adamant he did not seek to sign either of the boxers nurtured by Brian Hughes.

'I've never approached a fighter in my life,' Graham says. 'I didn't want any more fighters. I was quite happy with what I'd got. I wasn't looking for any more money. I don't regret taking them, but I've never been into nicking anybody else's fighters. I've never shafted anybody in boxing. I'm not like that. I'm probably the only trainer who isn't. A lot of trainers try to get more fighters because it's more money. Boxers have always come to me. I even told Ricky he could go somewhere else if he wanted, but he wanted to come to me. Why do the others want to come here? We must be doing something right.'

So what does he make of Farnell and Gomez and how is he handling them? He pauses and weighs up his response.

'With Arnie [Farnell] . . . you don't always see it at the time. Once you know the answers, you can pass the exam, can't you? When you're doing something that's physical you've got to explain to him what you want from him. Even then he's still got to practise and practise to get it right. And then he's got to do his sparring, and then he's got to do it in the ring. It comes in stages. He knows an awful lot more about boxing now than he ever knew before. He's really trying, but it's not all going to happen overnight. He's getting steadily better all the time. It's taking him back to basics.

'It's basically the same with Mike. We can make their punches that little bit more correct, to get them nearly perfect. That's what you've got to work for. And, of course, I had to lay down the law with Mike. We weren't looking to take on fighters and we certainly weren't looking to take on fighters with problems. That was the first thing I told him – "It's a no no." I know Mike and we'd known for ages that he was going off the rails. With Bognar, he shouldn't have been in there, he was ill, but that night with Kevin Lear was an accident waiting to happen. We all knew it was coming sometime. The thing is, Mike's been really good for Manchester boxing. He's only young, and he deserves another chance.'

Gomez has been driven to work by his girlfriend, and since they live at the other side of Manchester she sits in the gym, with baby Louise, until he has finished. Graham operates an open-house policy. People wander in, watch the training for a while, and wander out again. A female reporter from the local newspaper chats with Graham and his boxers.

'Our doors are always open,' Graham says. 'Phil Martin used to lock up his gym, everything was done behind closed doors, but it's the public who buy the tickets for the fights and we always encourage them. We get crowds in here when I've got the body belt on, doing 15 rounds with Ricky. As gyms go, it's okay. We could do with more equipment, but all trainers say that.'

Graham is about to have a stint in the ring with Hatton, although he plans only a few rounds. Hatton looks chunkier than he does on a fight night. It must be the shorts. Instead of the familiar long trunks that have been *de rigueur* in recent years, he is wearing a much briefer pair that affords a rare glimpse of his muscular thighs.

The revelation is not lost on Graham. 'I say to him, "Why don't you wear short shorts for fights and show them your muscles?" He'd terrify them. They don't realise how muscular his thighs are. He's a nice guy, but he's clinical in the ring. He wants to knock them out. He wants to be dramatic.'

Hatton may not be seeking to knock out his trainer, but the action is dramatic enough, accompanied by the din of a local radio station. He pounds away at Graham's body belt in his characteristic, all-action style.

Hatton strips off his T-shirt after the second round as Graham paces the ring, taking in gulps of air. And then they go to work again, Graham holding up his gloves to give Hatton a different target, then indicating he wants him to resume his assault on the body belt. Graham grimaces and tries to stand his ground, but is inevitably forced back by the torrent of punches.

They call a halt and Graham asks to be helped off with the body belt. Hatton grasps a bottle in his gloved hands and takes a long swig. Graham is drenched in sweat. You could still wring out his clothes. He is offered an orange and steps outside, into the rain, to eat it, piece by refreshing piece. Hatton discusses technique with Gomez, illustrating his point with a dip and sway of the body. Gomez nods but seems disinclined to prolong the conversation. Graham's latest recruit drops his skipping rope and tries the weights, with a little guidance from a stable-mate. Garrulous, often aggressive, sometimes confrontational at Moston, Gomez is noticeably subdued here. He is more restrained, even coy, as if he is steeling himself to be on his best behaviour. He is still a new boy at Hyde, of course, yet he knows he is not the star of this gym. They are all overshadowed by Hatton who has the banter, self-confidence and aura of the No. 1.

Gomez leaves the weights and walks towards a poster for the forthcoming show at the MEN Arena. Hatton's name is in large, bold lettering at the top of 'The Body Snatcher' bill. Farnell's revenge mission against Groenewald has second-top billing. Gomez's name is almost lost, in small print, down among the undercard matches.

'It hurts when I see my name down there,' he confesses in a low voice. 'I want to get my name back up to the top again. I've got to get it right now. Billy told me straight. I won't get another chance. I've got to do it for Alison and the kids. We're looking for a house nearer to the gym. I sold those I had at Moston, but I'll need a lot more money to get the one I want. I still fancy Rossendale, but we'll have to see.

'People keep telling me they hear I've been in trouble again and that's something I have to put up with. I'm the first to admit my faults, but I've not been involved in any trouble recently. Honest. I did have a problem over my community service. There was a bit of a misunderstanding with Brian, but it's all sorted out now. I must admit I do miss the Moston gym – even Brian, for all that's gone on between us. I was with Brian for 16 years. I still keep in touch with the boys. I've spoken to Robbie, Mike and Thomas. It's difficult to leave all that, but sometimes you have to. Brian didn't really want to be in it any more.'

A heater blasts hot air into the room on the right and Farnell works up a sweat on a punch bag. There are no signs forbidding swearing here and that licence has plenty of takers. Somehow, you cannot picture the original Billy 'Preacher' Graham in this environment. Hatton is on a mobile phone, trying to organise southpaw sparring partners in preparation for his fight against Stephen Smith. He is talking to David Barnes, from Hughes' gym.

Farnell, the self-proclaimed 'Warrior' of the ring, is a mild, polite, seemingly vulnerable figure away from the battle lines. 'As Billy says, I needed to get back to basics,' he concurs, turning away from the punch bag. 'He's working on my stance. He said I'd got my feet all wrong, the body movement, everything. And I'm thinking about my boxing more. I've not lost my aggression, no matter what anybody says. I've still got that. I'll always have it. But the higher you go, the more you have to think about it. I'm not going to go rushing in any more, the way I did against Takaloo. That night I was so emotional, I built myself up so much. I've never known an atmosphere like it, even at the MEN. I was singing to myself as I came into the ring and almost crying with the emotion. I threw my face into his face, and everything I should have been thinking about went out of my head. I went straight for him and he got me. No complaints. The best man won on the night. I wanted to wipe him out and got caught.'

He permits himself a laugh about it now and shakes his head in disbelief as he recounts his folly. 'When I think about it, oh, it was just . . . At least I realise why it happened and I'm not going to let it happen again. My aggression is more controlled now. I'm learning when and how to use it. You can't just blow people away. I've got a big fight coming up, but we all have. It's a big show and we know what we've got to do.'

Wayne Shepherd has that other kind of show to focus on, the small-town kind of show that mainstream boxing will pass by with scarcely a sideways glance. Britain's oldest boxer is off to the North Wales seaside resort of Rhyl to face a local man, Neil Bonner. Shepherd will be cast as the opponent, a role he knows well, even if he is reluctant to play it. However, he has had plenty of notice for the fight and, with almost a month still to go, travels down from his home in Carlisle to polish up his ring work at Jack Doughty's gym.

He bounds into the gym, a short, muscular man with a shaved head and a boxer's trademark nose. At the age of 43 Shepherd is twice as old as some of those he exchanges blows with and he takes an obvious pride in his fitness. He was 32 when he turned professional, belatedly realising he could earn money by doing precisely what he had been doing as an amateur.

'We lived in Padiham, near Burnley,' he says. 'A trainer down there called Bert Myers told me I ought to go professional. I thought I was too old, but I'd been knocking his pros about and he said I was in good shape. So I decided to give it a go.'

Shepherd has stayed in shape by faithfully following his training schedule. He begins his day with a run along the beach and around a golf course near his home. In the afternoon, he concentrates on bag work and, in the evening, he gets to grips with weights, unless he is sparring at Shaw. But he believes psychological preparedness is equally important.

'I'm training to be a hypnotherapist,' he says, a bolt out of the blue that would catch any opponent off guard. 'I work as a nightclub doorman at the moment, but I've been interested in hypnosis for 25 years. I picked up a book about it and thought, "I'm going to get into this." I'm really interested in the subject, everything about the mind. I believe I use mind over matter now, training as I did more than ten years ago. I don't leave my training alone. When people leave their fitness alone and follow a normal lifestyle, they put on weight and get out of shape. I don't allow myself to get out of shape.'

It appears Shepherd has something of a problem getting his head around his place in professional boxing.

Doughty joins the conversation, saying: 'He is known as a journeyman.'

Shepherd screws up his face and interjects: 'Terrible name, that.'

Doughty: 'I don't think it is. Boxers don't seem to like it, but it means afraid of nobody, take anybody on. Consequently, his record is a bit lop-sided.'

Shepherd: 'Do you know something, and this is perfectly true, I would not know what my record is.'

Doughty: 'He's had 50-odd fights.'

Shepherd: 'It does put me off knowing I'm going to lose more than I win because half the time I think I've won my fights, and then the referee puts up the other boxer's hand and I get so frustrated and annoyed when I know I've beaten the other person. I had a fight up in Newcastle. I didn't get the verdict, but I knew I'd beaten him. After, in the shower, he asked me how I thought the fight went. I said, "I beat you and you know I did." He said, "That's the way it goes in your home town." His friends came up and congratulated me, but he never came up afterwards for a drink. He went out the back door and I drank with his friends. So that said it all.

'That really frustrates me, and the only reason I'm continuing is because in my amateur career I had a terrific right hand and left hook, and I knocked out nearly every opponent I fought. In my pro career I haven't done that, for some reason. I don't understand. Maybe it's a psychological problem. But I believe it will come back all of sudden. I think that's why I'm continuing, just to show what I'm capable of doing.

'It is possible age has caught up with me, but if I thought it had, without realising it, I wouldn't be able to do the physical things I can do now: the five-, six-mile runs, training continuously and having the stamina. I fought a ten-round fight two months ago and I finished the fight stronger than my much younger opponent. And that was at a week's notice.'

Doughty: 'He fights more often than most. He'll turn out anywhere, at the drop of a hat. He averages about a fight a month, which is quite a lot these days. I think he carries on because he loves a scrap; he must love the atmosphere and being there. He hasn't got a lot of nerves. Every fighter must be on edge before he goes in, but he just loves the whole thing.'

Shepherd: 'I don't have any nerves whatsoever. I do like the money, everybody does, so extra money is welcome.'

Doughty: 'I think the money is secondary for him. I think he loves the fight. Am I right?'

Shepherd: 'I think they go hand in hand. Why not fight for something – money? I've also met some good people in the gyms that have become good friends. I treat everybody individually. When I was younger, I never used to bother. I used to think, "I'm going to be fighting you," so I never made friends. Now I talk to people.'

Doughty: 'That camaraderie is obvious when we travel around and meet other fighters. Everybody knows him. They all respect him. Especially so because he's older, he's been in with tough opponents, opponents of a higher class as well. I tell my wife such and such a boxer is a nice lad and she says, "You always say that. They can't all be nice lads." But they are. Well, most of them are. They can knock hell out of each other and then afterwards love each other. Take Gary Dixon, a lad I had fighting in Glasgow the other night. It was a 50–50 contest, but unless you knock them out up there you're not going to win. Sure enough, the points decision went against us and he said to me, "I've let you down, haven't I? I told him he hadn't, but he's not one of those who grumbles and makes excuses. I will never blame the fighter. I would never tell a boxer he was terrible and got it all wrong. That would be so discouraging.

'As for this question of how long Wayne wants to go on, it's definitely all in the mind. If he's got doubts, he should stop, but while he thinks he can do it, he'll carry on.'

Shepherd: 'I don't even think about how long I will go on. As long as I enjoy it and can do it, that's the answer. I thought about managing, but now I'm not 100 per cent sure. Maybe when I'm not actually fighting I can look at it in a different way and may become involved.'

Two of Shepherd's three brothers have boxed. Glyn, four years his junior, never fulfilled his promise. Charles, 33, won titles but a combination of cut eyes and the scars of a broken marriage derailed his career. Now he has decided to give it another go. Wayne has two sons, Wayne Jnr, 24, and Lee, 22. The younger son had a brief flirtation with boxing.

'Lee wanted to fight to prove he could do it,' his father says. 'He had a couple of fights and packed it in. Wayne's into weights and body-building. I've told them if they want to box, they can, but I've never pushed them. I would worry for them, although I'm never worried for myself. I've never had any problems with scans or anything. There is a risk from the accumulation of blows as you get older but, touch wood, I try not to get hit that much. I've got a style that seems to stop me from getting hit as much as other boxers. If I felt I was really hurt I would call it a day. I've never actually been knocked out. The only time I've suffered at all was when I jumped up a weight and got stopped. I think, by coming in late, I possibly appreciate it more. I've learnt a lot from boxing, watching great fighters, as well.'

Doughty: 'In days gone by, fighters went on and on, with flat noses and cauliflower ears . . .'

Shepherd laughs self-consciously and clutches his re-shaped snout. 'I had a perfect nose till I sparred with a heavyweight and got it broken,' he explains. 'I had an operation so I could breathe at one side of my nose and they didn't tell me to lay off the running. I went training and it happened to go this way.'

Doughty: 'It's a great nose.'

Shepherd: 'People have perceptions. They think because you've got a broken nose you must be a rough and ready guy. In some respects it helps on the door because it puts people off. They think, "I'm not messing with him!"'

Doughty: 'They say you can't teach an old dog new tricks, but he's still learning. He tends to be tense, burning up energy, which is why he's not punching hard enough. I'm trying to relax him so that he can get better leverage into his punches. He can be out-boxed by somebody quicker, cleverer. I have him get in close and rough them up. In Belfast once, he was up against an unbeaten boxer, Danny Ryan, who was picking him off easily at distance. I told him to get in close, rough him up, anything. Well, Wayne went beyond that. He even brought his knee up into his groin and butted him, and in the end the referee disqualified him. Wayne blamed me. He said, "Jack told me to do it." I didn't mind that.

'A lot of journeymen go in with champions and people who are in a far higher class. If he got a few defeats on the run they'd stop him boxing. So, I try to keep him at a lower level, and he's had a few wins in the last year or so. He should do OK in his next one. The only thing is, we're the away fighter, we're going into Neil Bonner's territory. The last time we went to North Wales, Bonner was fighting somebody else and at the end of the first round he butted him, blatantly, but didn't get disqualified. We'll have to watch out for that.

'It was a Sunday evening show, at a nice hotel. We were the last fight. Wayne lost on points and, as we came out of the ring, all hell let loose. The supporters of one of the other boxers had been drinking all afternoon and suddenly this mass fight broke out in the bar. I led Wayne to the dressing-room and the doormen rushed in. They threw out the two main culprits, but everyone followed them out and they carried on fighting in the car park. This time it's an afternoon show, so they won't have had as much to drink.'

It's time, now, for Doughty and his fighters to get down to business. Shepherd is in one of the rings, loosening his limbs and shadow boxing. Choi, one of Doughty's Mongolians, is throwing punches at his imaginary opponent in the other ring. Circuit training is testing the resolve of a motley-looking crew in the main body of the gym; the weights are straining a pair of aspirants at the far end. Doughty strides towards the rings, pads at the ready. 'Of course I still do the pads,' he responds indignantly to the obvious and reasonable question. 'I'll always do the pads.'

He climbs into the ring with Choi, instructing the boxer to throw the left, then the right, then clusters, then combinations. Doughty is content and Choi steps down to take his pick of the punch bags. Doughty beckons Shepherd, who goes through a similar routine, peppering the pads and dutifully following every order. He plants his feet and delivers power. His head is glistening with sweat and suddenly he looks his 43 years.

They take a breather and Doughty nods his satisfaction. 'If he could punch like that in fights, he would knock people out.'

13 ☆ COLD SWEAT

'THE BODY SNATCHER' SHOW IS JUST A FORTNIGHT AWAY AND THE body snatcher in chief is missing. Ricky Hatton has not trained for three days because he has a cold, and Billy Graham is becoming anxious. In normal circumstances, Stephen Smith ought to pose little trouble to Hatton, but suddenly the circumstances have changed and that could make an important difference. This fight is supposed to be another step towards bigger, more lucrative things. Slip-ups don't feature on the agenda and Graham is reluctant to take any chances with his prize asset.

'This cold's going through the gym and now I've got it,' Graham says with a confirming snivel. He goes on, a tad confusingly: 'It's a pain in the arse. Michael's got it, as well. Arnie seems to be the only one who hasn't. Luckily Matthew Hatton is sparring in Birmingham. You would expect Ricky to be all right. It's amazing how so many finely tuned athletes go down with bugs. They don't like to be anything less than 100 per cent. He can't afford to miss another day's training from now on. I'm supposed to be doing 15 rounds with him on Friday, but I don't think I can. I did it once before when I was ill and it killed me. This is a disaster.'

Graham may not be fit enough to climb into the ring, but he still has much to impart and a wide-eyed Farnell hangs on to the 'Preacher's' every word. Farnell departs in his England football kit, smiling broadly, and Graham admits this affable side to the boxer's nature has taken him aback.

'I used to think he was nasty and vicious,' Graham confides. 'That was the way he always came across, but he's a really good lad. It's like his dad. You wouldn't think he was such a nice bloke when he is in there with Arnie's Barmy Army and all that, but he gets tanked up because he's so nervous at fights. We still laugh about the night Arnie hit somebody in the privates and his dad shouted, "Hit him there again – he can't take it there!"

'In this game it does help if you can scare your opponent. That's the best way. Or you can let them underestimate you, which Ricky has done with some of his opponents in the past. I think Arnie and Michael have tried too hard to try and scare their opponents. I don't want them getting themselves psyched up. That's a waste of energy. I want them to use their energy in the fight. Arnie and Mike shouldn't have to be learning the basics at this stage of their careers. They should know every move, every punch. We've got to work on Arnie, especially. We're just scratching the surface with him. Ideally, he could have done with a long break after he lost to Takaloo to concentrate on learning, but, hopefully, we'll get there.'

Those words would rub salt into Brian Hughes' gaping wounds. According to boxing's bush radio, he may lose another of his fighters to Graham's gym. It is said David Barnes is considering following Farnell and Gomez.

'I hear something else is happening,' Hughes groans. 'I don't know for sure, but I need to sort it out. I don't believe any of them when they say they don't want any more fighters. They want to take the ready–made, finished article. I stopped Barnes sparring with Hatton. They should come to me first and ask me if they want him to spar, not the boxer. There's no loyalty these days. Some of these younger blokes in the game think we're dinosaurs, they do. I think this may be the time to go, now. I don't need this.'

The enmity between the Collyhurst and Phoenix camps is increasingly tangible, yet Hughes echoes his rival's claims when he says: 'I have never, ever criticised Billy Graham in the press or on TV. Why should I be jealous of anybody? Life is too short.'

Ten days to the fight and Hatton is making up for lost time. He managed to arrange sparring sessions against southpaw opposition and now he is pounding away at the body belt, worn by one of Graham's assistants, Gary Booth.

'This is the first time Ricky's been on the body belt with somebody else since I've had him,' Graham says ruefully. 'I hate it because it's like an admission that I'm getting old, past it. I got hit on the button once doing it. I've also had my ribs broken, but it still hurts more being on this side of the ropes.'

It is just another source of anxiety for Graham, who admits he will suffer from gut-wrenching tension as fight night draws closer.

'Doing this is like going on a roller-coaster ride,' he says. 'It's only when you get off that you really enjoy it. On the morning of a fight I'm all knotted up inside and wonder why I do it. Then when you walk to the ring, there's so much pressure. But when it's over and you've won again, it's the greatest feeling and I relive it all on video.

'The trouble this time is that Ricky's not done enough training, really, and we did think about cancelling the fight. But he thinks he'll be okay and I just hope he is. We finally got him some southpaw sparring. I hate southpaws. They never look right against southpaws, they're never smooth. David Barnes wanted to spar with Ricky, but I think Brian Hughes was afraid he'd want to come over here.'

Graham, in any case, preaches against over-training and over-sparring. He has taken his boxers out of the foot-slogging era yet declines to venture too far down the road of sports science.

He explains: 'The body and heart need the rest, so I like to give my boxers weekends off rather than have them running up hills, and I don't go in for the long dawn runs. My lads run in the evenings, but the routine involves a lot of sprinting. I also think a lot of the new ideas with sports science are over the top. They're gimmicks. I don't like a lot of sparring for the simple reason that it's dangerous. Every blow to the head sends the brain swimming around. If I thought other fighters were sharper than mine I would spar and train more, but I don't think they are. Too much sparring also leads to too many wars in gyms. We've had some. I've stopped some but, generally, I don't. I let them sort it out themselves. If someone is getting too much crap it's better to let him give the other one some back. That's the way it is in boxing.'

Hatton, wearing a vest bearing 'The Hitman' slogan, is watched by his brother, Matthew, recently returned from his stint in Birmingham. Slogans, like tattoos, appear to be obligatory. Matthew's message reads: 'Fear is in the eye of the beholder – don't let it be you.' Farnell is next in the ring as Gomez, wearing a Manchester City shirt with his name on the back, follows his girlfriend, daughter and cousin through the door.

'I've had an easy day today, but I had a hard one yesterday and I'll have another hard one tomorrow,' Gomez is eager to point out.

Matthew is beckoned by a Sunday newspaper photographer to pose in front of a white screen, erected in the other room. Ricky, too, is asked to step forward and looks puzzled by the photographer's arty ideas, but co-operates without complaint.

A handful of onlookers applaud at the end of Farnell's ring session with Booth. Farnell stands beneath a shower of water and then slumps to the canvas, grinning with satisfaction. Booth also finds respite on his haunches. One of the on-lookers turns away, almost into a stream of shower gel, playfully squirted from above. A sheepish Ricky Hatton bounds down the stairs and rubs away the gel with his foot before disappearing into the shower.

A few minutes later he steps out into warm, early autumn sunshine, zipping up his Manchester City jacket with one hand and gripping his Manchester City bag with the other. The back window of his black Jaguar is a display of Manchester City favours. He is still coughing and spluttering, and admits:

'It's been a bit worrying, taking three days out of the gym, right in the middle of my hardest and most important work, so we thought of calling the fight off. When I came back in the gym, Billy said, "Let's see how it goes", because there's too much at stake. But it was like I'd never been away. Everything's gone perfectly, apart from the cold, and that's turned out to be not much of a problem.'

What is at stake for Hatton is the passport to a fight for the undisputed world crown. The Russian-born Australian, Kostya Tszyu, is acknowledged as the No. 1 and the New Yorker, Zab Judah, former IBF champion, is another potential target for the Mancunian.

'I'm happy to be patient for those fights because I know I'm not at my peak yet,' says Hatton, who is approaching his 24th birthday. 'I'm not far away from my peak but I'm not there yet. Those fighters are already signed up for fights, but another year will definitely be better for me. If I wasn't improving I'd be a bit more gutted, but that's not the case. Kostya Tszyu's one of the best, pound for pound, in any weight division. You want to be at your peak when you're fighting these fellas.'

FIGHTING CHANCE

Richard Hatton still seems like the boy next door. He was raised just up the road, in Hattersley, which will forever bear the stigma of association with the Moors Murderers, Myra Hindley and Ian Brady. That Hyde should now have found infamy through the serial killer, Dr Harold Shipman, is an unfortunate and macabre coincidence. Hatton lives just up another road, in Gee Cross, with his parents. His father, Ray, a former Manchester City player, and mother, Carol, follow his every punch and move from ringside. The contrast with Gomez's family background could scarcely be starker.

'I come from a good, stable family and I still live at home,' he says. 'I never get in trouble outside the ring. My father brought me up in the right way. My friends are the same friends I've always had, from the council estate. Even though I'm doing better now and mixing in bigger circles, my best mates are still the ones that I went to school with. They're typical Jack the Lads, off the estate. Well, that's what I am, really. They don't let me get too bigheaded and carried away.'

Hatton might have followed in his father's footsteps and pursued a career in football. He joined City as a schoolboy and, by all accounts, had above average talent. However, he had already made an impression in boxing and most reliable judges of that sport considered his talent exceptional. He realised that, too.

'I was on City's books when I was 13, 14 years old, but at the time I was winning national amateur boxing titles left, right and centre. I won nine in all. Although I had a talent for football I was just better at boxing. Everybody could see that was my game. Dad never tried to steer me to football because it was clear I was something special in boxing. I turned pro at 18. My mum definitely worried when I took up boxing, but I've been doing it for as long as she can remember now and, touch wood, she's not seen me seriously hurt yet. Hopefully, she never will. It's something she's got used to.

'I was never a tearaway at school or anything. It's strange, really. You'd have thought I'd have gone for football because nobody in the family had done boxing. And it's probably even stranger the way I fight because it's not the way you'd expect from somebody with my personality.'

They call Ole Gunnar Solskjaer, the Manchester United striker, the 'Baby-faced Assassin' and the moniker could apply to the one-time City youngster.

'I think that does work in my favour,' he acknowledges. 'A couple of times I've fought more experienced fighters, who have been in there with all the champions, and they've thought, "Oh, we've just got a youngster here. No problem at all." Then the bell goes and they get a bit of a shock. And the best is yet to come from me.'

Hatton has had his more familiar moniker (the original 'Hitman' was Tommy Hearns, from Detroit) since he first walked into a boxing club and put on a pair of gloves.

'I sparred with some of the other lads and started knocking seven bells out of them,' he recalls with a relish that gives a clue to the other side of his character. 'The coach there said, "Look at him, he's a little Hitman," and it stuck. I was about ten. I think it just came from natural strength. At that age I didn't know Tommy Hearns or anything about him, but I definitely became a Tommy Hearns fan. A hitman goes out and kills people and I suppose because of my style, which is so aggressive, it's the obvious choice.

'I don't really change in the ring, but I suppose I do want to hurt my opponent – till the count of ten. And then I hope he gets up, he's in full health, and we can go and have a drink together and be mates for the rest of our lives. I don't particularly hate opponents. The only thing that drives me on is the thought that the fella across the ring is taking my livelihood away from me, he's standing in the way of a better life for myself and a better life and future for my son. He's standing in the way of all the sacrifices I've made in the previous weeks of training, all the hard work, all the road work, all the sparring.

'I've never been badly hurt and never been stopped. I don't worry about being hurt. If you do, you're in the wrong game. I'm sure I'll know when to get out. I've been brought up the right way. I've got good people around me. With my style, I think I'm always going to be in exciting and probably tough fights. To say I get stuck in is a bit of an understatement. I'm not really destined for a massively long career. It's more likely I'll have a short, exciting career, hopefully make plenty of money and get out. Most of the people who continue past their time do so when they've not achieved what they hoped to, but I'm well on the way to achieving what I want.'

Hatton's son, Campbell, is 21 months old and lives with the boxer's former girlfriend, just up yet another road, in Broadbottom.

'When I leave the gym here, I'll be going straight up there to see him, and he stays over at my house three times a week. It's funny because his mum and I kept having arguments, splitting up, then getting back together again. Eventually, we said it wasn't working, we weren't for each other, and we decided on a full stop. Then we found out she was pregnant. So it was a bit of a strange one. But we get on fantastic now. It couldn't be better, really. And, not being with her, I don't get no aggro like you normally expect from your missus. You never know if we'll get together again, but at the moment, I'm concentrating on my boxing, doing my best, and I like things as they are.

'I wouldn't encourage Campbell to box if I could help it. But if he wanted to, I wouldn't have a choice in the matter. I'd do what my parents did with me. Whatever I could see his strengths in life were – boxing, football or an everyday job – I'd support him and push him. If he wanted to do boxing, I couldn't stop him, but I'd sooner have him kicking a football in front of 40,000 at Maine Road – and not for United, that's for sure!'

Hatton's younger brother, Matthew, has decided boxing is his game also and takes another undefeated record into the MEN show. However, like many sportsmen with outstandingly gifted siblings, he may suffer by inevitable comparison.

'Matthew is realistic,' Ricky says. 'He knew what he was coming into. He knew that when he turned professional, everybody would say, "He's Ricky Hatton's brother," rather than, "He's Matthew Hatton," but he's not the jealous type. He's dead proud of me, just like I'm dead proud of him. Now I think he's beginning to leave that label behind because he's getting a reputation off his own bat. He's 13 fights unbeaten, he's impressing everybody in the press, and now it's gone from "Ricky Hatton's younger brother" to "Matthew Hatton", which I'm dead chuffed about.'

Hatton may be the star of the team, but he never overtly flaunts his status. He doesn't need to. It hits you in the face like one of his punches. He constantly offers advice to his gym-mates, although he rarely appears to hold back in sparring, even against his brother, and much to the anxiety of Graham. Like all good stars of teams, Hatton goes out of his way to talk up his colleagues. Gomez and Farnell were hardly strangers to him when they arrived at Hyde.

'We trained together and sparred together as amateurs,' Hatton says. 'Although we went to different gyms as professionals, we've always got on well. Now, being in the same gym, we all buzz off each other. Everyone can see how hard each one's working. There was a big thing when they both left the Collyhurst gym, but it wasn't because Brian Hughes did anything wrong. Brian Hughes is one of the best trainers in the country. They simply reached points in their careers where they needed a different outlook, something to give them an extra kick, something to go for. They've come into a new gym, working with Billy Graham, also one of the best trainers in the country, bringing in the knowledge of Brian Hughes. Billy is just adding to what Brian Hughes has already taught them, so they've got the best of both worlds.

'Billy is a fantastic conditioner, a fantastic coach. He's had so many different champions – world, European, Commonwealth, British, right across the board – and they've achieved that through training with Billy. It's certainly not just a business relationship that I have with him. He takes every punch with you in there. He's like your best mate as well.'

Yet it takes a selfish, blinkered approach to reach the summit in any sport, and if mates slither down the slope into oblivion that's just the way it is. Only the very few go all the way and by then envy is likely to have replaced genuine friendship.

Hatton accepts: 'Some jealousy is always going to be part of it. If other lads from other gyms are getting all the publicity from all the papers and television, I'm sure something in the back of my mind would be saying, "Phew, I wish I was like that." But in most sports, and certainly in boxing, they're all very respectful. When they see my name in lights, they're possibly a little peeved and think, "I wish I was there," but like all boxers, they give you respect where respect is due. I'd do the same.'

Hatton has earned respect not only for his boxing but also for his humanity. He has been accompanied regularly in the ring, before and after contests, by a boy called James Bowes, who has had a far more daunting fight of his own, against serious illness. That James has survived until now is testimony to his courage and, his family is convinced, the inspiration he draws from his hero and friend.

'It's a miracle he's still with us,' Hatton says. 'He should have left us about four months ago, but he's battling on. He has his good days and his bad days. The really sad thing is that his mum has died. If it had happened to James we would have been prepared for it, but this is a real tragedy. He'll be there with us next week, as long as he is fit enough. His mum, God rest her soul, was always adamant that because I kept having him in the ring and at the gym it gave him a bit of inspiration. That's like winning a belt for me.'

A couple of his Jack the Lad mates have pulled up in the gym car park in a van and Hatton jumps out for a chat with them before driving off in his sleek black Jag to see Campbell.

The start of the final week before the show finds Hughes a changed man. He is the buoyant, genial, gregarious figure of old. He vowed to 'sort out' David Barnes and he has done. The boxer has, along with Michael Jennings, Thomas McDonagh and Matthew Hall, signed a contract tying him to Hughes.

Hughes says: 'Frank Warren told me I should become a manager as well as a trainer and I've taken his advice – after 40 years of handshakes. I feel sad, having to work like this, but times have changed.'

Nothing, it appears, will be allowed to deflate Hughes now. He has had to cope not only with defections but also with what has amounted to character assassination on the Internet.

'I feel happier now than I have for the last three years,' he says. 'These are the last I'll bring through but I'm even more determined now, after certain things that have gone on. I'm no egotist. And, on my life, I've not been a thief or done anything wrong. I've got a three-year plan with my boxers and I follow it through. Others have copied my methods because they know it works. We start them from amateurs and try in three years to get to British or other titles. If people want to leave and try something different I can accept that, but to slag me behind my back and not even come to me and tell me why, I can't understand that. I've still not spoken to Farnell, face to face, since he left.'

Those at the gym maintain it is no coincidence that Hughes' mood and the atmosphere in the camp have lightened since the departure of Gomez. One says: 'Michael could be nasty and jealous. He caused problems. Things are a lot better without him.'

Gomez, wearing his City shirt, is the first boxer to appear at the Lowry

Hotel, an ultra-modern, simple-is-beautiful new Manchester landmark, although it stands on the Salford bank of the River Irwell. This is the venue for a press conference, two days ahead of the MEN show. Gomez was not scheduled to be here. The media have been invited to interview the men on the main events and place names have been put out for Ricky Hatton, Stephy Smith, Ruben Groenewald and Anthony Farnell. That, too, hurts Gomez. He yearns for the attention, the stature, the respect. He peers out onto an unseasonable, sunlit scene, hunches his shoulders and throws a flurry of punches.

'Two more fights and I get a shot at the title,' he says. 'It's my third and last chance, but the good thing is that all I've got to worry about now is in the ring. I've seen people in a different light in the last couple of months, and that includes Brian.'

Proceedings are held up because Smith is late. A journalist informs his colleagues that Hatton's opponent has gone to the other Lowry, the art gallery and theatre, out at Salford Quays. As soon as Smith arrives, Frank Warren, wearing a three-piece suit and sitting at the centre of the line-up, begins the promotional spiel for a 'cracking night of boxing'. He announces that he has agreed an extension of his contract with Hatton, whom he describes as 'the most exciting fighter in Britain'. He contends Smith will give him a tough fight and stresses that Ricky cannot afford to slip up because 'he has greater fish to fry down the road and we're keeping him busy till that happens'.

Hatton is asked why he turned down an offer from the BBC and says he had no intention of parting company with 'the best promoter in the country and one of the best in the world'. Warren comes in to dismiss the BBC's strategy in boxing as a joke, citing the on-going case of Audley Harrison. 'They've got no promoters. I have 12 million reasons why I don't like Don King [knowing laughs from the assembled media] but promoters do have a role to play. They put bums on seats and it works. What's kept boxing alive in this country is Sky. The proof of the pudding is the man on my right [Hatton]. He's sold more tickets than Lewis or Naz in this country. The guy is a genuine star and he's come through with Sky. We will sell 13,000/14,000 tickets for Saturday and it's a genuine fight. The BBC coming in is great, but let's have some competitive matches.'

The recurring charge levelled against Hatton and Warren is that they are ducking competitive matches. Junior Witter, the British champion, claims Hatton is ignoring him, while it is generally recognised that Kostya Tszyu represents the ultimate test. Warren, conscious of the growing cynicism, states that Hatton will fight both.

Smith's trainer is also his father, Darkie, and he is palpably unimpressed with Warren's assumption that Hatton can look beyond this fight. Smith Snr points out that his son is also a world champion (the IBC version) and argues that his one defeat, against Bobby Vanzie, wasn't really a defeat. 'Ricky is good, but Stephy is better,' he grunts. 'Ricky has got to prove he can land this fish first!'

Hatton, the consummate professional, takes the opportunity to express his appreciation for the nutritional and dietary guidance he and his colleagues have been receiving. 'All the lads from the gym have had the benefit of it.'

Farnell, a spectator for much of the press conference, finally gets the chance to have his say and delivers his message in a few words: 'It's the most important fight of my life. I've trained 200 per cent for this and I'll put it together on Saturday night. Ruben is a good boxer, but I'm so much better. What's happened in the past has happened.'

The formal conference breaks up and the fighters and trainers are ushered to quiet corners for TV, radio and one-to-one newspaper interviews, as well as pictures. Ray Hatton looks on as his son stares into yet another lens and then copes assuredly with yet another reporter. Ray, who made a handful of first-team appearances for City before injury cut short his career, has had two pubs and now works in the carpet trade, but mostly, it seems, his life is consumed with guiding, fetching, carrying, encouraging and worrying for his sons.

'I would have loved Ricky to play for City,' he says. 'It would have been a much easier life for him. All boxers deserve respect. There's no hiding place in the ring. You know your job's on the line every time you go in there.

'My wife and I are far more nervous than he is. We'll lie awake the night before the fight till three o' clock, looking at the ceiling, while he's snoring away in the next room! Things have turned out well for him, though. He wanted to watch City play Liverpool on Saturday afternoon, but we put the block on that. He'd go 12 rounds by half-time! Matthew was also a good footballer and now it's working out for him in boxing.'

Hatton Snr is slightly amused by his son's talk of diet and nutrition. 'It's really just energy drinks. Ricky eats normally except in the last week. He just has to be sensible. Food is your fuel. You need it.'

Warren, too, undertakes his round of personal interviews. The sell comes easily to him. He is straight and never patronising. He knows better than most that, as a promoter, he is there to be shot at. He has survived a gunman's assassination attempt and a number of intimidating skirmishes, let alone more routine, occupational hazards, to reach the top of his business. He accomplished that by changing the landscape of boxing in this country.

'I'm a London boy, from Islington, but what I've done in my time in boxing is basically taken it out of London,' Warren says. 'If you look at the Mickey Duff era, his big fights took place at Wembley and the Albert Hall. Occasionally, you had a fight in Manchester, but it had become a bit of a graveyard for boxing. I've taken boxing to places like Sheffield, Manchester, even Newcastle, and regenerated it, especially with the talent we've found. There's a lot of talent in Manchester at the moment. We've made it a success story.

'Guys like Mickey Duff had it pretty easy. The Board of Control operated a policy where no major shows could take place within 14 days of each other, but nobody could define what a major show was. I wrote to the Board asking them for a definition and couldn't get it. In the early days, I couldn't even get a show on because in the course of a month there would be one show at Wembley, one at the Albert Hall. You also had a situation where all the Duff fights would take place on a Tuesday and they would broadcast on the Wednesday, on *Sportsnight*, with highlights on *Grandstand* on the Saturday. They allowed only two live TV shows per promoter, I think it was, which I took them to court over and we settled out of court. It was restraint of trade and I got TV to take the live boxing. That ended their monopoly, I got ITV involved and it took off from there.

'My policy then was to take it around the country. I just thought, "Why has everything got to take place in London?" There was a population of 56 or 57 million people and they didn't all live in London, so we took it out there. We had a series, *Seconds Out*, in which we put on young talent. We featured people like Nigel Benn and Chris Eubank. A lot of the young talent came through that system.'

The role of the promoter is a subject he touched on earlier and he readily comes back to it: 'In the early stages of boxers' careers, all the investment in their development is made by the likes of the promoter or the manager. We put our money up. They're not the main events, they're on the undercard. I've got a couple of fights here this week that typify what I'm talking about. David Barnes and Matthew Macklin are two good young fighters, but they're on the undercard and they'll learn their trade. We have to pay to develop that. TV are not coming to film them, they're coming for the main event, and that's the point I was making about the BBC. Audley Harrison fighting some stiff in a six-round fight is hardly main-event material. I don't blame Audley Harrison for that, I blame the BBC.

'A good promoter will recognise two important things. Firstly, if I'm at home, watching on TV, I want to feel the atmosphere. If it's an empty hall, you know it's an empty hall. Secondly, if you're commentating or reporting on the fight and the place is full and it's exciting, you get caught up in the atmosphere. If it's empty and a bit hollow, you're going to feel low-key. The atmosphere at the Velodrome last year is what it's all about. That's what we're good at doing.'

Warren's investment in Manchester and its boxers has proved particularly productive and rewarding.

'Ricky Hatton started boxing at Wythenshawe, 600 seats. That's where we got it going and worked at it. You've also got Anthony Farnell and Michael Gomez. Brian Hughes has been very instrumental in the process, as has Ricky's dad, Ray. They've all helped to make this work, because they'd get out, they'd sell tickets, they'd get behind the promotion. It's the same old story: whether you're a manager or promoter in sport, or the manager of a pop star, you're always seen to be taking advantage of the athlete or the artiste. That's the public perception and it won't change. The boxer has got to do the best he can for himself, but most boxers these days have accountants and lawyers, and you're negotiating with them. Some of these lawyers fancy themselves as super sports agents and don't know which day of the week it is, but that's what you have to deal with.'

Surely one of boxing's fundamental PR problems is the egregious Don King? The image of the electric hair and the eccentric megalomaniac convicted for killing overwhelms all else.

Warren responds: 'You've got to remember that Don King came into this business when he was 40 years of age, a guy who had been to prison; he's a product of the streets, he's a black guy. In his lifetime blacks didn't have the vote. He's a hustler, so he hustled, and he didn't know any different. It's cost people, and that's life. The world goes on and the world changes, and when Don King is dead and gone boxing will carry on. It's not called "Don King", it's called "boxing". Don King is probably the hardest-working man I've ever met. He's got tremendous vision, tremendous foresight. He's brave in a deal, he's fearless when he makes a deal, but sometimes he lets himself down. But then we all do that now and then.

'America is a different type of boxing to here. Don King is really into heavyweight boxing. There are two types of boxing. There's heavyweight boxing and there's boxing. Heavyweight boxing generates millions and millions of dollars at the top level. In the '70s and '80s I don't think it was too good for the game, the way the heavyweight division was operated, and he was basically in control of it. However, I think Larry Holmes made a very valid comment, saying he got screwed, but if he'd been promoted by somebody else he still wouldn't have earned as much money. I don't know how you take the rights and wrongs of that. It depends which way you want to look at it. But also, I know there are deals where he's done his money. At the end of the day, he's got a totally different style than I've got, and he's a different animal to me.

'You have to be everything, a jack of all trades, to do this job. To some boxers you are a father figure, sort them out with all the things that go on behind the scenes. A lot of boxers, especially the good ones, are pampered from an early age – like soccer players. Because they're a special talent they get the best treatment. Some of them don't know what the real world is all about. I came from a humble background. Islington, where I grew up, was a tough old area, so I understand. I left school when I was 15. One day you're dealing with a boxer who can't afford to pay for his car, the next you're dealing with the chief executive officer of Sky TV or *Showtime*. That's how diverse this business is.'

Few boxers in recent times have had more serious or persistent problems behind the scenes than Michael Gomez.

'Michael's got self-inflicted problems,' Warren says. 'He's a super guy. He came from a very tough background, poor childhood. In some ways it's a credit to boxing that he's got his house and his family and that, but he's let himself down on a couple of occasions. It's annoying, it's frustrating, and for him on Saturday it's make or break. We've given him another chance, but you can have only so many chances in life.'

The fall-out from Gomez's defeat to Laszlo Bognar caused deep embarrassment for Warren. Reports claimed Gomez was coerced into fighting, despite the fact he made it clear he was unwell.

Warren replies sternly: 'I've got letters in my office saying that's untrue. He was not coerced or anything. I didn't speak to him till the day of the fight. Certainly he was not coerced by me, because I never had any conversation with him. I never knew he had anything.'

What about Gomez's claim that he was removed from a ringside seat?

'Oh, I don't know about that. If somebody gets moved out of a ringside seat that's because he's sitting in somebody's seat. You can't just go and sit anywhere you like. If he's got a problem with that then that's his problem. You cannot live and sleep with these guys. Like your kids, you hope they are going to do the right things in life, but once they're outside the front door you don't know what they do. He's supposed to be responsible, he's a father, but he's been out on the piss, he's been overweight for fights, I know that, but all I ever hear is afterwards. You never hear about it before, you always hear about it after they've been beaten. Then it's, "Oh, I've been on the piss." Well, why are you telling me now? I don't want to hear these excuses. Tell me before and I'll pull you out of the fight.

'You look at Ricky. He's a professional. He likes to be out with his mates, and why not? He's a young man. People have to understand that as a boxer you've got to sacrifice a lot of your youth. It's a team sport till the bell goes and then you're on your own. Once the fight's on, Ricky is up for it. He trains properly and gets himself ready. Plus, he's got a good family around him. It's easy to criticise Michael but you've got to remember he was born in a car, he lived in a [children's] home. What you going to do?'

Naseem Hamed's falling star leaves something of a void in the firmament of British boxing. Perhaps Hatton can fill it, or how about Vanzie, a more flamboyant showman?

'Naz was an exciting fighter at one stage of his career. Now he fights once in a blue moon, once a year, and he's a bore. In his last fight, he was booed out of the ring. I've never seen a show where people were booing after three rounds of a guy who was a good puncher, and walking out of the venue. Ricky's the best value now, without a doubt. Vanzie's not a bad little fighter. He blows hot and cold. He can look great and he can look crap. He's with me now and he'll get an eliminator for a world title. If you're with me, you'll make money and, providing you do the business, you'll do well.'

Warren has transparently done well for himself and has no plans to seek another outlet for his considerable business acumen.

'My only ambition, and it's an old joke, but it's to eat my prawn sandwich without any of the prawns falling out. I'm okay; we've done all right. I've built the London Arena, the largest purpose-built arena in London, and I've been involved in various other things, but deep down I enjoy my boxing. Sometimes the politics are a pain in the arse and some of the people you deal with are a pain in the arse, but we're good at what we do. I've managed and promoted all the big names in the sport and I still get a kick out of looking at the Barnsies and the Macklins, and thinking, "Hang on, these are the guys of the future." And maybe it's a bit of ego. You want to be proved right when you say, "This guy is extra special."

'Outside the ring, you have as tough a fight as they have in it, but I still get a buzz on big fight nights, when the job's all over and you can sit down. It can be frustrating, such as when you see Farnell lose his common sense and a fight he should have won, but then that's part of boxing. More than anything, I enjoy boxing.'

Gomez and Warren appear at ease with one another now. They chat briefly and part with an exchange of smiles. Each knows it is in their common interests to put any differences behind them and make this last chance work.

Richard Maynard, who handles media matters for Warren, offers this balanced version of events leading up to that first, ill-fated fight against Bognar. He says: 'Michael told me he didn't feel so well and thought he might have a cold coming on, but there was no suggestion that he wanted to pull out. It was almost a casual remark.'

14 ☆ BLOOD AND THUNDER

THE *MANCHESTER EVENING NEWS* ARENA, APPROPRIATELY RUBBING shoulders with a refurbished Victoria Station, is a symbol of a city going places as well as a monument to reaffirmed cultural and sporting status. The IRA bomb that exploded only a few hundred yards from here in the summer of 1996 galvanised Manchester's defiance, which in turn spawned a spectacular renaissance. This area has been rebuilt and reinvigorated, and the ripple effect has enhanced commercial and leisure regeneration across the cityscape.

Stores and boutiques are still busy when the first fighters on 'The Body Snatcher' bill arrive at the MEN Arena. They almost outnumber spectators for the opening exchanges, but nothing can dull the sense of occasion for Matthew Hall, making his professional debut. The 18-year-old from Middleton, groomed by Brian Hughes, calls himself 'El Torito' (The Little Bull), just as Tony Ayala, a hard-punching American light-middleweight, once did. However, the youngster's idol is Mike Tyson, which is readily apparent in his physique and style. He is short for a light-middleweight, a chunky figure with a shaved head. He wears black trunks and boots. He hustles forward menacingly, swarming his opponent – the lanky Pedro Thompson, from Nobby Nobbs' camp – and wins in 2 minutes 15 seconds as the referee, Phil Kane, steps in to call a halt. Hughes' satisfaction is tempered by the conviction that, with a little self-control, his protégé could have recorded a clean knock-out. That, he has no doubt, will come. Two of Hughes' other boxers, Thomas McDonagh and Michael Jennings, also enjoy quick success against Birmingham veterans. McDonagh wins in one round against Brian Coleman, Jennings in four over Karl Taylor.

The schedule is in danger of getting ahead of itself, so there is a lengthy delay before Billy Graham leads one of his young hopefuls, Steve Foster Jnr, into the ring for a super-bantamweight contest against Cardiff's Jason White. Graham is wearing a black beret, his lucky charm and an emblem of revolutionaries from Che Guevara to Robert Lindsay's Citizen Smith.

Robin Reid, a spectator this evening, is preoccupied with business outside the ring. He hovers pensively, biting his lip and glancing in the direction of Frank Warren. He catches Warren's eye and they retreat to seats three rows from ringside. Warren talks intently. Reid listens intently. This is patently more than casual chit-chat. Foster, the son of a famous fighting father from these parts, Steve 'the Viking', has completed two rounds of jousting with an awkward opponent before Reid and Warren split, the boxer joining Jennings and other members of the Collyhurst and Moston contingent in seats on the other side of the VIP divide.

In the third round Foster delivers a blow on the low side of the target divide and White doubles up. The referee, Phil Edwards, almost pleads with the reluctant White to stand and continue. White finally complies and, in a state of frenzy, seeks retribution. Foster responds in kind and White reels away, to be rescued by the referee.

Warren is sitting in the front row to watch one of his tips for stardom, Matthew Macklin, take on Estonia's Leonti Voronchuk at welterweight. 'Jab, jab, then the right,' Warren yells. More instructions come from his corner and supporters. His head must be aching more from the bombardment of advice than from anything Voronchuk can throw at him. Macklin's patience is rewarded in the fifth, when his left to the body floors Voronchuk and referee Kane stops the fight. Voronchuk's protests are in vain. Warren is on his feet, another job done.

Warren is still on his feet, applauding the introduction of his next big welterweight hope, David Barnes, who has to negotiate a Russian, Sergi Starkov. Barnes, displaying the Cross of St George on his flamboyant outfit, wields a sword-like left to cut down his opponent late in the first round. Starkov is undaunted and forces Barnes to demonstrate his dancing and jabbing skills. Ricky Hatton's parents take their places at ringside as Warren shouts: 'Underneath, son. Body shots. That's it.' Starkov earns Barnes' respect, and although he goes down again in the sixth and final round, the Mancunian cannot stop him. Barnes gets the verdict, 60–54.

Hughes' night's work is over. He has four wins out of four and heads for home, leaving the stage to his former fighters and the Billy Graham camp. Michael Gomez, bare-chested and ready for action, climbs into the ring with none of the old fanfares or regalia: no Mexican Hat Dance, no sombrero, no shamrock, no 666. Only the shin-tickling long, black trunks, trimmed with the Irish tricolour. This is an eight-rounder, one of the supporting acts, and Gomez has been made aware of his place in the grander scheme of things. But some habits die hard and he confronts his opponent, Jimmy Beech, in a familiar show of sneering aggression. The man from Walsall laughs dismissively and carries on his warm-up routine as Graham steers Gomez to his corner, doubtless reminding him to channel his energy more purposefully.

At last, the tension begins to bite and the temperature rises, testament to the expectation – or perhaps uncertainty – Gomez generates. He makes a convincing start, working to Beech's body. Graham preaches calmly to his latest disciple at the end of the round and Gomez gives his full attention. Another good round for Gomez has Warren bellowing his support. Beech retaliates in the third, drawing blood from Gomez's head. The ex-champion, roused to more furious conflict, is warned for a low punch before putting down Beech. The bell intervenes but nothing can constrain Gomez in the fourth. Beech bleeds from the nose as Gomez assails him like a thunderstorm. An uppercut virtually lifts Beech off his feet and referee Kane decides to end the deluge after 2 minutes 15 seconds of the round.

A contented Warren stands and applauds as Gomez reaches out of the ring for his crowning glory – a sombrero. He poses with his new trainer for the photographers and leans into the MC's microphone to assure the audience: 'I'm back for good!'

Anthony Farnell, too, makes an understated entrance. The Roy Keane shirt has been discarded and, although he glares at Ruben Groenewald as the referee, Ian John-Lewis, issues his final instructions, he is heeding

Graham's warning. The South African pointedly ignores Farnell's eyes and is palpably untroubled by the chants of 'Manchester, la, la, la, Manchester, la, la, la'. There are still yawning gaps in the gallery, but the home backing is raucous and committed. Gomez, on an adrenaline-pumping high, has no problems finding a seat to his liking tonight, and adds his vocal support.

Groenewald is a cool and durable, if unspectacular, customer and he picks off Farnell with his jab. Farnell is less inclined to deploy that rudimentary tactic, much to the dismay of a camp follower, who tells his friend: 'He's punching so much harder in the gym. I can't understand why he doesn't use the jab more.'

The camp follower is happier in the third, as Farnell delivers more power and Groenewald bleeds from the nose. Gomez is on his feet, screaming. Ray Hatton leans forward for a better view. Carol Hatton's eyes and thoughts are wandering elsewhere. By the sixth, Groenewald is threatening to take charge of this grim encounter and the Hattons join Warren in imploring: 'Come on, Arnie, come on!'

Farnell responds with a more measured approach in the seventh. Among the approving on-lookers is Phil Taylor, the darts world champion, who shares his thoughts with a TV roving reporter. Farnell swings wildly in the ninth, desperately seeking the decisive contact. He puts together a more constructive attack in the tenth, but Groenewald is apparently indestructible and returns the blows with interest. He leaves his ugly calling card under Farnell's left eye and, early in the 11th, the camp follower is again perplexed. 'He gets it right in the gym, but he's reverting to type.'

Farnell gives him what he wants, a big right that hits the target. Ray Hatton is standing, urging on his sons' stable-mate to give more of the same. Farnell answers the final rallying call of his fans, and although he is reduced to an undignified sprawl in his endeavour to nail Groenewald, the champion is left gulping for air.

Groenewald's corner claim victory in the din at the end. For a fleeting moment Farnell looks bewildered. Graham, to his angst, is not here to offer reassurance. He is already back in the dressing-room, preparing Ricky Hatton. Farnell's face is red and now contorted. He could be smiling. He could be crying. It is difficult to tell. Someone hands him a white baseball cap and he raises an arm in salute, inducing another roar from the arena. Both corners put on a show of bravado but, at ringside, few are bold enough to call it. One judge has Groenewald the winner, the other two go for Farnell. The new champion is carried shoulder high to soak up the adulation. It has been a tough, dour struggle, but this time, Farnell has kept his head and reclaimed his title.

The main event is imminent and still much of the seating on the top tier is empty. Predictions of a 13,000- or 14,000-strong audience may have been a tad optimistic. Seasoned observers at the arena reckon the figure is closer to 10,000. One says: 'People are seeing through some of these fights. They're not stupid. Hatton's got to have a proper fight. This won't last three rounds.'

Whatever the crowd figure is, the noise from the gallery is hugely impressive. A chorus of boos greets the challenger for the WBU light-welterweight title. Stephen Smith, robed in shimmering silver, prances into the ring with the air of a man unconvinced of his 'Stunning' moniker.

Carol Hatton takes a drink from a bottle before her son is summoned, to a deafening eruption. Hatton's young and tragic friend, James Bowes, is already in the ring, parading the belt. Smith closes his eyes as the strains of 'Blue Moon' bring a paradoxically melodic lilt to the frenzy. Hatton, in his familiar blue and white, dips through the ropes and the decibels go up again. The muscular thighs are covered by the long, tassled trunks. He punches the sides of his face in ritual final preparation as Mickey Vann, the referee who has been in charge all the way through his title campaigning, calls the combatants together. Ray Hatton is back on his feet, clapping vigorously with the throng. Carol Hatton reaches down for her drink and takes another sip.

Hatton's fan club clear their throats for more cries of 'Manchester, la, la, la'. The champion, mindful of the early shock in his last fight, respectfully sizes up his opponent from a distance and the early punches, albeit ineffectual, come from Smith. Recce accomplished, Hatton unleashes his artillery. The speed, accuracy and power of his punching are awesome and Smith suddenly realises this is a proposition unlike any he has previously experienced. Carol Hatton shuffles to the edge of her seat, shouting on her son. He scarcely needs the encouragement. He knows he has an inferior fighter at his mercy, and mercy is not in his ring vocabulary. Whichever way Smith sways or ducks, the rapier-like punches catch up with him. A straight right sends Smith back and down, blood glistening from a cut on his cheek. He takes a mandatory count of eight and Hatton moves in again. His mother is on her feet. Somehow, Smith stays on his feet to the bell.

Smith attempts to fend off the champion in the second, but it is a hopeless cause. Hatton piles on the pressure again, pinning him into a neutral corner. Smith goes down and Vann steps forward to begin the count. Blood gushes from a cut above Smith's right eye and he gets to his feet, indicating the damage has been inflicted by an elbow. Before Vann can digest the claim Smith's trainer, and father, Darkie, clambers through the ropes with a white towel. He shoves the referee, reiterating his son's complaint of foul play. For a few moments the surreal scene seems frozen. A stupefied Smith Jnr tries to restrain his father and Vann orders the trainer out of the ring. The bellicose Smith Snr, still protesting and motioning with his head to suggest a butt, returns to his corner, but the contest is over. Vann has no alternative but to disqualify Smith Jnr. Hatton has retained his title in 3 minutes 28 seconds. Hatton leans out of the ring to kiss his mother and leaps on to the ropes to take the acclaim of the crowd. Smith Jnr isn't quite sure what kind of filial reaction would be appropriate. His embarrassment is compounded by the abuse raining down on his father. The feeling at ringside is that Smith Snr knew exactly what he was doing, that it was a calculated intervention to spare his son further punishment. As the disgraced Darkie Smith retreats from one corner, Ray Hatton walks away from the other, clutching his son's yellow gloves.

Hatton says, as he steps down from the ring, that he is 'mortified' the fight ended as it did. He goes on: 'I was really disappointed for the fans. I'd have finished him in the next exchange.'

In the dressing-room, Smith Snr maintains: 'Boxing used to be a clean, decent sport. Tonight, I saw Stephen nutted twice and everyone saw him [Hatton] walk forward and smack Stephen with the elbow. What do you do? Do you stand there and take it? I'm fed up. If they want to ban me, they can ban me. I'm finished anyway if this is the kind of people in boxing.'

Along the corridor in a press room, a photographer is calling up a sequence of pictures, recording the extraordinary events, on a laptop computer. Warren is anxious to speak to the media. Hatton, still bare-chested, joins him, facing the assembling journalists. 'Are you all right there, son?' Warren asks. Hatton says he is, but the promoter asks someone to bring the boxer a dressing gown. Warren whispers in Hatton's ear as his Manchester City top is handed to him. He drapes it over his shoulders. Graham completes the press conference line-up and Warren begins:

'I'm disgusted with what's happened. Darkie's trying to justify his actions. There's no justifiable reason. It's irresponsible. They called for this fight. It looked a matter of time before the fight was stopped. It took the gloss off what would have been a great win. [Paolo] di Canio did it in soccer and got a long ban. Darkie Smith should be banned. He could have caused a riot. The purse will be withheld, apart from expenses. I've criticised referees in the past but there's no place for that. The crowd showed their feelings but were well behaved. It's not been a good night for the sport. It's a shame for Ricky. Now we'll look to the future. Ricky will have a fight before the end of the year.'

Hatton concedes he needs to see a tape of the fight to be sure he did not elbow Smith, but is adamant it could only have been accidental. 'You could tell the way the fight was going I didn't need to use my elbow,' he maintains. 'I've been robbed of a fantastic finish. It's very disappointing for the fans and they behaved really well.'

Warren is certain Darkie Smith's act was a conscious ploy to stave off Hatton's onslaught. 'Without doubt, it was deliberate, to stop his son taking punishment. I thought he was playing for time. All he's done is cost them a lot of money. He and I have never really got on but his son is a super kid and it's a great shame what has happened. It's just terrible. He knew it would be a matter of seconds before it was stopped.'

Hatton: 'And I wanted a good finish, especially after City losing 3–0 to Liverpool today!'

Graham: 'It was going to be one of those wicked finishes.'

Warren: 'His next fight will be before Christmas. We'll look at taking him to the States.'

Hatton: 'I definitely fancy going to the States. All the great champions are over there. They like exciting fighters and I think they'll like me.'

Warren: 'Economics is what it's all about. He's now one of the highest-paid fighters in the country and we have to generate the income. If the figures add up, we'll do it. Witter will happen some time next year.'

Back in the ring, the show goes on in front of a drastically diminished audience. Eamonn Magee, who took Hatton the distance last time out, finds himself on the undercard, fighting Northampton's Alan Bosworth in an eerily anti-climactic atmosphere. Bosworth, cut above the left eye and overwhelmed by the man from Belfast, is rescued by the referee, Edwards, who steps between them midway through the fifth round, declaring: 'That's it, that's it.'

Among those still in their seats are Ray and Carol Hatton, but then they have another son to watch. Gomez is standing in an aisle, signing autographs. 'Just one more fight, then I get a re-match with Lear,' he says. 'There'll be no slip-ups this time.'

Ricky Hatton slips quietly, largely unnoticed, into a seat next to his parents as his brother, Matthew, and Graham, report for business. The opponent in this six-round welterweight contest is David Kirk, from Mansfield. Farnell, wearing a white tracksuit, is also at ringside. Phil Taylor has joined the Hattons on the front row.

Now, in a becalmed and nearly empty arena, Carol's calls can be clearly heard. 'Use that jab . . . Combinations . . . Come on, Matt, you're stronger than him,' she calls.

Her husband is no less vociferous: 'Come on, Matthew, work, son . . . Put it on him now, Matt . . . You're getting to him now . . . Push him off, he wants a rest.'

Kirk goes down in the fourth but it is a slip, as referee Kane confirms. A clash of heads leaves Kirk with a gash and in the sixth Hatton, too, is cut, on the right eye. They go the distance and Hatton looks expectantly at the referee. Instead, Kane lifts Kirk's hand and the Hattons are stunned, staring ahead in disbelief. The referee scores it 58–57 in Kirk's favour, ending Matthew's 13-fight unbeaten run, and ringside pundits share the family's incredulity.

Farnell is beckoned by fans to shake hands and sign autographs. 'I can't understand that,' he says. 'I had Matthew winning by at least two rounds.'

Farnell's face still looks contorted, red and swollen. But now, as he reflects on his fight, he is undoubtedly smiling and contends: 'I feel great. I really enjoyed that. It's been a brilliant night for me. Brilliant.'

It is 11.35, but the night is not yet over for Nobbs, who brings another of his journeymen, Leeroy Williamson, to the ring for the final bout, at middleweight. Every impact of leather on flesh, every grunt and groan, echoes around the vast, deserted arena. Williamson is swamped by Belfast's Mickey Quinn and when he is floored in the second, referee Edwards calls an end to proceedings.

It has been a long, eventful show, and for most of the winners hugely satisfying. However, the shambles of the main event has left an inevitable pall over the MEN and Ricky Hatton is as frustrated and dismayed as his brother. It is scant consolation to him that Darkie Smith faces disciplinary action. It is thought Stephen Smith will eventually get his share of the purse, but he fears his career now has nowhere to go. Some of the more seasoned observers reckon old Darkie might actually have got Hatton and Warren off the hook, deflecting attention from what they contend was a sham of a match.

The gloom and recrimination inside the arena is put into its unseemly context by a poignant scene outside. A small group of people are huddled in conversation. The smiles and body language radiate affection. In their midst stands James Bowes, beaming contentedly. Did he enjoy it? 'Yeah,' he says excitedly.

A woman wraps a caring arm around him and says softly: 'He always enjoys it.'

Wayne Shepherd's next fight is four days away and he has driven down to the Shaw gym to train under Jack Doughty's tutelage. With him this evening is his brother, Charles, who has decided to attempt a comeback.

'I'm having a go at getting back,' the younger Shepherd says. 'I've done a few rounds' sparring tonight and it was OK. I felt all right. I packed it up because I had a messy marriage and divorce and all that. Now that's out the way, so I thought I'd give boxing another go and see how it works out. I'll probably try for a fight before Christmas and take it from there.'

Two sparring partners, in trunks and boots, hands wrapped, are waiting to work with Bobby Vanzie, who has called to say he is held up in traffic. Gary Hibbert, from Oldham, is leaning against the wall, chatting. Scott Martin, from Stoke, is sitting on the edge of the ring, swinging his legs, and chatting.

FIGHTING CHANCE

The main topic of conversation in every gym is the Hatton–Smith debacle. Doughty recalls Smith's only other defeat, also in a controversial fight, against Vanzie: 'He complained Bobby hit him with low punches. It was down in London and Smith had a lot of his supporters there so we had to sneak Bobby out of the back door – just in case. A lot of people can't get on with Darkie Smith, but I've never had a problem with him. He seems to think I can be trusted,' Doughty adds with an enigmatic grin.

Doughty confesses that his normally sanguine demeanour can be deceptive. 'I'm controlled in the corner because you have to be,' he says. 'But I do have a temper. It's the Irish in me. It explodes and then it's gone.'

Vanzie arrives, half an hour late, in a black Toyota Celica, the registration arranged to read: 'BOBBY'. He parks outside the door and dashes in to avoid the rain. He is wearing a black tracksuit, with his name on the back. He apologises for being late and exchanges pleasantries before placing his bag on a table at the side of the ring. Towering above him is his regular trainer, Maurice Core, a tall, lean, languid figure who looks more like a West Indian fast bowler than an ex-boxer. Vanzie, too, is of Caribbean stock. He takes off his earrings, and chunky gold chain and bracelet. He removes his top, revealing a black vest, and pulls on a black T-shirt. Emblazoned on the front is his name, on the back 'Team Viper'. He takes a white headguard from his bag. Core wraps his hands and puts on his gloves. The slow, meticulous process has taken 20 minutes.

Vanzie's first sparring partner is Hibbert, a respected boxer in these parts, as well as a friend and trusted accomplice. Vanzie has a reputation for being unorthodox, flashy and inconsistent. He is all those things in this session. He is a southpaw, yet frequently switches stance. He winds up an exaggerated, round-arm, viper-like strike. Sometimes he connects; often he does not. He sways, arms by his side, teasing his opponent, before launching himself into attack.

Martin is a tall, upright boxer, presenting a different proposition for Vanzie. Initially it seems Martin might be out of his depth, but by the second round, he is warming to his task and ruffling Vanzie's feathers. Core calmly issues instructions from the corner. Doughty surveys all. Martin draws Vanzie into a scrap that has a discernible edge to it. Some of the exchanges carry genuine weight and venom. They shake hands at the end, but Vanzie turns to lean on the ropes. He looks shattered after his double stint. Martin looks thoroughly pleased with himself.

Vanzie talks with Core and then with Doughty, who still cannot give him the name of an opponent for his next scheduled fight, at the York Hall, Bethnal Green, in ten days. It was to have been a WBO lightweight title eliminator, against a Brazilian, Antonio Mesquita, but that has gone out of the window following three attempts to put on a European Championship contest. The only fight Vanzie has had this year was an innocuous affair against an anonymous Eastern European. Vanzie cannot hide his exasperation.

'It's been my *annus horribilis*,' he says, sitting on the table at the side of the ring and reaching for his jewellery. 'I thought things would be on the up and up after leaving my former promoter. I don't want to sound like a spoiled brat, but I do think that bad luck has been following me around. It's like somebody's had a voodoo doll and been sticking pins in. I'm feeling it this year and, to tell you the truth, I was considering packing it in after the third pull-out by the Italian from the European title fight.

'If you saw how hard I train . . . This is sparring. I train at the gym, in Bradford, and it brings you to tears. You know, a grown man crying and all that. If you saw what Maurice has me doing, day in, day out, the seven-mile runs, the sacrifices. People talk about how hard they train, how much they sacrifice, but they fight and they win or lose. I train and there's no fight. I've had so many e-mails from people asking me what's happened to me. It's like I've been in limbo all year. I used to think trouble came in threes. For me it comes in fives!

'Jack will tell you, I'm 100 per cent mentally strong, but there's only so much the human mind can take. So I've had hypnotherapy to try and get me back, to try and pretend that never happened, but it doesn't work. At the end of the day, I know it did. I've put my body through all that and gone nowhere. I've seen the physio countless times for different injuries sustained through the hard training, and it's been for nothing. In the past year, I've had one low-key fight and I'm glad it was low-key because, having been out of the ring, I'm not going to be at my best. There's going to be some ring rust there.

'That's definitely a fear and the guy I was supposed to be boxing next week, Mesquita – 25 fights, 25 wins, 20 KOs – is obviously a dangerous opponent, a puncher. We questioned Frank Warren's choice of opponent as a route back, but he pointed out that he'd fought some boxers a few times. All the same, he was a devastating puncher and I had to be up for it. I trained like a madman. Now I'm left in the lurch.

'Tonight just showed that it has had an effect on me. That wasn't me in there at all,' he says, nodding his head in the direction of the ring, 'and I know that. Halfway through that I thought, "Why bother?" Not with the sparring but why bother going through this when you know you're not right? I only ever perform when I'm 100 per cent right. If you'd seen me the last two times I was in here, you'd know that wasn't me at all in there.'

He talks intensely, passionately and eloquently. He is often interviewed at ringside for television – too often for a supposed active fighter, he feels – and delivers his comments with equal fluency, usually accompanied by a flashing smile. His style, inside and outside the ring, is stamped 'Potential star quality'. His head is shaved, but a sliver of whiskers has been shaped down the side of his face. He lives near Bradford, in a small town called Queensbury. This self-styled Marquis of Queensbury has devised his own, distinct version of the noble art.

'My style has just developed,' he says. 'It was always awkward, anyway, because I'm a southpaw, but the unorthodox skills come with that. I wasn't taught that. I'd try out different things in the ring, like changing stance. Apparently, there was a poll on the Internet that said the person most likely to break through on the world scene this year was Bobby Vanzie, which is quite flattering. I was told about it after the European fiasco, when I was feeling quite depressed and it made me think maybe I should carry on, maybe there would be light at the end of the tunnel, but I can't see it. I've missed a peak year of my career and I just hope that if I do carry on, next year will be better.

'Everybody keeps telling me to keep my chin up. There's never a day goes by when I'm not stopped in the street in Bradford by people telling me to keep my head up. It's easy to say that, and no disrespect to any of them, but it's really, really tough. My two girls are my inspiration. They are five and three. I fight to give them a better way of life, but I've had one fight this year and I didn't make a lot of money from that. I'm doing this for my family, to give them a decent way of life. I'm doing this to pay the bills, to pay the mortgage. I'm the main money-earner and this year I've not earned hardly anything. I find it very hard to make ends meet, which is why I toyed with the idea of getting a more stable career, something where I would be paid every week or every month.

'Before boxing I worked in various clothing stores, but since I was ten years old I always wanted to become a professional boxer. When you know what you want to do, you have your blinkers on. I've got my education. Without blowing my own trumpet, I feel I've got a lot to offer. I can do things other than the sport of boxing.'

Vanzie is still British champion, but he is not the top-ranking boxer in the country and that irks him. 'The most frustrating thing for me is to go to sleep at night and know that no matter what I do, I'm always going to be No. 2 in Britain to Colin Dunne. He knows, his trainer knows and obviously I know that I've got the beating of the guy, and yet I'm still at No. 2. I'm not really interested in Colin Dunne's title, I'm interested in the scalp, to be recognised as No. 1, the best. That's all I've ever wanted. I thought that if you'd got the talent nobody could stop you from going all the way. But, obviously, there's a lot more to it than that.'

Perhaps Vanzie is too unorthodox, too flash and too opinionated for his own good?

'I don't think my style has hindered me,' he maintains. 'It might have done as regards getting fights. Jack had nightmares getting me fights early on because I was a strong counter-puncher. I'd knocked out a few early on and was hard to match, and I was a southpaw to boot. But as soon as I'd won the Central Area title I knew I was on my way. I didn't think the train would stop. I thought that, so long as I kept winning, it would roll on and on and I'd ultimately get to the top and one of the recognised world titles. That was all I wanted for myself, to be recognised as the best, then pack it in, my aspirations in the game fulfilled. I just don't know how I'm going to get those wheels going again.

'It looks like there's no opponent for the title eliminator. It could be just another Eastern European. With me, it's 80 per cent mental, 20 per cent physical, and if I'm not mentally right, then I can't perform right. If I'm in with somebody I know doesn't deserve to be in with me, then I'm not going to perform well.'

Doughty wastes no time with words of reassurance, preferring to confront reality head on and remind Vanzie he is not the first boxer – or trainer, or manager, or promoter – to encounter the darker side of the business.

'I just tell him what's happening,' Doughty says. 'We'll get there. Bobby feels this is happening only to him and I know he's not concerned with other fighters, but this is typical of boxing. Boxing's a rotten, horrible game. As I've said before, one day you feel like packing it up, the next you're on a high again.'

Vanzie comes back: 'But Jack, what you've said there, it's not true. Or I'd say it's incorrect. You find me one fighter that's gone through what I've gone through this year. It's been a joke. I'm talking about getting up for a fight three times, the same guy pulling out three times, changing camp and being messed about yet again. That's what I'm talking about, Jack.'

Doughty: 'Bobby wanted to be with Frank Warren because he knew he was the top promoter in the country and Bobby always said he could get the fights. He can get the fights – it's just that, unfortunately, things have worked out wrong. We'll come through it, and he'll box, he'll win, he'll be on top again, and really it's time for a turnaround.'

Vanzie: 'I'm not getting any younger. I'm 28 years of age and lightweights tend to pack in pretty early. I said to you, Jack, a while ago, that I had only two years left. I try not to take any punches, I'm not that kind of fighter. My style shows that. So I'm not shop-worn and I feel I can come back, as soon as I get over this hurdle.'

Summer is reluctant to take its leave, even now, in early October, bringing an improbable Riviera-like glow to the North Wales coast. Rhyl, traditionally a holiday destination for workers and their families, is grateful for the unseasonable bonus. Weekenders and day-trippers are bringing welcome trade to the stalls and arcades, hotels and bars. A short car ride inland, the Marina Holiday Park is preparing for some brisk Sunday-afternoon trade. A boxing ring is taking shape in a function and entertainment room. Caravans are being made ready for their short-stay guests. This is boxing of the small-hall variety.

Wayne Shepherd has driven the four hours from his home in Carlisle and now stands with his girlfriend, Joanne, at the back of his four-wheel drive Mitsubishi, eating a sandwich. 'They've not got the ring up yet, so there's no rush,' he says.

Shepherd's father – his only other supporter here – has joined Jack Doughty and his two corner assistants, Eamon Vickers and Ray Ashton, by the indoor pool. Doughty, too, has brought a packed lunch with him. He looks across the pool as the first of the spectators, a group of young white males with attitude, march by. 'They are typical of boxing fans these days, and have been for a few years now,' Doughty says, mindful of the mayhem that marred their last trip to this part of the principality. 'I'm not suggesting there's anything wrong with them, though, not at all.'

It seems a far too relaxed and agreeable ambience for a riot, and Doughty is more anxious to avoid hearing what happened in Audley Harrison's latest fight. It was shown on television at a time that reflected the appeal of yet another mismatch involving the Olympic super-heavyweight champion and Doughty chose to record it rather than miss his sleep. A two-round demolition job over the hapless American, Wade Lewis, awaits his belated attention.

On a normal autumn day, the tropical heat here would provide a welcome haven. Today it is intolerably oppressive to all but the bathers. Shepherd takes a seat with the rest of his entourage and closes his eyes. 'Must be hypnotherapy,' Doughty mischievously surmises.

Whatever it is, it is no answer to the unbearable temperature. 'I bet I've lost three pounds in here already,' Shepherd says. The unanimous verdict is to decamp to benches outside. The sunshine is warm but the air is invigorating compared with the sauna-like atmosphere inside. They still have time to while away, because the show will be starting late. The boxers have weighed in, but the referee, Roddy Evans, from Pontypool, and other officials have been held up by roadworks on the main road into the area. Even the ambulance is having trouble getting through.

Inside the hall, the ring is in place and the seats are filling. A little boy carrying a bucket and first-aid box scurries by. Phil Williams, one of the co-promoters, looks harassed and checks his watch. Richard Jones, the Central Area secretary, looks perplexed and he, too, checks his watch. They cannot hold up proceedings much longer so Jones, who last refereed 20 years ago, agrees to step into the breach. An audience of about 450, many of them standing at the back, are commendably compliant each time the organisers beg their patience and understanding, although the ear-splitting disco music would drown any intended protest. Not all of them are 'typical of boxing fans these days'. Young women, middle-aged couples and children make up the gathering.

More than an hour after the scheduled start, the MC, Simon Goodall, son of Mike Goodall, the more familiar MC and the other co-promoter of the show, climbs into the ring. He informs the audience that one of the five contests has been cancelled because of a half-stone difference in weight between the two fighters. Another contest will be a mere exhibition because they have been unable to find an appropriate opponent for the local cruiserweight, Spencer Wilding. Again, the response in the hall is remarkably muted.

Jones is joined in the ring by two featherweights, John Simpson, from Greenock, and Ellesmere Port's Lee Holmes, for a contest of six two-minute rounds. In Holmes's corner is Steve Goodwin, much travelled as one of Brian Hughes' assistants. Holmes has the backing of the hall against the Scot, whose unsophisticated style matches his hirsute, sinister countenance. Even these little men seem to almost reach the ceiling. Holmes is eager to jab, but Simpson wants a war and Jones has to warn them to clean up their act. An aggressive final round stirs the audience, but cannot swing the decision Simpson's way. Jones stands back to satisfy himself he has his calculations right before turning to Holmes. Simpson flails the air in irritation. The referee has a word in Simpson's ear as he dips through the ropes, but still the vanquished boxer shakes his head in disdain.

Jones remains on duty for the exhibition bout. The large frame of Paul Buttery, Hughes' latest heavyweight hope, appears in the opponent's corner. He answered an 11th-hour SOS call to bolster the sagging show. Wilding, tall and willowy, leaps over the ropes, just about the limit of his exertions for the afternoon. The sound effects as Wilding reaches forward are more menacing than the punches, which rarely make any semblance of contact. It is reminiscent of the old *Top of the Pops* classics that were distinguished by the abysmal miming.

These guys really are scraping the ceiling. Cynics might contend they are also scraping the barrel with this one, yet still the audience are extraordinarily accommodating. One wag urges: 'Come on, Spence, I want to eat,' and Wilding quite forgets himself, connecting with a genuine punch, and duly apologises. They produce more robust action in the fourth and final round, and receive a warm ovation at the end. The audience are told that both boxers can be seen fighting for real at StarSports Promotions' next show, in Preston.

Fighting for real resumes here with a super-middleweight contest under the control of the originally designated referee, Roddy Evans, who has finally extricated himself from the traffic jam. Worcester's Harry Butler, stocky and stern-faced, has the dubious honour of being local man Craig Winter's first opponent for four years. Winter, appropriately attired in candy-striped red-and-white trunks, is given a rousing reception. As Winter begins his comeback, loud bangs on a side door induce a puzzled silence in the hall. More, louder bangs have the desired effect and three gruff customers, who look as though they could handle themselves in the ring, are allowed back inside without question. The audience settle down again and a middle-aged man on the front row contentedly tugs on his pipe.

Winter, the leaner and quicker boxer, does the banging in the second round as Butler tries to figure a way through the jab. Butler, hungry for a brawl, has some success in the third and fourth rounds and both appear to be running out of steam in the fifth. Winter re-imposes his authority in the last round and although Butler stares hopefully towards the referee, it is Winter's arm that is raised. Butler's rueful expression turns to a contemptuous laugh as he hears the score, 60–54, or 6 rounds to none. Winter leaves the ring with a smile of victory and handshakes from his supporters.

Shepherd climbs up to the ring for the final contest, at middleweight, against Neil Bonner, and scans the room. He spots his girlfriend at the back and waves. Doughty and his assistants look the professional part, wearing shiny emerald-green tops. Shepherd, in black trunks, amuses himself by dancing to the disco music as he awaits the local boxer. Bonner enters the arena to enthusiastic acclaim and touches gloves with Shepherd.

Bonner, elaborately tattooed on the left breast, shoulder and arm, is much the taller and immediately sets the pattern of frustrating Shepherd's endeavours to get in close. Bonner lands a punch after the bell and apologises. Shepherd graciously acknowledges. So much for a dirty fight! Bonner knows he has the measure of Shepherd and cleverly outmanoeuvres the veteran.

Doughty dispenses grease and sagacity between the rounds as Shepherd pants for air. 'Breathe deep,' he tells his boxer and asks his assistants to give him a drink. 'Come on Wayne, get in,' Doughty calls in a low, calm voice as the action resumes. Shepherd obeys and finds his target, but at a price. Bonner retorts with a more sustained offensive.

'Step back and finish him, Bon,' yells one of his fans. Bonner seeks to do just that but Shepherd avoids his haymakers. Doughty instructs his man: 'If he's going low, you go high.' Whichever way Shepherd goes, it makes scant difference. Doughty wafts him with a towel before sending him out for the final round. 'Wayne, give it everything,' Doughty implores. Shepherd gamely wades in, but the bell has no one in suspense. Shepherd looks for Joanne as Bonner goes to the referee for confirmation of his win. Bonner has been awarded five of the six rounds, with one even. Shepherd departs to generous applause and the show is over. It has lasted less than two hours.

Shepherd and his cornermen walk out of the back door and meander through the caravans to trailer No. 232. It is actually a mobile home, spacious and far more luxurious than the average small-hall dressing-room. Shepherd slumps onto a bench seat, sweat streaming from his shaved head and body.

Doughty smiles a resigned smile and says: 'We can have no complaints about the verdict. They usually try to give the opponent a share of one round and that wasn't difficult today.'

Shepherd reaches out his hands to have the tapes cut off and grimaces as he says: 'I didn't get my shots in. He kept beating me to the punch. He made his height advantage tell.'

Joanne arrives and sits opposite her boyfriend. 'I had to ask his [Bonner's] people where you were,' she says, smiling lightly. 'They were going on about how strong you are.'

If that is meant to console Shepherd, it does not have the desired effect. 'Were they going on about my age?' he wants to know.

'No, not your age. Just how strong you are.'

'What was I like? Tell me. I value your opinion.'

Joanne coyly ponders her reply.

Shepherd knows the look. 'I was crap, wasn't I?'

'No,' she says, earnestly.

'What then? Lacklustre?'

FIGHTING CHANCE

'Well, yes.'

'I know. I might have been better at light–middle. I drove down, four hours. I could have done with a sleep, but I'm not going to make an excuse of that, or my age, or anything. I'll drive back.'

Joanne tilts her head as she responds: 'He won't let me drive his four-wheel drive.'

'Pull my boots off, will you, Joanne?'

A few yards away, behind another caravan, the promoters, referee and officials are counting out money. The paying customers have dispersed quietly and orderly, without a hint of dissent, let alone riot. The setting sun is about to spread its saffron shroud over the distant hills and the late afternoon is still a balmy delight. Williams, alas, is still agitated.

'I haven't enjoyed it,' he says dolefully. 'I thought the show was crap, to be honest. Boxing is hard work. People are so ungrateful. The tickets for this show were £20, but the boxers sell most of them and they get £4 commission. Twenty-three paid on the door, that's all. We had to pay a referee who did only two fights, as well as a referee who stood in for him. The boxers get £600, plus expenses. We have a budget of nine grand, so it doesn't take rocket science to work out there's not much money to be made from it. I prefer Thai boxing. It's more fun.'

15 ☆ THE UNENDING FIGHT

AUTUMN HAS REVERTED TO TYPE, ITS FIRST FROSTS STIFLING THE LIFE
and dimming the glow of summer's lingering blooms. The North Sea
breakers pound the Yorkshire coastline in dramatic and forbidding
rhythm. Most of those who succumb to the enduring allure of
Scarborough's bracing charms this October day are content to stand in
awe at a safe distance. But some will always rise to the challenge, and
skilled surfers venture into the chilly waters to indulge their exhilarating
passion.

Paul Ingle's passion almost killed him. It is nearly two years since his
fateful attempt to retain the IBF featherweight title against South Africa's
Mbulelo Botile, at the Sheffield Arena. Ingle collapsed in the 12th and
final round of a brutal contest. He was saved by the efficiency of the
emergency procedures and an operation, performed by Robert Battersby,
consultant neurosurgeon at Sheffield's Royal Hallamshire Hospital. Mr
Battersby removed a blood clot from Ingle's brain and took out the side
of his skull. In another operation, 11 months later, Mr Battersby replaced
the discarded bone with a titanium plate.

An L-shaped scar on the right side of Ingle's head bears graphic
testimony to the surgery. He sits on a sofa in the lounge of his
unpretentious but impeccably kept home in Newby, on the outskirts of
Scarborough. His mother, Carol, has moved in with him since his
girlfriend left.

'We were planning to marry next year, but she said she couldn't cope, or something like that, and she's gone,' says Ingle, now 30. 'The person she's living with now, a lass, is bad news. She got tied up with her and that was it. Four years down the drain. I've got my mam, though. She's No. 1. She's there all the time for me.'

Ingle's speech is slow and slightly slurred, but he is coherent and alert, and is sustained by a resilient sense of humour and an unshakeable determination. He is determined to build a new life and a new career in boxing, as a trainer. He is determined to shed most of the unwanted weight he has put on and to become less dependent on his devoted mother. He maintains his passion for boxing is undiminished and all about him are pictures and mementoes of his boxing days. The EBU belt is prominently displayed on the mantelpiece. But Ingle says he recollects nothing of his last fight and very little of his previous fights. He will be eternally grateful for the care and attention he has been shown by the medical profession and those in his own trade, especially his trainer, Steve Pollard, his manager, Frank Maloney, and his conditioner, Neil Featherby. However, his appreciation is tempered by the uncertainty surrounding that contest in Sheffield.

'I can't remember anything about the fight at all and my other fights are just vague,' he says. 'I can't remember getting weighed in or anything for the Sheffield fight. To me, that's a good thing because it was a defeat, a bad defeat, against somebody I thought I would beat. I wouldn't have taken the fight if I didn't think I could beat him. It was only my second defence. I can't really understand why it went wrong. If I'd thought it was going to be a hard fight I could, as champion, have said, "Wait a bit, let's take somebody else." If I thought there was anything wrong I would have said I felt a bit funny and wanted pulling out – like I've always said. If I'd felt funny before the fight, had a bit of flu or anything, I'd have pulled out, definitely. I wouldn't risk my life for boxing.'

Carol does remember the events leading up to the fight. She says: 'He'd been training and I said, "Don't go 12 rounds with him." He said, "I won't, I'll knock him out." If he's not 100 per cent he will not fight. He's pulled out of fights because he's not felt right. Mr Battersby said it could have happened in the first round, when he got hit and that lump came up. I wasn't there. The first I knew was when I got a phone call from my brother, who was at the fight. He told me Paul had gone to hospital. I got a lift through to Sheffield that night.'

Pollard and Maloney were inevitably challenged over the wisdom of sending out Ingle for the final round. Both were adamant their boxer was lucid and aware he was trailing on points, but insistent on trying to salvage his title by knocking out Botile. In a first-person newspaper article two days later, Maloney said: 'I could see after two, three rounds that Paul was not himself . . . There have been certain things I have not been particularly happy about in Paul's preparations, not just for this fight. I believe he should have gone to a training camp. Paul's a young man. He likes to live a social life . . . When a young fighter's not in training it's hard for him to live the life he's supposed to.'

Ingle now responds: 'As far as I can remember, I trained well. It went all right. Weight was not a problem. When I'm in training, I'm in training, and that is the only thing in my life.'

Carol confirms: 'From eight weeks before the fight, he trained hard.'

Ingle resumes: 'Then, after a fight, I'll enjoy myself. Not where I get blathered every day, I just go out once or twice a week, just like the lads. I don't know whether I over-trained or did too much, but from talking to people who saw the fight, all I can do is put it down to over-training. I've tried a training camp. I went out to America and it was absolute rubbish. There was nothing that I wanted. Everybody is an individual and if you're 100 per cent happy you'll train harder. I don't believe everybody who is forced to go to a training camp will be a champion. You've got to be happy doing it.'

Ingle could, of course, judge for himself what went wrong that night by studying a tape of the fight, but so far he has not been able to face it.

'I've not looked at it, not yet,' he says. 'I want to do because I want to see what I think of myself. I might see that I'd over-trained, or done something wrong. I think I'll be able to tell. But I'm not going to look at it yet because I'm still cheesed off that I can't fight any more. It might be a few years before I can look at it.'

Much clearer to Ingle is his indebtedness to the safety regulations and medical care he received that night and after.

'Absolutely brilliant, from what I understand, straight after and in hospital,' he says. 'I would do anything I could for them, to raise money, whatever, I'd do it.'

Carol, of course, recollects everything with harrowing clarity. Her son was in hospital in Sheffield for six and a half weeks, and in Hull for a further five and a half weeks' rehabilitation. The road to recovery could go on for several more years.

She says: 'He had three mild fits while he was in hospital and they said he could have had a slight stroke. He gets pins and needles down his right side, but that's the same side as the damage to his brain. Usually, it's the opposite side. It also affected the vision of his right eye. He's got short-term memory loss. He can't remember coming round, or anything. They said he could get back to 90 per cent, but there would be 10 per cent short-term memory loss. They said he'll get better in two to five years, and he is getting better every day. His treatment is finished now. He had his last visit last month. The main thing is he's here.'

A side effect Carol had not catered for was her son's voracious appetite, as she explains: 'The extra weight was the drugs to start with, but he had this tendency to want to eat. He kept saying he was hungry all the time, so we were feeding him sandwiches and all that. They said that would go gradually, which it has. He's got to keep to a strict diet.'

Paul verifies: 'I can't understand why, but I was always hungry. When I came out of hospital I thought I was going to pop. I got to nearly 14 stone, nearly 5 stone over my fighting weight. Between fights, I usually put on a stone or a stone and a half, but that was just being out of training, a bit of over-eating and fluid. That's the way it is. But I mean, I couldn't believe this. I looked in the mirror and thought, "Is that me?"'

Carol: 'He won't get on the scales now until he's down to something like his proper weight.'

Paul, who is just 5 ft 5 in. tall, adds: 'I'd like to come down to 10 and a half to 11 stone. If I eat any more salad, I'll look like a rabbit! I'm also getting through the multi-vitamins. I've been to the fitness gym a few times. I just do a bit of walking, then have a go on the stepping machine. I get out with my mam and go for a walk around town. The more I can get out the better I feel. The trouble is I can't walk for long because of the pins and needles. It's frustrating. I don't like being in the house, closed up. I was always hyperactive, wanting to do things. I'd go off for a run, do my training, come home, have my tea and then go out again. I'd never stay still. When I'm sitting here, I'm thinking I wish I could do this or that. That's the hardest part. I know it's going to come so I just take my time, build on it.'

FIGHTING CHANCE

His fitness schedule was interrupted by another operation, earlier this year, which was unconnected to his brain surgery.

'I had a hernia,' he says with an it-never-rains-but-it-pours expression. 'This lump kept growing and growing. I thought, "Hey up, am I eight months pregnant?" Sky asked me to commentate on one of their shows, but I had to pull out because of the operation. They say they'll have me on another show soon, though. I'm looking forward to that. I'm getting better every week and the more I can do, it brings me round even more. I play snooker. It isn't a fitness game, but it's an indoor, safe game! You're just hitting balls and hopefully you're not going to get hit back! I really enjoy it and it helps. It brings me on more when I see people I know.

'I hear from boxing people I was involved with, like Steve Pollard and Frank Maloney. They've been really good. So has Neil Featherby. He's been brilliant. When I go anywhere everybody's really glad to see me and speaks to me. I've been to a couple of shows. But I don't want to phone people up and ask them to come and see me. You can't do that, can you?'

Ingle has mapped out a future in boxing as a trainer of aspiring youngsters from the Scarborough area. He maintains he wants to give something back to the sport but admits he also needs an income.

Carol says: 'Paul got £7,000 from a fund-raising effort, but we're still waiting for the Board of Control. It's taken them nearly two years. The insurance people say it should be coming through but the waiting has made it worse. They said they wanted to wait a year, to see how he comes on, but what's that got to do with it? It should be there. It's tucked away.'

Paul: 'They are insured and we pay the tax, so I must be entitled to something. I've not quite made enough from boxing to be comfortable. Boxing is what I've done all my life, so I'd like to stay in it. I want to get into training. I want to keep involved because I know everything that happens now. I know everything that goes on because of what I've experienced, what I've heard and seen. And I don't want kids, people I'm involved with, to get hurt or injured. I'll make sure they're looked after properly. So I'm going to give them advice. If they don't want advice, fair enough. I'm not going to pester them. It's up to them. I just want to make sure everybody's safe and well. I feel I can give something to the sport.

'I definitely feel I can make a living out of training. I would like to go on my own because Steve's got his way of training and I've got mine, so I don't want to mix them and have an argument. That's the way I'd prefer it. If I can't handle the kid, I'll tell him to go to Steve. I'll work from Scarborough. There are lads at the amateur gym here, where I used to go, who are good and, hopefully, I'll take them on. I've spoken to Frank Maloney and he's interested.

'I'm here to help others and I'd like them to have what I've had, because I know how good it is to win. I don't like to see people ripped off and tret the wrong way. It is a hard sport and fighters do get ripped off. I'd like to think I never did, but if ever I found out I had been there could be a few more boxing lessons! Steve Pollard has always been brilliant with me, giving me good advice as well. He told me he'd look after me. People he has in boxing know what it's about. People on the outside, with the money, all they want is the money. They aren't bothered about the boxers.'

For all Ingle's loyalty to Pollard and Maloney, he now reveals a nagging concern about that night of 16 December 2000, and the days and weeks leading up to it.

He says: 'I don't know whether Steve and Frank found a difference in me in the build up to the fight, but I hope they didn't see anything different, because if I'd felt different I wouldn't have fought. And if they saw something different and made me fight, persuaded me, then I think they were out of order.'

Carol, too, wishes to express her feelings. 'They shouldn't have let him go all those rounds,' she says. 'You can't tell me they never knew there was something wrong in that ring. Mr Battersby said Paul would have known nothing. He was that fit, that's why he went all those rounds. But I think they should have stopped it. I wish I'd have been there because I would have done something about it.

'That wasn't Paul in that ring, not after the first round. But that could have happened when he was training, Mr Battersby said. He said Paul wouldn't have known anything was wrong in the ring. He was missing punches, but Paul would have thought he was hitting. You can't tell me Frank Maloney and Steve Pollard didn't know there was something wrong with him. They knew that wasn't Paul in that ring. Everybody did.'

Paul: 'If I had known it wasn't me, or I wasn't performing right, I'd have said, "That's it, I don't feel very well, sack it," but I never. As far as I was aware, I was all right. Whether it was just the fitness, I don't know. The fighter is not the man to judge. If Frank said during the fight that something was wrong and they were pulling me out I'd have said, "You aren't," but at the end of the day he's my manager and if he wants to pull me out it's not for the sake of it, it's for a reason. And that reason could have prevented what happened.

'Steve and Frank are on the outside, round the ring, watching the fight and seeing how it's getting on. Any boxer's trainer, or manager, should always say, "I'm sorry, we'll fight another time." Otherwise, we'll have accidents if everybody carries on doing that. I'm lucky I'm here to say it. If I was in a bad way, they should have pulled me out and said, "It's in your contract, you'll fight again in six months, against the same opponent. You'll have rest and look at everything that was wrong, we can readjust and do it again." I might not have been here.'

Like the Hattons, Ingle was a useful footballer. Jonathan Greening, Middlesbrough's former Manchester United player, who also hails from Scarborough, recalls: 'I used to play with Paul in five-a-sides. He was good.' Again like the Hattons, however, Ingle knew his talent lay in boxing and he remains devoted to his chosen sport.

He is adamant: 'I have no regrets about getting into a boxing ring. If I could box next week I would. If they said I could box when I'm fit again, I would. Not a problem. I don't regret anything I've done. It's just unfortunate it's happened. I would always defend boxing. When I went to those two fights, I felt it was where I wanted to be, but I was just a bit gutted because I couldn't be involved any more in the ring. I can be involved around the ring and outside, but my place is in there, doing it. I'd love to be back in there, 100 per cent. Even if I could do it again, knowing something bad could happen, I'd fight because I love it. I'd take that risk.'

There was a time when his mother willingly countenanced his pursuit, but she could no longer do so. 'No,' she says unequivocally. 'Not knowing what I know now. I was happy for him to when he started, even when he turned pro. I was with him all the way. You never think it's going to happen to your son. But I've been through hell these last two years. It's been awful, travelling to Sheffield every day, and when he came home, it was worse. But I had to cope with it. His girlfriend never coped with it.'

Paul: 'You never think it's going to happen to anybody. It just happens and you can't believe it. When it's happened to other people, I've thought, "Flippin' 'eck." It's unbelievable it can happen to anybody. And it has. You're just unlucky. If I'd ever struggled with anything in boxing, I'd have packed in. I'd never go in there thinking money was at stake. Your life's more important than the money. It's only a sport. It's your job as well, fair enough, and you're getting paid for it. But you don't chance it. Never. I'd always go in thinking I was going to win first. To win the belt.'

Ingle now has an entirely different fight to confront, and to win. Reclaiming his mobility, in more senses than one, will put him on the road to his new goal.

'I'm hoping to be driving again soon,' he says enthusiastically. 'I've had 14 assessment lessons and the instructor says he can't teach me anything. I've just got to concentrate. Another month or two and I should be all right. That will be a big thing for me.'

Maloney, who says he raised £16,000 from a football match and dinner for Ingle, stands by the comments he gave two days after the fight against Botile.

Ingle's manager now reiterates: 'He wasn't the same fighter who won the title and then defended it the first time. There was a lack of sharpness. He was getting caught. I wasn't the main cornerman, though, I was outside the ring. He was clearly losing the fight. When he came back at the end of the 11th, I said to Pollard that he'd lost. He'd got to knock him out and Pollard told him that. I'm satisfied that he was aware of the situation. With hindsight, I'd have pulled him out, but the doctor said the damage could have been done earlier. He could have gone home, had a drink, gone to bed and then had the problem. What happened could have saved him!

'Training camps don't suit everyone, but when you reach a certain level, it is the best way to prepare. You've got to do it right. Lennox Lewis did it; lots of my fighters have done it. I tell them all it's got to be done. Ingle didn't want to do it. I employed someone to go to Scarborough and I know exactly what went on. I don't want to blacken the kid's name, but he should have gone to a training camp.'

Pollard sides with his boxer on this issue. 'For Paul Ingle, the training camp didn't work,' he insists. 'We went to New York and tried it, but it was an absolute waste of time. Boxers are individuals. At home Ingle was happy. It depends on your definition of a training camp. We had our own kind of training camp.

'Training for the fight went all right. He was psyched up and ready to go. We both thought he'd win in four rounds. Maybe he was complacent, I don't know. I've looked at the fight since and it was just one of those things where something went wrong. He couldn't fathom how to go in but, on the night, I didn't think I should pull him out. He was always responding when he came back to the corner. Before the last round he was speaking back to me. Everyone in the corner thought the same – that he had to go and win it with a big punch. Even he said, "I know, I've got to knock him out."

'I want him to be involved in training now and I'm helping him with that. We're setting up a promotional organisation together. I'll be in Hull, at my gym, and he'll look after the boxers in Scarborough.'

Robert Battersby is still consultant neurosurgeon at the Royal Hallamshire Hospital, in Sheffield. For reasons of confidentiality, he is unable to speak specifically about Paul Ingle's case. However, he does offer his thoughts about boxing and current medical precautions. Asked whether he approves of boxing, he replies:

'I have no strong feelings either way, but there is a case for saying consenting adults can do what they like providing they do not harm other people. That is not to say I condone boxing. I'm a neurosurgeon so I don't approve of people hitting other people and damaging their brains. But boxing has a unique position in law. My concern, as with abortion, is that if you make it illegal, you'll drive it underground.

'If boxing comes on the television, I will watch it. I used to box at school. I was knocked out when I was 15 and didn't wish to box again. You will not see a single boxer who has not been permanently injured to some degree. What is wanted is a change in the rules governing ringside precautions. I find it incredible that, outside the ring, the type of precaution is so derisory. Compared with the sums of money in boxing, the cost of an intensive-care facility and scanner, along with properly trained people, at ringside would be peanuts. It would actually save boxing money.

'The whole matter needs to be discussed and examined. I don't think that a referee is in any position to make a judgement on a boxer's state of health. Nor, for that matter, can any doctor at ringside. In the Paul Ingle fight, both boxers' brains would have been damaged. Unfortunately for one of them, he almost paid the ultimate price.'

FIGHTING CHANCE

The Phoenix Camp is in one of those limbo periods. A big show over, the next one not for several more weeks. The atmosphere is relaxed, almost casual. Anthony Farnell is here but will not be training for perhaps another couple of weeks and will have a longer lay-off from fighting than his stable-mates. He discovered he had sustained three broken ribs during his second hard fight with Ruben Groenewald.

Farnell, inevitably clutching his mobile phone, says he received a call from an evidently giddy Tony Oakey, the Portsmouth fighter who retained his WBU light-heavyweight title in another hard fight, against Andrei Kaersten, of Estonia, at the York Hall, Bethnal Green. 'He said to me, "I love you, you fight like me,"' a giggling Farnell reveals. But then the fearsome 'Warrior', removed from the battlefield, does seem an amiable softie.

Ricky Hatton is in training, as if he needs the regular diet of aggressive activity. He yelps with every ferocious punch he buries into the heavy bag. The bell sounds and he breaks off, clutching a drink bottle in his gloved hands. Hatton, along with his brother, Matthew, and Farnell, played in the benefit match for Paul Ingle and is happy to hear he is making progress, albeit slow progress. 'He is a good lad and he was a good fighter,' Hatton says. 'And he was just at the stage where the big fights and the big money were coming.'

Hatton is at the stage where he and Billy Graham are seeking even bigger money. He is now earning hundreds of thousands of pounds for fights and Graham is confident he will move into the seven-figure bracket next year. The trainer says: 'I tell boxers to be in it for the glory and the money will come. But it is about money, and the higher up you go, the bigger the risk of a fall. So make sure you've got enough before you take the really big risk for the really big money – and then get out. Everybody's going on about the Junior Witter fight and they both want it, but the money has to be right.'

Matthew Hatton shadow boxes in front of a mirror, which runs the length of the wall at the far end of the gym. Not that he can see much. The mirror is steamed up in the sultry atmosphere. Matthew, his pride hurt by the defeat against David Kirk, is eager for a re-match to put the record straight. 'There's no way I should be losing to him,' the younger Hatton says. 'I want him next and get it out of the way.'

Michael Gomez impressed his new camp with the victory against

Jimmy Beech, but his absence from training has puzzled Graham. 'I don't think he'll have gone off the rails again. Not now. Not after that win.' Graham calls Gomez and leaves a message, asking the boxer to ring back.

The message from the Boxing Board is that Stephen Smith has lost 10 per cent of his reported £70,000 purse following a disciplinary hearing into his fight with Hatton. That cut represents the share his father, Darkie, would have received but for his intervention. Smith Snr's licences have been withdrawn. Frank Warren has been awarded £2,000 compensation and the other £5,000 will go to the Board's charitable trust. Smith Snr had written to *Boxing News*, apologising for his actions in Manchester, saying in mitigation: 'The father in me took over from the cornerman.'

Boxing News has become something of a wailing wall for fight people of late and Bobby Vanzie, who was as bad as he feared he would be against another modest opponent, Russian Andrei Devyataykin, responds in writing when the paper asks what has gone wrong with him. Vanzie scraped a points win over eight rounds, but Frank Warren described the performance as 'dreadful', adding: 'I walked out in the end.' Vanzie details every blow of his tortuous year and concludes: 'Frank didn't make a mistake when signing me . . . doubt me at your peril.'

Over at the Collyhurst and Moston gym, Robin Reid is cooling on the offer to rejoin Warren's ensemble. He feels more inclined to stay with Jess Harding. There is a growing concern on the ground that the influx of cheap ring labour from Russia and other republics of the former USSR is impacting on the home market.

'I'm not so sure it's a good idea to move over,' Reid says. 'The money's not as good as I thought it would be. The trouble is he's got so many fighters now. It's getting so big. I might be better off staying where I am. I've been promised I'll get better projection.'

Michael Jennings is assured support and attention when he joins Paul Buttery on the Preston show, later this week. 'I'm top of the bill,' Jennings says with the wide-eyed wonder of a little boy on Christmas morning.

Gomez still craves a return to main-event status and, to his trainer's relief, he is back in training. Everyone has to endure the wind and rain of life, but Gomez is interminably confronted by hurricanes. He had to take time off to help look after the family of a half-brother, who has just begun a six-year jail sentence for fire-arms offences. He and the gym's other big names, Ricky and Matthew Hatton, Anthony Farnell and Stephen Foster are all here. Farnell, still not fully recovered from his ribs injury, joins his colleagues on the punch bags but opts out of the punishing vaulting exercise. Ricky Hatton again sets the standard, punching with awesome power and bouncing over the metal beam, one side to the other, like a rubber ball. 'Me and Ricky have done 50 of those jumps in a minute,' Farnell says, watching his stable-mate.

The healthy rivalry inside the gym will doubtless intensify. The Manchester derby is eight days away. 'Come on, City,' Hatton roars.

'Come on, you Reds,' Farnell retorts.

Foster, the other Red, smiles meekly. So does Gomez. He is still unrecognisable from his old ebullient self. In any case, he needs all the breath he can muster. He has nothing like Hatton's spring-heeled vault and takes the occasional break. His punching, too, is tame by comparison. They switch to the weights and Hatton ribs Gomez as the effort shows on his strained red face. The rest join in the fun and Gomez takes it on the chin. The acquiescent smile is another sign of the changed circumstances.

Hatton has learned that he is to share top billing with Joe Calzaghe in Newcastle, before the end of the year. The MEN is unavailable and Graham groans: 'The place holds only 10,000. The Geordie fans are good, but with both Ricky and Calzaghe on the show it's not big enough. Ricky could sell it out on his own.'

Gomez joins Farnell on a show in the New Year and, again, he knows he cannot afford to blow it.

'That was more like me at the last fight and I'll be up for this one,' he says, sweating profusely. 'I'm not fit at the moment because I had to miss training for a bit. Well, we had to try and help my half-brother's family. It's tough on them. These things just seem to happen around me. But I've always come through the problems and I'll get back up there. I never doubted I'd come through it, even when I was at my lowest. I'll be around for another five years.'

So much for the 'I'll quit at 26' pledge, then.

He grins and says: 'That was just for the publicity. I'm a fighter, aren't I?'

FIGHTING CHANCE

Martin Jolley has come to terms with life after boxing. His romance with Joanne has been rekindled and she has moved in with him, evidently giving him the stability he had yearned. He was made redundant by his long-time employers, but has another job in printing, and is working the door at an Italian restaurant in Chesterfield town centre. He has also found a way of keeping any boxing pangs at bay by giving fighters – male and female – the benefit of his knowledge and enthusiasm.

'I can't really be described as their trainer,' he says. 'I just help out. Give them advice. You never lose that love of the sport and I like to be involved. I know how people can get hurt, so if I can do anything to prevent that then I'm happy.'

That concern for others was put to the test at a show in Alfreton, where he was watching a woman boxer he helped prepare for her fight. He recalls: 'She won all right, knock-out in the third round. But then trouble started in the crowd. There were busloads of them, looking for trouble, fighting, throwing chairs. It was mayhem. We had to lead women and children to safety. They were terrified.'

It is news concerning the two children he always treated as his own, yet feared were not, that may prove a defining development in Jolley's turbulent life.

He explains: 'DNA tests have shown that both kids are mine. It's great news and a great relief. I had to know, one way or the other. I couldn't go on with the uncertainty. After all the bad times, I feel that things are going my way at last. I'm very content and settled. Joanne is good for me, especially after I had to give up boxing. She's totally different to me, but that's probably what I needed. I can't blame anybody else now for losing my temper and blowing up. It's up to me to prove I can be a good person. I've got another chance and I'm going to take it.

'I still go to the gym and still keep reasonably fit, and I like to keep in touch. Well, once you've been in boxing it's a part of you. But I'm not really sorry I've finished fighting. You see so many shows spoiled now because people pull out and they end up with exhibitions, which are just a waste of time and the punters' money. I had my time in the ring and they can never take that away from me.'